D1519874

Félix d'Herelle and the Origins of Molecular Biology

Félix d'Herelle and the
Origins of Molecular Biology

William C. Summers

Yale University Press

New Haven and London

Printed in the United States of America.

Library of Congress Cataloging-in-Publication Data

Summers, William C.
Félix d'Herelle and the origins of molecular biology / William C.
Summers.
    p.   cm.
Includes bibliographical references and index.
ISBN 0-300-07127-2 (alk. paper)
    1. D'Herelle, Félix.   2. Microbiologists—Canada—Biography.
3. Molecular biology—History—20th century.   I. Title.
QR31.D44S84   1999
579'.O92—dc21
[b]   98-44302
                                                                CIP

A catalogue record for this book is available from the British
Library.

The paper in this book meets the guidelines for permanence and durability of the
Committee on Production Guidelines for Book Longevity of the Council on
Library Resources.

10   9   8   7   6   5   4   3   2   1

Contents

Preface

The early twentieth-century French-Canadian biologist Félix d'Herelle is best known today for discovering bacteriophage (or phage), one of the crucial entities for fighting disease early in the century and still important to molecular biologists today. Yet he was an unusual person—an autodidact, polymath, and outsider to the scientific establishment—in unusual times.

What can one hope to learn from the life story of one individual scientist? Inductive generalizations from specific instances are risky, but only when one examines the life and work of one particular scientist in detail can the reader see themes that have counterparts, parallels, and similarities in other instances, and thus contribute to a larger general understanding.

From my study of the life and work of d'Herelle, several such threads appeared to be of broader historical interest. One major theme in his life, recognized even by d'Herelle, himself, is that of the role of the outsider in science. D'Herelle's case is particularly interesting: his work was highly influential, indeed, seminal in twentieth-century biology, and he received many honors (but not the Nobel prize). Yet he held a permanent position in the scientific establishment only during his five years as a professor at Yale. He had no graduate students and only a handful of collaborators, and he was dismissed from key temporary positions and even declared persona non grata at the place where he did his most famous work, the Pasteur Institute. Surely, here is a case where scientific authority and institutional power relations appear to be totally divorced.

Another interesting feature of d'Herelle's career is the extent to which the absence of mentors and role models (to use the current jargon) shaped his development as a scientist. D'Herelle was almost entirely self-taught and had no teacher or senior colleagues from whom to learn the social and political structure of science. With the possible exception of a few summer courses, his formal education ended with the French baccalaureate (high school diploma) at age seventeen. He read widely, experimented in his home laboratory, and boldly took on jobs in which he could both learn and practice his scientific skills. His experimental and technical talents far exceeded his abilities as a scientific negotiator in the complex social world of international science. It is perhaps in this domain of scientific activity that one sees most clearly d'Herelle's lack of experience as a student and junior researcher under the tutelage of successful teachers. He often failed to appreciate the nuanced and complex structure of the scientific community, insisting instead on a formal structure, bluntly ruled, as he saw it, by a common and universal commitment to reason and logic.

A third theme in d'Herelle's science is the tension between holism and reductionism. He was a avowed Lamarckian in the tradition of French biology. He resisted chemical explanations of immunity advanced by Paul Ehrlich, Richard Pfeiffer, and Jules Bordet in favor of his original ecological ideas about the importance of bacteriophages in natural immunity and recovery from infectious diseases. Yet his views on the origin and the material basis of life were profoundly reductionistic. Indeed, he devoted an entire monograph to his "colloidal theory of life" as a challenge to the "cellular theory of life." This tension made him an enigma to the early molecular biologists, who adopted his organism (bacteriophage), his conception of it as an ultravirus, his experimental techniques but went far beyond d'Herelle in their use of phage as the quintessential genetic organism.

In his late-life memoirs d'Herelle claimed that he consciously modeled his career on that of Pasteur, and it is not unreasonable to take him more or less at his word. In his choice of problems (fermentation, insect epizootics, animal and human disease prevention) and his bravura in moving to new and challenging problems, he imitated Pasteur. His drive to bring his science from the laboratory into practical application in the field is a key Pastorian trait. The alacrity with which d'Herelle entered into disputes with colleagues and competitors, as well as his rhetorical flair, rivaled that of Pasteur. Indeed, more than ten years of d'Herelle's career were devoted to experiments and polemics driven by his priority claims in the discovery of bacteriophage.

D'Herelle was born in Montreal but was a citizen of the world. His politics were liberal if not actually left wing, and in his view science was just as applicable to the social as to the natural realms. He travelled widely, and worked in North, South, and Central America, India, Indochina, North Africa, Algeria, Tunisia, France, and the USSR. He often identified with the subjugated native populations where he lived and investigated their histories, cultures, and customs. As with many western liberals, d'Herelle was attracted to the great experiment in a scientific society taking place in the USSR. He went to Soviet Georgia in 1934 only to be disillusioned with the Stalinist Terrors of 1936.

His initial work was on fermentations and the "engineering" problem of producing industrial alcohol from agricultural byproducts, first in Canada (excess maple syrup production) and then in Guatemala (unsold bananas) and Mexico (sisal residues). A chance observation led him to investigate the epizootic infection of locusts, and he soon applied this knowledge to fight locust plagues in South America, North Africa, and Cyprus. For this work he became quite famous and is the acknowledged pioneer in the field of biological insect control. Important as this work on insect pathogens was, it has been overshadowed by his second major discovery, that of viruses that infect and kill bacteria, the virus he named bacteriophage. Before antibiotics and specific chemotherapy, bacteriophage raised hopes that the cure for infectious diseases was near at hand. The simple and elegant methods d'Herelle devised to study phage appealed to a new generation of biologists with more fundamental aims. Thus, phage became "the right tool for the job" for the founders of molecular biology in the 1930s. To the present day, phage and the experimental techniques devised by d'Herelle are central to molecular biology, as well as to the new fields of biotechnology and genetic engineering.

Acknowledgments

The following people provided critical information and help for this project: Revas S. Adamia, Teimuraz Chanishvili, Marion Davis-Amesbury, Edouard Doucet, Emory Ellis, Raymond Latarjet, Denise Ogilvie, Annick Perrot, Robert B. Schultz, the family of George H. Smith, Antony Twort, and Elie Wollman.

The following libraries and archivists were of immense help: Silvia Vermetten (Leiden); Denis Plante (Montreal); Judith Goodstein, Charlotte Irwin, and Bonnie Ludt (Caltech Archives); Carlos Denis Ceballos and Margarita Peraza Sauri (Mérida Public Library); Victoria San Vincente (Mexican National Archives); Liisa Fagerlund (World Health Organization, Geneva); Rockefeller Archives; New York Botanical Garden Archives; Yale University Library, Manuscripts and Archives; British Library (India Office Records); National Library of Medicine; Wellcome Institute, London.

Many people responded with helpful advice and information: Hans-Wolfgang Ackermann, Daniel A. Alexandrov, Donna Duckworth, Leonard A. Dobrovolski, Gerald Geison, Ferenc Georgyi, Harold Harrison, Guy Lacroix, Esther Lederberg, Salvador Luria, André

Lwoff, Nicole Mazure, Steven Peitzman, Nathaniel Rakieten, Kirill Rossiyanov, Jann Sapp, David Shrayer, Maxime Schwartz, Bruno Serignát, Mabry C. Steinhaus, Jean Théodoridès, Barbara Tunis, and Louis Weinstein.

Illana Murcia and Irina Gordienko provided translations of crucial Russian documents. Permission to use previously published or unpublished materials have been generously granted by the following: Académie des Sciences (Paris); BMJ Publishing Group; Chapman and Hall, Ltd.; Masson, Editeur s.a.; Institut Pasteur; *Journal of the History of Medicine and Allied Sciences;* The Lancet Ltd.; Hubert Mazure; Mosby-Year Book, Inc.; Royal Society of Tropical Medicine and Hygiene (London); *Scientific American;* Société de Biologie (Paris); Mabry C. Steinhaus; and the *Yale Journal of Biology and Medicine.* H.-W. Ackermann, T. van Helvoort, and H. Mazure each read the entire manuscript and provided many useful comments and much helpful advice.

This project owes its initiation as well as its completion to the constant support and advice of my colleague and friend, Professor F. L. Holmes, who provided wise counsel, constant inspiration, and gentle criticism. Two other colleagues in the Section of the History of Medicine at Yale were also especially helpful along the way: Joseph Fruton, another biochemist-historian, by his example and advice, and the late Arthur Viseltear, by his enthusiastic encouragement. Colleagues in other places, too, were both helpful and encouraging to me in this project: I am especially grateful to Ton van Helvoort and Daniel Kevles. It is with special gratitude that I acknowledge Hubert and Michèle Mazure, who provided immeasurable help in this work. Without their assistance and generous hospitality I could not have completed this book.

My wife, Wilma P. Summers, and my daughter, Emily A. Summers, put up with my devotion to this project over a long period of time. Although I acknowledge their sacrifices, I cannot sufficiently repay them, but dedicate this work to them in partial recompense.

Chapter 1 Peregrinations of Youth

Félix d'Herelle later attributed his interest in the nascent field of bacteriology to a chance conversation while on a school holiday excursion through the north of France, Belgium, and the Rhine valley. Sixteen-year-old d'Herelle, touring that summer with one thousand francs from his mother, was visiting an inn where he overheard a conversation about a boy who had just been bitten by a rabid dog. The distraught parents were making plans to take their son to the nearby village of St. Hubert, where he would be treated by the monks at the abbey. A cult had grown up around St. Hubert, an eighth-century bishop, which claimed miraculous cures of rabies at the abbey. Having heard of Pasteur's work on rabies, d'Herelle wondered why the boy was not being taken to Paris for treatment, and when he inquired further was told that "for time immemorial, the monks have treated individuals bitten by rabid dogs with such success that of the numerous inhabitants of the country who have gone there, none have failed to experience relief of symptoms" (*PM,* 12). Since the village was less than sixty kilometers away and he was not pressed for time, d'Herelle decided to visit the abbey and inquire about the treatment offered there.

At the abbey they told me that the monks inserted under the skin of the forehead of the patient a thread from an old stole, worn, it was said, by Saint Hubert himself, a bishop of Liège, who lived in the seventh [*sic*] century, and prescribed the recitation of certain chants for nine consecutive days, after which the patient was provided with tranquility, the hydrophobia [victim] was cured . . . on one condition, however: he cannot look at himself in a mirror or in a brook for the next 40 days; this evidently to excuse failures. Not believing in miracles, I thought at the beginning that the "thread" developed into a medicine which was analogous to that which Pasteur inoculated, but this hypothesis collapsed immediately, when one [of the monks] remarked to me with an air of bruising superiority, that if the patient is unable to come to the area of St. Hubert, the monks send to him, by letter, that which is called a *répit* [respite, relief], which they employ as a cover for seven years. Besides, previously bitten persons, cured by the monks, have the authority to give these same *répit*.

Then, for a very long time afterward, I made inquiries into this subject. I heard that the fame of St. Hubert extended to past centuries, and by the turn of the nineteenth century, throughout a great part of Europe. I have found it mentioned in several medical books published in Paris in the early part of the nineteenth century . . . with strong sarcasm, besides. (*PM*, 12–13)[1]

D'Herelle noted that the monks reported a failure rate of about one in two hundred, the same as that found by those who used Pasteur's new method. Even in later life, he remained perplexed by the concordance of the success rates claimed for the two treatments, and observed that "furthermore, it is very strange that the confidence [in St. Hubert] has continued since the ninth century [*sic*] (an epoch when miraculous so-called treatments were inaugurated) if the victims had succumbed, since among other reasons, rabies is a malady which is unforgiving and which does not pass unnoticed" (*PM*, 13).

By his later recollection, this chance encounter in a rural hostel "was a decisive influence on the course of my life: it oriented me toward medicine, toward microbiology" (*PM*, 14). Although he may have been inspired, it was several more years before he set about acting on this inspiration. Between completion of secondary school at age seventeen and his beginning scientific work nine years later, d'Herelle led a peripatetic existence of international travel and self-education.

Félix Hubert d'Herelle, with only a high school education and self-taught in the sciences, would go on to international fame and notoriety for the invention of modern biological pest control as well as the discovery of the microbes upon which the science of molecular biology would be built. For all of his career, d'Herelle remained the vagabond scholar, an outsider in the institutional world of twentieth-century science. How he was able to command an audience for his work, how he was able repeatedly to obtain support for his work, and why he remained an outsider even while his ideas and results were adopted and celebrated at the very center of the scientific establishment are the matters which are illuminated by an inquiry into the details of his personal and scientific life.

Félix was born on 25 April 1873 in Montreal. His father, Félix Haerens d'Herelle, was a French-Canadian free-thinker, and his mother, Augustine Worms-Mect, was a devout Dutch Catholic from near Maastricht. D'Herelle's father was thirty years older than his wife, and was, apparently, a widower with older children prior to his marriage to Augustine (*HM, PM,* 5).

The family name, Haerens dit Herelle ("called Herelle," contracted to d'Herelle) may reflect a minor honorific title acquired by an ancestor who distinguished himself in the siege of Metz in 1552 when Henry II of France was defending the Protestant city against the forces of the Holy Roman Emperor, Charles V. The honorific d'Herelle was often dropped by Félix's mother and brother.[2] D'Herelle's grandfather was born in France in 1760 and emigrated to Canada in the early nineteenth century. His father was born in 1811 in Canada and was in the circle of friends of the liberal Québec leader, Sir Henri Gustave Joly de Lotbinière.[3]

When Félix was five years old, his brother, Daniel, was born. The next year their father died at age sixty-eight, and Augustine Haerens returned to Europe with her two young sons. The family fortune appeared to be intact, as Félix attended a lycée in Paris and spent his summer holidays in the countryside.[4] When he was sixteen his mother gave him a bicycle and 1,000 francs for his vacation travels through the valley of the Rhine, the occasion of his youthful epiphany at St. Hubert. The next year, following completion of his studies at the lycée, she gave him the rather lavish sum of 3,000 francs, enough to allow him to spend three months traveling in South America, a trip that took him to Buenos Aires, Paraguay, Brazil, the Cape Verde Islands, and finally back to Paris.[5] The romance of travel became ingrained in the young d'Herelle, and for the rest of his life he never passed up an opportunity to travel and indulge his curiosity about other peoples and cultures.

His first port of call on this South American adventure was Tenerife in the Canary Islands, and d'Herelle recalled "It was my first contact with exoticism: I was enchanted" (*PM,* 14). He later recalled that since he had his pistol with him, in Asunción, Paraguay, he decided to indulge his passion for the hunt. While he did not kill any large animals, he did bag some small partridges and many ducks. It was on this trip as well that d'Herelle learned to speak Spanish;

to occupy his time on board the ship, he studied a Spanish grammar he had brought along. Later he recalled that he was able to get along in this language in the cities, but was utterly lost when he got out into the countryside.

On the return leg of his trip, just after his ship, *Royal Mail*, left Rio de Janeiro, yellow fever broke out among the passengers and crew. Within eight days about twenty passengers and crew had died. "One morning, very early, seven bodies, one-by-one, slid into sea," d'Herelle wrote (*PM,* 21). This drama deeply impressed the seventeen-year-old. He attended the talk given by the ship's doctor who noted that "we are totally ignorant of yellow fever, the cause, the mode of contagion, the treatment, in spite of many scholars who have studied this disease" (*PM,* 21). D'Herelle later recalled that he was among the more calm and detached passengers: "It is probable that I have, by birth, the first required quality needed to make a good microbe hunter; most of the passengers were in anguish: I was perfectly calm, I thought I was invincible. It is such a feeling of security in the face of danger, that for me, comes from my inveterate optimism; the pessimist is necessarily upset because he thinks that the misfortune will, by preference, visit him; the optimist is courageous, and it is not entirely vanity: he is persuaded that the misfortune is not for him" (*PM,* 21).

This intimate brush with epidemic infectious disease may have had some subtle influence on d'Herelle, but when he returned from South America at the end of summer 1890, he showed little inclination to settle down to a career, vocation, or further education. He immediately embarked on a visit to England, where he stayed eight months, the winter of 1890–91, while learning English. He found England a country "of gray monotony"; "English comfort is very uncomfortable for a Canadian" (*PM,* 22).

Probably in the fall of 1891, d'Herelle went to Bonn where he attended lectures at the University of Bonn "for several months." Which courses he followed is unclear, but he described attending an autopsy where he was particularly impressed by the way the professor held forth in a pontifical manner (*PM,* 23). In the spring of 1893 d'Herelle set out for Turkey, again on an excursion of adventure. One of his fellow passengers was Marie Adèle Caire, daughter of the French consul in Istanbul. Apparently young Félix and Marie fell in love quickly because they were married on 11 July 1893. He was twenty and she was fifteen; in d'Herelle's words, "we did not have 36 years between us" (*PM,* 23).

The young couple spent several months in Turkey visiting historical monuments, talking politics, and enjoying a leisurely life of idleness. They then spent four of the winter months (1893–94) in Athens, again being idle tourists (*PM,* 30). Apparently, they returned to Montreal in the middle of winter, however, for the birth of Louise Marcelle on 19 March 1894.[6] In the winter of 1896–97 they again visited Greece for several months, but by the spring of 1897 d'Herelle realized that he had to find direction: "I was 24 years old, it was time for me to make some choices: the conclusion was that it was wiser to return to the country where I was born, and then I would see what happened. I was, moreover, always thinking about bacteriology, so on my arrival I set up a laboratory and began to experiment, all alone because at this time there were only two French Canadians who were interested in microbes, Dr. Bernier, who was later the first professor in this subject at the University of Montreal, and myself" (*PM,* 38bis).[7] In his home microbiological laboratory, d'Herelle worked to educate himself in the techniques of bacteriology. At the same time he subscribed to key journals in the field: *Annales de l'Institut Pasteur, Comptes Rendus de la Société de Biologie de Paris,* and *Centralblatt für Bakteriologie.* In addition, he took some summer courses in Europe during this period (*PM,* 51).

While he continued to amuse himself with his laboratory exercises, he was approached by an old friend of his father, Sir Henri Gustave Joly de Lotbinière, who offered him a scientific commission on behalf of the Canadian government. As the Minister of Inland Revenue for Canada, Sir Henri was concerned about the falling prices in the United States for Canadian maple syrup. He asked d'Herelle if he could explore the feasibility of fermenting, and then distilling, the excess maple syrup crop into a whisky for sale to the Americans. "Pasteur made a good beginning by studying fermentations, so it might be interesting for you, too," said Sir Henri when trying to convince young d'Herelle to accept the job (*PM,* 51). Apparently, the appeal to Pasteur was just the right touch, and d'Herelle went to work enthusiastically.

His account of his first research project suggests themes that would be carried through his entire life. He decided not to obtain a yeast for the fermentation from an institutional source, that is, from someone else who had worked on fermentation. Instead, he wanted to isolate his own. Thus, he obtained samples of fermentable fruits from many sources, even writing to New York for samples of fresh sugar cane from a tropical fruit market. These materials were used as sources of yeasts for fermentation of the maple syrup. By trial and error he eventually isolated a yeast that yielded an alcoholic product that could be distilled to give *eau de vie* or "spirits."

These experiments were carried out, at least in part, while d'Herelle and his family were living in Beauceville, a small town about fifty miles southeast of

Québec City. This region of Québec is well known for the high quality of its maple syrup, and this fact may have drawn d'Herelle to settle here. A diary kept by d'Herelle and his wife during this period gives a very sketchy outline of his initial work in fermentation. The month of March 1898 was given over to the sugaring operations, in which d'Herelle apparently took part or at least supervised. The entry for 31 March 1898 notes "received permission to make a study of alcohol." He bought his first still (alembic) on 16 May for four dollars, and it presumably arrived by freight or mail. On 2 June he "commenced the study of fermentation" and on 14 June "commenced distillation." Also on 14 June he recorded that the "taste was delicious." The entry for 15 June was "continued the fermentation," but it may have referred to further distillations of the already fermented maple syrup. On 16 June he "rectified the product." The cryptic note for 20 June 1898 is "retour d'Alembic" with a postage fee of seventy-seven cents. After this there are no more entries relating to maple sugar, fermentations, or distillations. In his memoirs d'Herelle explained that by the time he had obtained an acceptable product, the American market in maple syrup had recovered and there was no need for his process to convert excess production to alcohol. This shift in economic outlook for the Canadian sugarbush thus abruptly ended his promising start as a fermentation chemist.

Around this time, d'Herelle and his brother, Daniel, had become interested in a scheme that would make use of d'Herelle's knowledge of chemistry and foodstuffs: they were going into the chocolate business. On 4 March 1898 d'Herelle obtained a book on chocolate-making along with a letter from his brother about their joint project. During the fall and winter of 1898 d'Herelle worked in Beauceville while learning about chocolate. Also, Marie gave birth to their second child, Huberte, on 19 October 1898.

Even though he was planning for the practical business of chocolate-making, d'Herelle continued to develop his philosophical ideas. His diary entry for 12 January 1899 noted that he sent off for publication in *La Patrie,* a widely circulated Francophone newspaper, an article entitled "How Will the World End?"[8] This piece, perhaps d'Herelle's first published writing, was a long response to certain millennarian predictions for the end of the nineteenth century which had been published in the newspaper on 9 January 1899. One such prediction by an Austrian scholar named Falb, had the world ending at precisely 3 P.M. on 9 November 1899. Another, calling the city of Paris a modern Babylon, predicted its imminent ruin. Not only did d'Herelle ridicule such end-of-the-century superstition, but he described in detail fourteen accounts of how the world might end. These included various catastrophes such as the collision of the earth and a comet, massive floods, and widespread disease and famine. This article appeared in two parts, on 14 January and 21 January 1899, and was signed "F. Hoerens" (FdH: 1a).[9]

During this period in Beauceville, Daniel and Félix were negotiating with Montreal bankers for support for their plans for a chocolate factory in Montreal. On 17 August 1899, apparently with their mother's help, they bought a large parcel of land in the Montreal suburb of Longueuil,[10] where they started building a factory for their chocolate business.

Construction of the factory went forward during the winter of 1899, but by early 1900 Félix was having second thoughts about spending the rest of his life as a chocolatier. There may, too, have been signs of business or financial problems to come. On 22 March 1900, Félix sold his interest in the factory to Daniel. Although he continued to be involved in the daily work of the chocolate factory, he was thinking of other possibilities.

In the spring of 1900 d'Herelle signed on with a geological expedition to Labrador. The purpose of the expedition was to investigate persistent rumors of gold deposits in the tributaries of the Moisie River, which empties into the St. Lawrence at the port town of Sept-Iles, Québec. Félix's assignment in the expedition was as a medic, but as there were no illnesses or injuries, except for mosquito bites, he had little to do except hunt and fish (*PM,* 39). Leaving Montreal on 30 April, he was accompanied by his family as far as Sept-Iles. He and his survey party roamed the course of the Moisie River in a vain search for the rumored gold. They returned to Montreal on 10 July and Félix continued his work at the chocolate factory.

Fall and winter 1900 must have been difficult for d'Herelle and his family. By spring 1901 the chocolate business had gone bankrupt, and Daniel and Augustine Haerens d'Herelle were forced to sell the factory and the property in Longueuil.[11] D'Herelle later philosophically referred to this venture as an "unhappy speculation" in which he "lost all which his parents had left him except $2000" (*PM,* 54).

Perhaps it was his earlier excursion to South America that suggested to Félix and Marie that they might seek a new start there. A list of fifteen South American cities with the notation "written to" appears on a blank page in his diary for 1898. The letter "R" (*réponse?, rejeté?, reçu?*) appears by three cities. Thus, it appears that even before his unhappy speculation in chocolate-making, he was considering other possibilities. By spring 1900 however, the South American option seems to have taken on a new seriousness, because on 10 June Félix and Marie started keeping their diary in Spanish. This effort to sharpen their language skills was maintained until the fall of 1900, when the diary reverted to a mixture of French and Spanish for several months.

According to his later recollections, d'Herelle noted a magazine advertisement of an opening for a microbiologist in the service of the government of Guatemala and applied for the position. He seemed rather astonished to receive the appointment in the spring of 1901, and made hasty preparations to leave Canada and move his family to Guatemala City.[12]

It was during this stressful period in the winter of 1900–1901 that d'Herelle published his first scientific research paper, a study of metabolism, clearly related to his research on maple syrup. This paper, entitled "De la formation du Carbone par les végétaux," was published in the May 1901 issue of *Le Naturaliste Canadien,* a journal edited and published in Chicoutimi, Québec, by one Abbot V.-A. Huard (FdH: 1). D'Herelle's paper is of interest for two reasons: it shows the level of d'Herelle's technical and scientific development, and it exhibits the bravura and self-confidence which marked his entire scientific career. The truth or falsity of his claim (that carbon is not an element itself, but rather is a compound of elements) is not of concern to us. This paper, as the first effort of a twenty-seven-year-old self-taught scientist, taken in this context presages the style and imagination that would characterize his work for the next forty years.

No less a question than the global balance of carbon in nature was the subject of d'Herelle's inquiry. He began:

> When one considers, on one hand the small quantity of carbon dioxide in the atmosphere and, on the other hand, the enormous quantity of carbon which is contained in the plants covering the surface of the continents, when one adds again the fact that, if it is true that plants absorb the carbon dioxide of the air, and they liberate also a certain quantity, one can ask oneself if plants do not get from somewhere else than in the atmosphere the carbon which makes up the largest part. It is well proven experimentally that plants do not assimilate carbonates which are contained in soil: therefore, where does the millions of tons of carbon formed each year by plants come from?
>
> These different considerations led me to conduct an experiment, which allows envisioning the formation of carbon in a novel way. This experiment is repeatable, it is conclusive, and the important deductions [from it] and where they lead in plant physiology, are more important than cells, in what they provide to the theory of chemistry. The conclusion of this experiment is this: carbon is not an element. (FdH: 1, 70)

Next, in the methods section, he described the experimental apparatus in great detail. D'Herelle assembled a long series of flasks, sixteen in all, which were designed to isolate a bell jar, in which he would germinate six radish seeds as his biological material, from atmospheric carbon dioxide. The first ten flasks contained water, several with solid potassium hydroxide, lime water (dilute calcium hydroxide), barium water (dilute barium hydroxide), sulfuric acid, calcium chloride, and soda-lime. This train of flasks was used to deplete the incoming air of carbon dioxide. The last flask before the bell jar contained a solution of lime water, which signaled (by the formation of a cloudy precipitate of calcium carbonate) any carbon dioxide that might be present in the air just prior to flowing *into* the bell jar. Just after the bell jar a second flask of lime water detected any carbon dioxide flowing *out of* the bell jar. Several more flasks with barium water, potassium hydroxide, and more lime water were placed in line just before a water aspirator to prevent any retrograde entrance of carbon dioxide. Many precautions and tests ensured the integrity of the apparatus and the condition that no carbon dioxide could enter the bell jar.

The six radish seeds were placed in a dish of silica gel, previously analyzed and shown to be free of carbonates, moistened with a nutrient solution containing ammonium phosphate, and ammonium and potassium nitrates, all analyzed and shown to be free of carbon dioxide and carbonates. The apparatus was flushed continuously for thirty days with air, scrubbed through the various solutions at the rate of fifty liters per day. The silica gel and seeds were moistened with the nutrient solution twice a day as needed by means of an internal sprinkling device built into the apparatus.

At the end of the experiment the seeds had germinated, and rather pathetic little radishes had sprouted. D'Herelle reported:

> The lime water in tube number ten before the bell jar was perfectly clear, but the bubble tube number eleven that the air traversed upon exiting the bell jar, having been in contact with the plants, was cloudy, however slightly, showing that they had liberated carbon dioxide.
>
> With all these facts, it means that the plants themselves make the carbon that they need, and therefore a conclusion of this experiment, a conclusion very important from the chemical point of view: carbon is not an element. (FdH: 1, 74–75)

D'Herelle cited the case of ammonia (NH_3), which behaves as a single combining entity in many reactions yet is composed of two elements, as a precedent for his interpretation. He boldly extrapolated: "If carbon is not an element, the two substances with which it has the best analogies, boron and silicon, may not be [elements] either."

This note, signed "F. d'Herelle, Chimiste, de Longueuil, P.Q.," was almost immediately attacked by an anonymous critic, who signed himself as "Naturaliste-Chimiste." This response, entitled "Les végétaux font-ils du Carbone?" appeared in the same issue containing d'Herelle's paper, which suggests that perhaps the editor, Abbé Huard, was the mysterious author. After a rather respectful and flowery preamble, the Naturaliste-Chimiste came to the point:

> In effect, in all fermentations, even in the cells of a germinating seed, there is the formation of carbon dioxide. And, the experiment shows this, in view of the traces of carbon dioxide in tube number eleven.
>
> To affirm that plants make carbon and to admit the consequences which are advanced, he [d'Herelle] must calculate if the quantity of carbon in the radishes is greater than that in the seeds themselves.
>
> The learned chemist from Longueuil would certainly render a great service to science if he would continue his experimental work a little longer and make this comparison between the two quantities of carbon.
>
> Until then, the plants will continue to absorb carbonic acid, and carbon will remain an element.[13]

D'Herelle may have never seen the article and the reaction to it in the May 1901 journal, for by this time he and his family were preparing for their move to Guatemala. In later bibliographies d'Herelle never listed this paper, nor did he mention the work in his memoirs. It is likely that he was content to let it rest in convenient obscurity in a provincial journal for naturalists. He was off on another quest. As Geison and others have noted in the case of Pasteur, an early belief in oneself seems to be part of the self-mythmaking of scientists.[14] Now d'Herelle was headed for the unknowns of Central America confident that he would succeed. At what, however, was still to be determined.

Chapter 2 Fermentations:

Guatemala and Mexico

Guatemala in 1901 was a country of two million people with a progressive, if authoritarian, government. The former president, José Maria Reina Barrios, and his successor, Manuel Estrada Cabrera, were committed to technological development, education, and science. It was a time when the nation's intellectuals had considerable influence and the regime was sometimes known as "los científicos."

When Félix d'Herelle, his wife, and two daughters, the younger only a year and a half old, arrived at Puerto Barrios on the Gulf of Honduras, they still faced a journey of several days to cover the 160 miles from the eastern port town to the capital, Guatemala City. His equipment, books, and supplies from his little personal laboratory in Montreal had been carefully packed and sent to New Orleans by train to be forwarded to Guatemala by ship while he and his family had sailed directly from New York.

After a leisurely trip by train and pack mule from Puerto Barrios to Guatemala City via Gualán, El Rancho, and Sanarate, d'Herelle presented himself to the British Consul (as he was Canadian) as well as the Guatemalan authorities.[1] An indication of the social conditions in

Guatemala at that time was the Consul's suggestion that d'Herelle carry a revolver for personal protection, at least outside the capital city. This advice was to prove useful later on (*PM,* 98). The capital had about 60,000 inhabitants in 1900 and was a relatively new city, having replaced the former capital city, Antigua, after its destruction by an earthquake in 1772. Still, Guatemala City had a stately appearance and grand buildings.

While d'Herelle had been engaged as a microbiologist, René Guérin, a French chemist, had been recruited a few years before by the former president, Reina Barrios, himself (*PM,* 98). D'Herelle and Guérin, who "made up the entire scientific personnel of the republic" (*PM,* 100), were ensconced in the Palacio de la Gobernación, and d'Herelle considered his first professional laboratory set-up to be very good. He was provided with a room to house experimental animals (formerly a Spanish chapel), a room for equipment, an office, and a small, well-stocked library (*PM,* 98).

As the government microbiologist he was responsible for routine bacteriological examinations for the General Hospital of Guatemala City. This experience must have provided d'Herelle with needed on-the-job training, since his past experience in bacteriology certainly did not involve routine hospital bacteriology. Although at this time bacteriology was receiving interested attention in Guatemala, and one of the best-known professors at the Medical School was a bacteriologist,[2] the physicians in Guatemala City probably had little experience with the use of bacteriological examinations in their daily practice of clinical medicine; d'Herelle indicated there were relatively few cultures to be studied (*PM,* 100). This gave d'Herelle a good opportunity to feel his way into his new position as well as to define his new duties to fit his interests and expertise.

He gave courses, unspecified in his memoirs, but probably related to microbiology, at the medical school of the University of San Carlos, and at the high school, as well as at the school for agricultural training.[3] He did not, however, have a regular faculty appointment, at least at the medical school,[4] but did function as an examiner for the baccalaureate in "botany, zoology, chemistry, physics, all the sciences . . . whatever . . . " (*PM,* 100). However, it was as the government bacteriologist "in charge of special missions" that d'Herelle carried out his most significant work in Guatemala. Three of these "special missions" appear to set the stage for much of his subsequent scientific work. The approaches he devised and the scientific successes he had in Guatemala helped him to mature and to develop a pattern of scientific investigation that he continued to employ and refine for his entire scientific career.

In 1902 the Minister of Agriculture requested d'Herelle to undertake a study of the possibility of fermenting bananas into a distillable alcoholic beverage, one which d'Herelle later called "mon banana whiskey." As in the case of Sir Henri and the maple syrup fermentation, Pasteur figured prominently in the discussion:

> The Minister of Agriculture called me in. He started the conversation in singular manner:
>   "Pasteur was a great bacteriologist."
>   "Certainly, the founder of bacteriology."
>   "Did not Pasteur occupy himself with fermentations?"
>   "Yes, it was the object of his first research concerning microbiology."
>   "Then every bacteriologist has to have research experience in the fermentation of a product as a source of alcohol?"
>   "Oh, certainly."
>   "I am happy to hear you say so. Here is what it is about. On the Atlantic coast are important banana plantations. Because of the spread of their culture to other countries, they sell very poorly, and perhaps soon they will not sell at all. It is necessary, then, to find a way to use them. You had told me that you were charged in your country with an analogous research project, therefore I thought of you. With these bananas one certainly ought to be able to make an excellent whiskey: Go, then, and spend a few months on the Atlantic coast and work out the process. A distillery will be put at your disposal, you will be able to construct the few special utensils you find necessary. This distillery is in Santo Tomas, near the plantations." (*PM,* 100–101)

D'Herelle, with his family, moved to Santo Tomás to commence his study of fermentation of bananas and to take his first steps following the path of Pasteur as envisioned by the minister. The village of Santo Tomás was pleasant; most of the founding families of the great plantations were of Belgian origin, and the d'Herelles seemed a welcome addition to this isolated little society. D'Herelle set to work and later recalled, "The problem of distillation of bananas presented no great difficulties, but in that country everything was long and complicated" (*PM,* 103). Although he had been provided with "a distillery" by the minister of agriculture, he still required specialized equipment, which took six months to arrive from New Orleans.

The main problem in fermentation of bananas seemed to be to find a suitable yeast strain. After acidification of the banana pulp with acidulated water, the material was pressed and two yeasts were added. One strain d'Herelle had isolated from overripe bananas, and the other was from a stalk of sugar cane. The fermentation proceeded smoothly and the product was then distilled to yield a colorless *eau de vie*. The product was aged a few months in oak barrels and to d'Herelle's French palate "resembled a good armagnac" (*PM,* 103).

A more complete description of this project was published in 1909 by d'Herelle's colleague, René Guérin.[5] Guérin described the need to find new, profitable uses for the oversupply of bananas. He noted the serious problem of spoilage of the fresh fruit between harvest and market and estimated the loss to be about 20 percent of the crop. One way to address these difficulties was to develop uses for bananas which resulted in more stable products. He described attempt to make a banana conserve by preservation with sugar. This product was considered "very good," but its preparation was "delicate." A dried meal, or banana flour, was also developed. This meal was stable, of exceptional digestibility, and had many perceived values, but as Guérin noted, "The truth is that the product does not please the public." In spite of being awarded a gold medal at the 1904 Louisiana Purchase Exposition (the St. Louis World's Fair), and in spite of testimonials from nutritionists, the banana meal did not sell to the public, and producers in Java, Jamaica, Costa Rica, and the West Indies all had stopped production. "The problem does not consist of augmenting the nutritive value of the banana meal, which is sufficient by itself, but to make a food tasty to the consumer," according to Guérin.

> It was at this moment that my colleague and friend, M. d'Herelle, currently chief of the Yucatán experiment station in Mérida, but formerly director of the distillery in Puerto Barrios (Guatemala), a longtime associate in my work at the central laboratory in Guatemala, studied a process permitting the direct production of drinking alcohol. The studies which we have made in the laboratory and in the fabrication of a distillery using the bananas rejected by the United Fruit Co. and destined to be thrown in the ocean or left to rot on the shore, has allowed us to obtain an eau-de-vie of very good quality, very similar to whiskey. Samples which had less than six months aging in the barrels were taken to the Saint Louis Exposition and were recognized for high quality taste. After analysis by the laboratory of the Department of Agriculture in Washington, it was rewarded with a gold medal.[6]

Guérin indicated that the banana whiskey approximated very much the taste of Canadian Club, a whiskey made from rye. With a palatable product in hand, the economics were then discussed: with a daily production of 150 cases of whiskey, the net cost of production amounted to seven to eight francs per case; at the same time an inferior product was selling wholesale in New York for twenty-two and a half francs.

From Guérin's account, the fermentation and distillation project was credited almost entirely to d'Herelle; oddly, however, he was not a co-author on the report of the work. This situation apparently did not bother d'Herelle, because in his reminiscences he recalled Guérin with friendship and affection. On the other hand, Guérin may have contributed more than he indicated and was trying to give special credit to d'Herelle as his junior colleague and protégé. Guérin noted that "we" carried out the laboratory studies, and as the Guatemalan representative to the Louisiana Purchase Exposition, he must have arranged for the promotion of the product there.

While he was attending to his banana distillery in the district of Santo Tomás, d'Herelle was frequently called upon for his medical knowledge, there being no physician in the region. Later he recalled that chronic malaria and intestinal diseases seemed common. As he was finishing his study of fermentation of bananas in his little laboratory in Santo Tomás, in early 1905,[7] he received an urgent message to return to Guatemala City. It turned out that a case of yellow fever had been reported in Belize, the capital city of neighboring British Honduras. The Guatemalan government feared that any epidemic in British Honduras would quickly spread to the adjacent Guatemalan highlands (*PM*, 114). As the government's microbiologist, d'Herelle was to oragnize the first line of defense against this dread disease, and after four days in the capital city, he started his return to Santo Tomás. Because Santo Tomás and Puerto Barrios, along with Livingston, were the Guatemalan Atlantic port towns closest to Belize, they were expected to be where the epidemic might enter the country.

Some idea of the difficulties involved in Central American travel at this time is reflected in d'Herelle's account of this journey. Since the railroad was incomplete for sixty-three miles between Guatemala City and El Rancho, this part of the trip was by mule train. At some point while riding his mule between Guatemala City and Gualán,

I saw a man, appearing drunken, coming up to me; when he was up to me, I was surprised by his aggressive motions, I parried a blow from his knife with my left hand which was injured by the point of the blade, while with my right hand, I pulled my revolver from its holster which I was careful to leave open, and I discharged it at the chest of the man who collapsed. I dismounted: the bullet had pierced his heart. After dressing my wound in a so-so fashion (I still carry the scar), I continued my trip: at that time, in such cases, it was preferable not to have dealings with the authorities; I certainly had nothing to worry about, but I did not want to be delayed for some time, under the pretext of an inquest. Several days later, in Gualán, some travelers who had arrived from the capital told me that they had found on the road the body of an escaped prisoner, who had been condemned for a capital crime. It was surely my man.[8]

Brigands on the highway were not the only perils. The day of his return to Santo Tomás d'Herelle contracted malaria, which was to recur many times in later life. Initially he did not respond to quinine, and he was immobilized for "a long month" by this illness.[9]

On 31 May 1905, six days after d'Herelle returned, yellow fever was reported in Puerto Cortés, the port of Honduras just to the south of Puerto Barrios. On 9 June, there was a case in Livingston, the port town of Guatemala near the border with British Honduras, and just to the north of Puerto Barrios.[10] With quarantine measures instituted and anti-mosquito campaigns under way, d'Herelle was well enough to get out of bed on 20 June 1903. Only two days later, the disease struck in Puerto Barrios and Santo Tomás with one case in each town. D'Herelle attended the patient in Santo Tomás. It was his first intimate encounter with this disease and he recalled with some understatement: "C'est une maladie impressionnante" (*PM,* 125). This patient recovered, not because of anything d'Herelle did, but as he recognized, because of the action of "nature." He continued to see patients; the usual fee was "a hen or a dozen eggs, double the rate at night" (*PM,* 126). In these two towns, from June through the end of the epidemic in October, there were twenty-five cases of yellow fever and eighteen deaths. In the interior villages of Zacapa, Gualán, and Chiquimula, the fever came later, between 15 and 20 September 1903. The mortality was overwhelming; within three weeks about one-third of the population of each of these villages had succumbed to the illness.[11] By November, however, the epidemic had run its course and the d'Herelles returned to Guatemala City.[12]

Beyond his work on yellow fever there is little indication of the nature of d'Herelle's work in Guatemala between 1903 and 1905. No doubt he continued to provide routine bacteriological and other support for the General Hospital. One such assignment illuminates the conditions in a country with endemic social unrest and incipient rebellions: in 1904 he was called upon to analyze a sample for "pathogenic spores," a sample of shrapnel from a bomb aimed at President Manuel Estrada Cabrera (*PM,* 88).

In July 1906 d'Herelle was given a problem that was to challenge his ingenuity and to provide new opportunities for his development as a microbiologist. Since before 1900, little by little, an insidious disease had been killing the coffee plants in certain Guatemalan plantations. It was spreading and threatened an important industry, so in 1906 d'Herelle was charged with the study of this malady with the goal of controlling or eliminating it.

The signs of this affliction included lesions of the bark at the base of the trunk consisting of black spots, followed a few months later by a slow yellowing of the leaves which then dropped off, and finally the death of the plant. Removal of the bark revealed a completely black layer of material in the vascular tissue. Microscopic examination of this black material showed it to be the mycelia of a fungus which had invaded the inner bark and cambium, but was never found in the outer bark or the woody fibers of the coffee plant. D'Herelle concluded that the coffee blight was caused by a parasitic fungus that mechanically obstructed the vascular system of the plant and eventually destroyed it. Early infections were limited to the roots, so he speculated that the infection spread mainly through the soil.

He first searched for descriptions of this plant disease in the existing works on the subject. A monograph by Georges Delacroix, *Les maladies et les ennemis du caféier,* described a similar disease of coffee plants, *pourridié du caféier* (coffee rot), observed in the Antilles but with somewhat different symptoms from those of the Guatemalan epidemic.[13] Furthermore, coffee rot was attributed to a fungus of the genus *Rosellinia,* which "it was impossible to confuse" with d'Herelle's new isolate (FdH: 4).

D'Herelle wrote to the directors of several agronomy stations in coffee-producing countries for advice and assistance. Only the director of agriculture in Java had any useful ideas. He suggested that the Guatemalan disease might be caused by the fungus *Corticium javanicum* Zimm., and he sent a sample of this organism to d'Herelle for comparison. Unfortunately, this fungus was a basidiomycete while the Guatemalan fungus was a pyrenomycete.[14] The staff at the Institute of Tropical Agriculture in Hamburg, to which d'Herelle sent a sample, replied that they could not identify the fungus and that "local study by a mycologist would be essential." D'Herelle noted later, "I was not a mycologist, but I had done many different things while I was in that country, so I did not hesitate to accept the challenge" (*PM,* 137).

He carefully studied this disease in the laboratory and in the field. This project is the earliest work of d'Herelle as a professional microbiologist to reach publication, and thus it gives valuable insight into his early development as a scientist. This publication, completed after he left Guatemala, reflected the logical and forceful style of presentation that characterized most of his published work. First he described the field of interest and surveyed the work of others that he thought relevant. After he had considered the theoretical possibilities, such as other known parasites, he compared them point by point with his own observations, using both microbiological information, such as the classification of the suspect organism, and the results of his field observations. Although the coffee rot from the Antilles was very virulent, the symptoms were different. Likewise, the magnitude of the epidemic in Guatemala, accounting for losses of 20 to 30 percent of the coffee plants in one or two years, seemed at variance with the lower virulence of the known coffee blights.

After a careful description of the course of the natural disease and the appearance of the plants at different stages of the diseases, he described how he studied the experimental reproduction of the disease by transmitting it from plant to plant with infected root cuttings. This allowed him to evaluate the virulence of the disease for species of coffee plants other than the most common cultivar *Coffea arabica var. Guatemala.* Once he had produced experimental infections in the natural host with the suspected natural source of infection, he was in a position to try infections with purified cultures of the suspect fungus. Thinking that the host specificity of the fungus might be related to some coffee-specific growth-promoting substance, he made nutrient agar plates containing an extract of coffee leaves. The fungus grew on this medium and would sporulate as well.

These fungal spores, however, were inactive, and he could not transmit the disease as expected: "I have already spoken of the experimental disease produced by deposition of the spores, coming from a plant attacked by the natural disease on the roots of a healthy coffee plant: I have nothing to add, other than that the experimental disease reproduces exactly all the phases of the natural disease, but that all studies of infection in a soil of distinctly alkaline reaction have failed" (FdH: 4, 182).

At this point in his discussion d'Herelle observed that the acidity of the soil could influence the growth of the fungus. Although it was known that fungi usually grew best in acidic media, he connected this knowledge with his field observations on the distribution of the blight:

> I wish to speak of the favorable action of the acidity of the soil on the growth of the parasitic fungus: a very fortunate circumstance has demonstrated the basis for this assertion: at the end of the month of October 1902, the volcano Santa Maria started to erupt and discharged a great quantity of cinders which fell on the neighboring plantations, covering the soil with a layer, in some spots, from one to ten centimeters thick; these cinders have a basic composition, the soluble portion composed of: phosphoric acid, 2.57 percent; lime, 4.60 percent; magnesium 2.32 percent; iron, 30 percent; and potassium 5.58 percent.

All these plantations which, in 1902, had been covered with a layer of cinders continued to be free of the malady, and were themselves, situated between two zones heavily infested. The planters did not suspect that what they considered as a disaster was in reality a providential safe-guard. (FdH: 4, 178)

This fundamentally ecological style of argument—that is, the correlation of natural phenomena with laboratory findings—was one that d'Herelle used repeatedly. He believed that nature's experiments should be incorporated into one's thinking and was always alert to such opportunities. Nature, in all its variations and seeming paradoxes, speaks to those who pay attention and gives hints and clues to basic facts.

The opportunity to contribute to the scientific literature and to name a new organism appealed to d'Herelle, and in this paper he followed the conventions of describing the fungus, its growth habits, and its spore forms in detail. He claimed such an organism had not been reported before and proposed a new genus, *Phthora* (devastation), and species, *vastatrix,* (devastator), for his organism. The paper concluded with a detailed technical description in Latin, as was conventional in taxonomic publications at that time.

In addition to the lesions of the trunk and roots which seemed to be associated with *P. vastatrix,* d'Herelle noted the prevalence of a condition he described as *grains noirs* (black seeds or specks) that seemed associated with the fungal infection of the coffee plants. About one-half percent of the coffee crop was affected, and the European coffee buyers were beginning to complain about the quality of the coffee. Since those plantations most affected by *grains noirs* were those most affected by the fungal infections of the trunk of the plant, d'Herelle speculated that there might be some relation between the two conditions.

Upon examination of the skins of the blackened coffee beans (*cerises noircies*) he found a bacterium which appeared closely related to that which causes a disease of grapes, gummosis of the vine.[15] He did not, however, find any fungi in the diseased coffee beans. He concluded, therefore, that there was not any direct relationship between the two diseases. However, he then raised the question: "Is there an indirect relation? It is very possible" (FdH: 4, 179).

In trying to understand the possible relationship between the prevalent fungal devastation of the vascular system and the less common bacterial disease of the beans, d'Herelle proposed an explanation which was, in several ways, the prototype for his later approach to infectious diseases in general, especially his investigations which led to the discovery of bacteriophage. Since the bacterial disease seemed restricted to regions where the fungal disease was prevalent, and since not all plants in such areas succumbed to the fungus, he suggested that many plants were infected with fungus but had a latent infection, either because they were partially resistant or because they had recovered. Such plants, under certain conditions of humidity and nutrition were rendered more susceptible to infection by the bacterial disease of *grains noirs*. This "ecological" concept of two associated organisms, which are interdependent on their interactions with the host and its natural resistance, as determining the outcome of the struggle between host and parasite became the analytical framework for d'Herelle's later work. It informed his research on the pathogenesis of intestinal diseases in locusts in Mexico, Argentina, and Tunisia, his work on dysentery in humans which led to his discovery of bacteriophage, and his approach to the study of cholera in India.

Practical action was always a primary goal of d'Herelle's research, and once he had identified a potential solution by laboratory study of a problem, he lost no time and wasted no words in advocating field trials of his remedies. He noted that the infection of coffee plants with *P. vastatrix* should be easy to control by avoiding acid fertilizers and adding lime or cinders to the fields to bring the soil to an alkaline reaction, unfavorable to growth or survival of the fungus. He even offered the practical advice to use the cinders from the burning of the dead plants to alkalinize the fields to protect the survivors (FdH: 4, 182). There is no evidence, however, to suggest that these prescriptions were ever put into practice.

It is unclear from the surviving records how long he worked on the problem of the coffee diseases, but this study began in the summer of 1906 and by early 1908 he was working in Mexico. In his autobiography he described the trip from Guatemala to Mexico as beginning in December, presumably December 1907. These dates suggest that he continued working in Guatemala for about eighteen months after taking up the problem of the coffee blight. Such a period is consistent with his observations that it took fourteen to eighteen months for coffee plants to develop symptoms after experimental infections (FdH: 4, 175).

The reason for d'Herelle's departure from Guatemala and the conditions under which he left are unclear. Thirty years later he recalled his time in Guatemala fondly: "When I think of Guatemala, it is always with affection. It is where I carried out my apprenticeship in life, where I commenced my scientific career. Obliged to occupy myself with questions of a great variety of interests, microbiology, hygiene, medical examination, mycology, fermentation, chemistry, botany, agriculture, all these constituted a training which were a great aid to me all my life" (*PM,* 143).

D'Herelle and his family left Guatemala in December 1907 and headed for Mexico City.[16] He had been engaged by the Secretary of the Department of Agriculture of Yucatán because of his expertise in fermentation technology. While Canada had a glut of maple syrup, and Guatemala had rotting bananas, in Mexico d'Herelle was to turn his attention to bagasse, the residue of the Mexican sisal plant remaining after extraction of the fibers.

During the Spanish-American War in 1898 the world price of sisal fiber, a major export from the Yucatán, dropped by 42 percent in that one year alone. Over the next ten years the industry showed no signs of recovery, and by 1907 the plantation owners from around Mérida formed a group which pressured the Yucatán's Secretary of Agriculture to rehabilitate the industry by seeking new uses for the Mexican sisal plant, known locally as henequén (*Agave four-croydes* Lemaire).[17] The owner of one of the largest henequén plantations, or haciendas, was also the Mexican Secretary of Public Works, Colonization, and Industry. Don Olegario Molina, owner of Hacienda Chochoh, not only invited d'Herelle to use a small experimental distillery he had constructed on his property, but also provided the d'Herelles with full accommodations.[18]

The trip from Guatemala City to Mexico City in 1907 was slow and tortuous. From the Pacific port town of San José in Guatemala the d'Herelles took a boat to the Mexican port of Salina Cruz. After a train ride across the Isthmus of Tehuantepec they boarded another boat at the Gulf port of Puerto Mexico (Coatzacoalcos) for travel to Vera Cruz, followed by another train ride to Mexico City.

D'Herelle must have started right to work in Mexico City because by 13 February 1908 he had already registered the first of his six patents for bagasse fermentations with the Mexican government.[19] After several rounds of consultations in Mexico City, he set out for Mérida, the principal town in the Yucatán, and started his study of bagasse fermentation. His work there was supported jointly by the Yucatán Department of Agriculture and the sisal growers' association. Initially, d'Herelle's laboratory was in the General Hospital in Mérida because there was no other suitable facility for scientific work in Mérida (*PM,* 176). After visiting many sisal plantations, he accepted the offer of Don Molina to set up an experimental station on his property, one of the largest plantations.

By March 1908 d'Herelle and his family had moved to the Yucatán and took up residence at Hacienda Chochoh: "I moved with my family into a house on the plantation Chochoh; two rooms were outfitted as laboratories. There were on the plantation two young Mayans who had worked as domestic servants on the property and who understood Spanish: they were provided to me as *garçons de laboratoire.* This was fortunate, since in addition to their other work, they were able to serve as interpreters, because the women I engaged as household help spoke only Mayan" (*PM,* 200). The plantation was a society in itself with about forty Korean families employed under a contract labor scheme, as well as many Mayans who, in d'Herelle's view, were to all intents and purposes enslaved.[20]

In his approach to his new assignment, we can again see something of d'Herelle's style as a mature scientist. For his work on sisal fermentation we have rather detailed accounts of his laboratory experimentation because he submitted progress reports to the Secretary of Agriculture of the Yucatán on a biweekly basis for the first six months. These reports were subsequently published as an appendix to a 1910 government document (FdH: 7). Close analysis of these reports, the next best source after actual laboratory records, reveals a logical style of experimentation, characterized by a focus on immediate practical problems.

The first report, dated 15 April 1908, described assays to measure the quantity of fermentable sugars in the bagasse of the sisal. This determination, in d'Herelle's view, was the most important first point to establish. On 8 April he obtained some juice made by pressing bagasse and determined the total content of sugars by polarimetry (a measurement of the degree of rotation, clockwise or counterclockwise, of a beam of plane polarized light). He was aware that potentially fermentable sugars (such as disaccharides, oligo- and polysaccharides) might be present as complex sugars, so he subjected the samples to "inversion." Although his report does not indicate in detail how this procedure was done, he mentioned the treatment of the samples with hydrochloric acid. Since he later employed hydrolysis by sulfuric acid for this purpose, it is likely that hydrochloric acid hydrolysis was the method used in these early analyses as well. The acid hydrolysis of glycosidic bonds was already a standard procedure to produce "invert sugar" from complex starches.

The deviation (i.e., rotation of the polarized light) before inversion was $+1.7°$ and the deviation after inversion was $+8.4°$ at a temperature of $33°C$. He then applied the formula of Landholt to calculate the percent sugar from the polarimetry data:

$$P = 100 \text{ (Difference)}/(142.6 - 0.5T) = 100 \ (8.4 - 1.7)/(142.6 - 0.5 \times 33)$$
$$= 5.3 \text{ percent.}$$

This value was the mean of eight observations for a sample prepared on 8 April. A similar assay with six observations on a sample prepared on 11 April gave 5.2

percent. These determinations were compared with those obtained by a second method based on the reduction of copper from a solution of copper and potassium salts, "a gravimetric method, more complicated but more exact than the volumetric method." The mean of seven assays before and after inversion gave a net yield of reducing sugars of 5.03 percent. In this report d'Herelle then discussed the possible sources of error in each method but finally concluded: "Besides, the correspondence obtained for the two methods: polarimetry (5.32) and copper reduction (5.03) is sufficient" (FdH: 7, 312).

Confident in this estimation of the fermentable sugar content of at least two batches of bagasse, d'Herelle went on to calculate the theoretical yield of alcohol from 100,000 henequén leaves. From records for the previous year at the plantation, he estimated the amount of juice produced from that many leaves to be about 30,000 to 32,000 liters. From the work of Pasteur and others, it was known that the theoretical volumetric yield of absolute ethanol from the fermentation of glucose is 0.61 l/kg. Thus, if 30,000 liters of juice contained 6.05 percent reducing sugar, a maximum of 1,107 liters of pure alcohol could be expected. This estimate was very encouraging and was roughly one-third that expected from cane sugar, a known and economically viable source.

Not content with his first attempts, d'Herelle noted that not all of the complex compounds may have been broken down to fermentable sugars in these experiments. He then tried to find ways to release more sugars for fermentation. First, the juice was heated at 120°C for twenty minutes, followed by the usual hydrochloric acid inversion. This heat treatment seemed to help: the total reducing sugars increased to 9.2 percent. Treatment at 120°C with sulfuric acid in concentrations from 1:1000 to 1:100 increased the yield, to 13.4 percent reducing sugars in the latter case.

At the end of this first report d'Herelle noted that while his results were promising, the next problem, which might not be so easy to solve, was the isolation of a suitable yeast capable of carrying out the fermentation. He was aware that the usual industrial production of alcohol did not involve decomposition of complex polysaccharides to fermentable sugars as a first step and that this problem would be an obstacle to economic application of his work.

His next report on 2 May 1908, however, started out: "During the last 15 days of April, I have been dedicated to selection of yeasts appropriate for fermentation of the juice of bagasse" (FdH: 7). D'Herelle outlined two possible approaches to the problem. Just as grapes harbor the optimal yeast strains for wine making, it makes sense to search for yeasts in the natural habitat of the henequén. Once a set of pure yeast strains has been collected, the next step should be to determine their characteristics in order to optimize the bagasse fermentation. But, he said, there exists another way: "Take an already well-known yeast and gradually adapt it to the special conditions of the [sisal] must." Here he firmly rejected the latter, rather Lamarckian, approach: "I think the first method is preferable. . . . I have taken these as the starting points, the yeasts from on the leaves, in the bagasse or in the juice which has undergone spontaneous fermentation."

In order to isolate yeasts from these sources, however, d'Herelle had to devise a solid medium which would allow growth of yeast but not of the bacterial contaminants in these samples. Slightly acid agar plates inhibited growth of all the bacteria while still allowing growth of yeast. With this medium he selected "eleven or twelve" yeast strains to save for further study. These strains were first grown on sucrose and later gradually "acclimatized" to the henequén juice before he compared their properties.

Another problem that attracted d'Herelle's attention at this early phase of his research was the effect of climate on the yield of juice and on sugar content. Because agaves store large quantities of water, they can withstand severe, dry conditions. Toward the end of April the plants became drier and, little by little, appeared to reduce their sugar content so that by 28 April 1908 total reducing sugars averaged 1.7 percent. The first rains of the season fell on 30 April and d'Herelle analyzed leaves collected the next day: he found 6.3 percent reducing sugars. This was quite remarkable: "As we see, only a single rain is enough for the plants to immediately elaborate a quantity of sugars sufficient to replace the decrease that occurred during the month of April." While the yield of sugars may be diminished during the last month of the dry season, d'Herelle suggested that from the point of view of commercial practices, sufficient supplies of high-sugar bagasse from the rest of the year would be available to keep production going. In addition, he observed, during the dry season at the end of April there was a reduced harvest of leaves with the workers only cutting them three days a week.

During the first two weeks of May 1908 he continued to study the yeasts he had isolated from the sisal sources in order to see if a suitable strain could be found. From the original eleven or twelve isolates, he described seven: five of these did not decompose the sugars in the henequén juice; the remaining two were almost equivalent in their behavior and were studied further. The first was inoculated into 100 milliliters of juice with 6.5 percent reducing sugars, and after fermentation he obtained a yield of 3.9 percent ethanol. This represented an amazing 98 percent yield. A similar fermentation with the second gave equally striking results. The principal difference in the fermentations with the two yeasts, according to d'Herelle, was that yeast 2 "imparted a very agreeable flavor to the product" that was lacking with yeast 1.

The next logical step was to test the yeasts strains on juice in which more sugars had been released by high temperature acid hydrolysis. He speculated at this point that such fermentations should almost double the yield of alcohol.

In his report on 1 June 1908 (FdH: 7), d'Herelle was able to verify his predictions: six experiments between 19 May and 27 May with acid-treated juice gave yields of alcohol between 7.4 and 8.5 percent. In this report he described his procedures in sufficient detail for eventual industrial application: The juice was held in the autoclave for forty-five to sixty minutes after acidifying with 2 milliliters of concentrated sulfuric acid per liter of heated, acid-hydrolyzed juice. A test fermentation was done on 250 ml. After cooling to 30–32°C, three drops of a pure culture of yeast 1 were added. Fermentation was active ten to fourteen hours after inoculation, and by forty to forty-eight hours it became very slow, almost complete. After sixty hours from the time of inoculation, the alcohol content was measured by distillation in a Salleron apparatus. The results were calculated to correct the temperature to 15°C and to give the yield of absolute ethanol. D'Herelle concluded this report again with a comment on the weather. "There has been no rain at Hacienda Chochoh after that on 30 April. The leaves are so dry that harvesting has been interrupted."

On 11 June it rained again, and after harvesting a few henequén leaves d'Herelle used this occasion to further his study of the effects of climate on the sugar content of the juice. For the first time he gave measurements of the specific gravity (grams/ml) of the juice as well as the reducing sugar contents. The administrator of the plantation, however, informed d'Herelle that they would not harvest on a large scale until the middle of August because of the dry weather. Under these constraints, he turned his attention to an analysis of the trunks of the henequén plants that were too old to produce leaves. Still, in the absence of rain, he was unsure of the value of these studies because of the previous sensitivity of the sugar content to the weather. D'Herelle's brief report covered the entire month of June 1908.

In the dry month of July he turned his attention to the chemical analysis of the henequén plant. This work did not require samples of bagasse or large numbers of leaves so it could be done even while the plantation was idle and waiting for the rains to come. D'Herelle analyzed both dry and fresh leaves for water content, fiber, soluble and insoluble materials, minerals, nitrogenous materials, reducing and non-reducing sugars, carbohydrates (classified as gums, pectins and analogous substances), and celluloses. Some of these analyses were compared to those previously published by a Professor Heim in *El Agricultor* 1 (number 8) in 1907. D'Herelle's numbers for the mineral content of henequén fiber (mean of 0.96 percent) disagreed with Heim's (8.02 percent). In a mild foretaste of some of his later scientific conflicts, d'Herelle called such differences "absolutely incomprehensible."

Additional determinations of both specific gravity and total reducing sugars in several more juice preparations led him to conclude that the specific gravity alone was not a useful measure of the sugar content. He also continued the fermentation experiments. In a series of four small test fermentations on heat-treated juice from leaves collected during July, d'Herelle reported yields of alcohol equivalent to between 1,245 and 2,160 liters of absolute alcohol per 100,000 leaves.

In his report dated 16 August 1908 (FdH: 7), d'Herelle gave a final summary of his chemical analysis of the fiber as well as the entire leaf of the henequén plant. In addition, he noted two positive microchemical color reactions— yellow color with iodine solution and dark red with concentrated nitric acid— reactions previously thought to be specific for the fiber of the New Zealand flax plant (*Ghormium tenax*).

By this time d'Herelle was beginning to think seriously about the problems involved in adapting his work for industrial production. His report of 1 September 1908 (FdH: 7) was principally devoted to devising methods for large-scale extraction of the juice from the sisal residues. The basic problem was that the industrial press at hand left the residue too wet, resulting in unacceptably high losses of sugar. The answer seemed to be the inclusion of a second extraction of the residue with clear water and combination of this second pressing with the first extraction. Analysis of a third such extraction showed that the additional recovery of fermentable sugars was low and hence economically unsound. Based on these double extraction experiments, which gave a total yield of reducing sugars of 83 percent, d'Herelle recalculated the expected commercial production of 95 percent alcohol for 100,000 leaves to be about 2,150 liters.

Although he continued his chemical analyses of various samples throughout the next several weeks, during early September d'Herelle was moving toward a final test of his work and began to carry out large-scale fermentations and distillations. While previous analyses were on small samples of 50–100 milliliters, he now undertook fermentations of twenty-four liters of juice. While he could ferment large batches, his largest still had a capacity of six liters, so he distilled the fermented must in three-liter batches. The product was described as "dry" with good color and an agreeable taste, much superior to rum or whiskey. D'Herelle speculated that "if refined in an adequate apparatus, it would surely give an alcohol of superior qualities." Presumably, he meant for drinking. The yields were still disappointing; as analysis of the fermentation reaction showed that the sugar had disappeared and that the crude yield of alcohol was near to the theoretical limit of 61 percent of the sugar content, d'Herelle attributed the losses to his inadequate still and batch operations.

From his report on 16 September 1908 (FdH: 7) until his final published report from Mexico dated 21 December 1908 (FdH: 7), d'Herelle focused on the final phase of his project, that is, demonstration of the feasibility of its industrial application. He had worked out the small batch operation of his laboratory equipment so that he was able to handle quantities of about 100 liters at a time, and he had obtained a larger still from the Department of Agriculture. In the middle of December it was arranged that a delegation from the Yucatán Department of Agriculture would visit his experiment station and observe it in action. D'Herelle started the process on 11 December with the cutting of one thousand henequén leaves. The delegation arrived on 13 December and the processing was begun. Two successive extractions of juice were carried out in twelve separate operations (necessitated by the small capacity of the press). The result was 432 liters of juice. After addition of 225 ml of sulfuric acid, the juice was heated at $120°C$ in the fermentation apparatus to hydrolyze the oligosaccharides and polysaccharides and the selected yeast culture was added when the juice had cooled. These operations were all carried out in the presence of the delegation from the Department of Agriculture. The fermentation finished on 16 December, and on 20 December the delegation returned to observe the distillation of the must. The still was a very old device that had been repaired many times, and its function was admitted by all in attendance as quite deficient. There appeared to be obvious losses during the distillation. The product of the distillations was a total of 15.057 liters of absolute alcohol. D'Herelle accounted for known losses of 4.6 liters of alcohol, so he estimated the yield obtainable with efficient equipment to be 20.7 liters per 1,000 leaves.

This performance appeared to impress the delegation of planters and government officials: according to d'Herelle's later recollection, "The day ended with a grand dinner; during dessert the governor gave a speech: he looked to the future when the Yucatán would become the great producer of alcohol for the world, there would be wealth for the planters, and for the famous scholar who discovered the procedure, a statue in gold built on the grand Place de Mérida.

. . . [but] vanity does not figure as one of my faults. Certainly I was happy, but because I had resolved a difficult problem, that fermentations held no more secrets for me, that the first part of my program, of bacteriological initiation, was over" (*PM,* 202).

Based on the favorable report of the site visit, on 2 March 1909 the Secretary of Agriculture for Yucatán officially requested support from the Mexican government to construct a model industrial-scale installation for the production of alcohol in Mérida. As planned it would be under the direction of d'Herelle (FdH: 7, 327). Inasmuch as the minister to whom this request was addressed was also the owner of the plantation where it was to be built, the plans went ahead as expected. D'Herelle agreed to oversee the construction and installation of the new distillery, but he was already beginning to look to new challenges. He planned to go to Paris in the summer of 1909 to arrange for the necessary equipment for the new distillery. While in the planning stages, he indulged other interests: with his friend Dr. Harald Seidelin, a pathologist at the Mérida General Hospital, he studied parasites in snake blood.[21] They described an unusual filaria in boa constrictors and published a note in the *Comptes Rendus de la Société de Biologie* (FdH: 5). In addition, he helped Seidelin cope with a yellow fever outbreak in Mérida. Later, d'Herelle said of Seidelin that he was the only person in Mérida with whom he could speak on topics other than agaves and sisal residues (*PM,* 204).

At the beginning of April 1909 d'Herelle and his family departed from Mérida and sailed for Paris via New York. While in Paris he worked with the

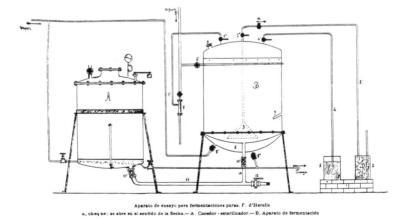

Aparato de ensayo para fermentaciones puras. F. d'Herelle
a, chequue: se abre en el sentido de la flecha.— A. Cocedor - esterilizador.— B. Aparato de fermentación

Figure 1. Diagram of distillation apparatus for production of ethanol from sisal bagasse (FdH: 15, p. 34 op.)

mechanics who were building the various pieces of apparatus he designed for the pressing, sterilization, and fermentation of the sisal juice (Figure 1). The capacity of this equipment was designed to process 6,000 liters each day and function without interruption for twenty days. At the end of the summer this equipment was shipped to Mérida. D'Herelle seemed to have a life-long instinct for keeping his work in the public eye, and while in Paris he conveniently arranged an invitation to speak to the *Société de Géographie Commerciale de Paris* on his study of agave in the Yucatán.[22]

In addition to overseeing the construction of his fermentation equipment, d'Herelle "obtained work as a free (i.e., unpaid) assistant at the Pasteur Institute" (*PM,* 206). This initial connection with the Pasteur Institute would soon lead to consequences of critical importance, not only for d'Herelle, but for his chosen field of microbiology, as well. That summer he worked on several projects: the effects of various yeast cultures on staphylococci, the further purification of the cellulose fiber from the sisal bagasse, and the examination of the Institute yeast cultures for strains active on henequén juice. In true Pastorian fashion, he kept one foot in the lab and the other on the factory floor.

D'Herelle and his family returned to Mérida in November 1909 and he went to work to set up the commercial distillery as he had planned. After many delays and much effort, the plant was finally operational in June 1910. Only the extraction of the juice still presented problems. Even so, the production in June averaged 1,200 liters of alcohol each day. D'Herelle later recalled that this initial ethanol was used to produce an anise-flavored *eau-de-vie* (*PM,* 207). Once he started to press the bagasse with a hydraulic press, the yield rose to 2,000 liters per day. By this time d'Herelle sensed that his role in the project was close to ending. Although he was offered the permanent directorship of the distillery, he declined and made plans to go to Paris and to associate himself with the Pasteur Institute. He did, however, agree to stay on until a suitable industrial chemist could be engaged to take over the operation of the distillery. This delay, however, resulted in an unexpected opportunity that would provide d'Herelle with his next challenge in his Pastorian quest.

Chapter 3 Epizootics: Locusts
in Argentina and Algeria

While he was awaiting the arrival of his replacement at Chochoh, d'Herelle turned his restless attention to another matter. At the end of August 1910 (29 August by his later recollection),

> a cloud of locusts descended on the little park near my house. My first thought was "if I would be able to find a disease of locusts." . . . Chance favored me, and what a chance! If, in retrospect, a genie of the thousand and one nights had asked me what sort of insect disease I wanted to study, I would certainly have responded: "a bacterial disease of locusts," because the locust is a destructive insect designated since the beginning of human-kind as enemy number one, and also because I hoped that governments would call me to use this disease as a means of control, which would give me an opportunity to study the phenomena governing the spread of epidemic diseases. (*PM,* 208)

D'Herelle's approach to this new problem followed the same pat-tern of his previous studies. His first step was to search for sick locusts: he asked the majordomo of the hacienda if he could find any locusts that appeared to be sick while he was out riding around the plantation. To d'Herelle's surprise and delight the man returned that evening to present d'Herelle with a match box containing three dead locusts that he had picked up that day. The majordomo assured d'Herelle that there were many more to be had if he were interested.

This account of the start of his work on the diseases of locusts is from d'Herelle's late memoirs; more contemporary sources suggest a more likely, if less colorful chronology. As early as 3 April 1908, two years before the possibly apocryphal locust hoard, d'Herelle seems to have been thinking about the locusts. Soon after they arrived in the Yucatan from Guatemala, his wife noted in her diary: "Félix wrote to [undecipherable, possibly Guérin] (coffee) and to Camara (locusts)."

In his first paper appeared on the subject, in the *Journal d'Agriculture tropicale* in August 1910, d'Herelle, in what was to become his typical style, presented a frontal assault on the existing views of the common disease of locusts. First he reviewed the state of the problem: in some infestations mortality among the locusts is so high that it is possible to scoop up the cadavers in sacks. "This malady resembles that which has been previously observed in different countries, notably the Republic of Argentina, and these epizootics [infections of animal populations] have been attributed to the fly related to the genus *Sarcophaga*." He then directly contradicted this conclusion on the basis of his observations: "I have received about fifty dead locusts, have dissected them, and have found the larva of the Muscidae, *but only in one out of fifty samples examined:* as the larva measures about four mm long, it is impossible that its presence escaped me in forty-nine cases! Furthermore, the forty-nine locusts did not have any interior or exterior lesions: thus the larvae had not escaped. I have arrived at the logical conclusion that supposing that the *Sarcophaga* to be the cause of death of one locust, the cause of death of the other forty-nine was different" (FdH: 9). D'Herelle did, however, observe that the dead locusts consistently had intestines distended with a blackish liquid packed with small bacteria, all morphologically similar. He lamented the fact that all his locust samples had been preserved in alcohol and that the locusts had disappeared from the Yucatán so that he was unable to culture the organisms, but he speculated that the true cause of the epizootic that was killing the locusts was the bacterial infection. Because there are more than thirty species of *Sarcophaga* and they are abundant in the tropics, he considered the flesh-fly maggot as just an incidental parasite, not the cause of the epizootic. He challenged his readers in Argentina to reproduce his observations and was clearly ready for the next locust plague to come his way.

This direct attack on current dogma did not go unnoticed: the journal editors sent his article to the leading authority on insect pathology, Jules Künckel d'Herculais from the Natural History Museum in Paris. Künckel d'Herculais, in a commentary on d'Herelle's note, observed that because the *Sarcophaga* larvae leave the locust several days before the insect dies and may exit at the small joints between the head and the thorax, the thorax and the abdomen, the ear cavity, or the abdominal rings, "it is therefore not surprising that M. d'Herelle was able to find locusts with no larvae and no apparent lesions." He continued, "In our opinion, the bacteria observed by M. d'Herelle will turn out to be saprophytic bacteria, in the same sense that certain mushrooms are saprophytes, which develop when the locusts are dying or are held in captivity with unfavorable nutrition."[1]

This preliminary note indicates that d'Herelle was interested in locusts earlier than he may have recalled later. This fact also supported by his next paper on locusts, published in 1911. This paper, which turned out to have a major importance to the field of insect pathology as well as beginning d'Herelle's work leading to the discovery of bacteriophage, described the next phase of his study: the isolation of the bacillus from the sick locusts and the demonstration that it is pathogenic for locusts. This work was most likely carried out in the summer of 1910 while he was casting about for projects once the sisal fermentation plant was up and running. Even as he was preparing to leave Mexico, he was looking for opportunities to study locusts. While the family was waiting in Mérida for the ship to France, his two daughters contracted yellow fever and were put under quarantine. At this time, d'Herelle was approached by a Mexican business syndicate to undertake a twofold study related to agaves: modernization of production of pulque (a fermented and distilled beverage derived from agaves) in Mexico and commercial uses for wild agave species growing in the north of Mexico. He was inclined to reject this commission until he came across a recent article in an American journal that attributed recent locust plagues in the southern states to invasions of locust hordes from across the border in northern Mexico.

Undertaking the mission to study pulque production and wild agaves gave him the opportunity and excuse to travel to the north of Mexico, where his personal aim was to look for locusts. While the work for the Mexican syndicate was apparently successful, his search for locusts was not: "From the point of view of locusts it was useless, I did not see a single one." Happily, his daughters had mild cases of yellow fever and completely recovered. They left Veracruz for Paris via New York in February 1911.

In the spring of 1911 the d'Herelle family took up residence in Paris, where

Félix "secured work as an unpaid assistant at the Pasteur Institute" (*PM,* 229). On 22 May Emile Roux, director of the Pasteur Institute, presented d'Herelle's final work on locusts in Mexico to the Academy of Sciences. D'Herelle wrote:

> The beginning of 1910 found me in Yucatán, where I observed an epizootic among the locusts (*Schistocerca pallens*). In all the dead locusts which I was sent, I noted the presence in the intestinal tube of numerous coccobacilli which I isolated. I have never found this microbe in the locusts captured in the flocks or without the presence of the epizootic, and always, to the contrary, in the dead or sick locusts, infected naturally or experimentally: often then one finds an almost pure culture in the intestines. These experiments serve to demonstrate the pathogenic role of the coccobacillus.
>
> On May 12, 24 locusts were inoculated with one drop of a 24 hour culture in bouillon. A needle was inserted between the second and third anterior ring. All died between 1 and 23 hours after injection.
>
> 24 controls were injected in the same manner with one drop of tap water: after 4 days none were dead.
>
> The same one drop of the same culture was deposited with a pipette on the mouth opening of 24 locusts: all died between 10 to 32 hours.
>
> 24 controls were again all living 10 days later.
>
> The digestive tube of all the dead locusts contained a blackish liquid or pulp of the specific microbe which was also found in the tissues. An inoculation of this material into bouillon gave in all cases an almost pure culture of the bacillus.
>
> On May 15 I placed 12 healthy locusts in individual dishes with one locust cadaver dead after ingestion of one drop of culture. Only 2 of the 12 locusts cannibalized the dead insects: one was dead after 9 hours after eating the carcass, the other was dead about 12 hours later. The 10 locusts which had not touched the cadavers were alive 10 days later. In one other experiment 5 of 10 locusts devoured the cadavers and were dead between 7 and 14 hours later. (FdH: 12)

After detailed description of the bacteriological characterization of the coccobacillus (*Coccobacillus sauterelle,* later *C. acridiorum*), and a careful study of its loss of virulence upon passage in laboratory culture and regain of pathogenicity upon repeated passage in the natural host,[2] d'Herelle concluded his paper with a proposal to move from the laboratory to the field, in true Pastorian style:[3] "It will be interesting to try to provoke these epizootics in the countries which suffer locust depredations by means of the bacillus from the Yucatán epizootic" (FdH: 12).

The promise of ending locust plagues was newsworthy enough that d'Herelle's claims were reported in the popular press. There they attracted the attention of Enrique Rodríguez Larreta, a noted man of letters as well as the Argentinian

Minister to France.[4] By the end of October 1911, d'Herelle and his family were on their way to Argentina. In an arrangement worked out with the government of Argentina, it was planned that they spend half of each year there while d'Herelle organized the battle against the locusts armed with his coccobacillus.

In 1911 Argentina was in the final phase of emerging from the shadow of the nineteenth-century political machine of the conservative followers of longtime president Julio Argentino Roca. The need for reform, especially electoral reform, was widely appreciated. The president from 1910–1914, Roque Sáenz Peña, although a representative of the old conservative order, worked for electoral reform and tried to accommodate the radicals who were continually gaining in influence. This period, from 1906 (the year of the election of Sáenz Peña's predecessor, Figueroa Alcorta) to the beginning of the war in 1914 and the first popularly elected government in Argentina, was a time of shifting patronage and political alliances. The organization of the Department of Agriculture and the campaigns against the locust hordes were, like most aspects of Argentine life, caught up in these political crosswinds. While d'Herelle came to Argentina with scientific goals, the outcome of his work there, in retrospect, is only fully comprehensible in the context of the rapidly changing political landscape as well as the scientific complexities of his project.

In the late nineteenth century the new sciences of bacteriology and tropical medicine were rapidly expanding in Latin America, partly because national governments were interested in modernization, and partly because colonial governments perceived a need to make the tropics more hospitable for newly arrived European colonists. Not only were Latin American scientists sent by their governments to Europe for training in bacteriology and tropical medicine (Oswaldo Cruz from Brazil, for example, was in Paris from 1896 to 1899), but European scientists were often invited to Latin America to assist with specific projects or to set up local scientific institutes. Félix Le Dantec from the Pasteur Institute in Paris went to Brazil in 1892 to set up an institute of bacteriology in São Paulo and later missions from the Pasteur Institute visited Brazil with the specific charge of investigating the causative agent of yellow fever.[5] In Argentina during the early twentieth century the bacteriological institute of the public health department was headed by an Austrian scientist, Rudolf Kraus.[6]

By a contemporary account, Argentina was an impressive place in 1911: "Buenos Aires is something between Paris and New York. . . . Nowhere in the world does one get a stronger impression of wealth and extravagance. . . . Every visitor is struck by the dominance of material interests and a material view of things: compared with the raking in of money and the spending of it in betting and ostentatious luxury, a passion for the development of the country's resources and the adornment of its capital stand out as aims that widen the vision and elevate the soul. A recent acute and friendly observer has said that patriotism among the Argentines amounts to a mania."7 This commentator, James Bryce, gives a vivid account of the situation in Argentina that led to d'Herelle's invitation:

> Agricultural prosperity, more general than almost anywhere else in the world, is tempered by two risks, either of which may destroy the profits of the year. One is drought. . . . The other danger is a plague of locusts. These horrible creatures come in swarms so vast as to be practically irresistible. Expedients may be used to destroy them while they are walking along the ground by digging trenches in their path, tumbling them in and burning them, but many survive these efforts, and when they get on the wing, nothing can be done to check their devastating flight. Did the swarms come every year, the land would not be worth tilling, but at present the yield of good years more than covers the losses both of droughts and locust invasions. Men talk of erecting a gigantic fence of zinc to stop the march of the creatures southward from the Gran Chaco [the northern province], for here, as in South Africa, they seem to come out of a wilderness.[8]

The resources devoted to the campaigns against the locusts probably reflected the importance of the Pampa agriculture to the economy and provided a significant opportunity for political patronage. The three major agricultural products of Argentina during this period were wheat, maize, and linseed, and the country ranked first in the export of all three in 1912. The economic progress of the nation was thus highly dependent on the continued development of the Pampas. Bryce observed, "The Pampa country has now been turned from a prairie of grass and flowers into huge fields divided by wire fences and intersected by straight roads, or rather cart tracks, marked by the line of brown dust that a drove of cattle or a vehicle raises."[9] Most of these large farms (*estancias*), which averaged six square miles in area, were owned by Argentine-born families of Spanish, English, or German origin. New immigrants from Spain and Italy made up the majority of the agricultural work force.

In response to the need to provide the large farms with protection against the locusts, a rather elaborate organization evolved: "In the Republic of Argentina there exists a special division in the Ministry of Agriculture charged with the destruction of the locusts, this is the Agricultural Defense, which is composed of more than three thousand employees. This administration has as its head the director of Agriculture, and is composed of an inspector-general, of a deputy inspector-general, of three inspectors for each zone, of first and second class inspectors, of commissioners and of deputy commissioners. In May 1913, it had no less than 200 employees" (FdH: 17, 387 n. 1). With such a substantial bureaucracy, it was not surprising that d'Herelle was entering a political thicket when he promised a quick, cheap, and sure cure for the locust problem.

In late October 1911 d'Herelle and his family arrived in Buenos Aires, a thriving city of 1.3 million people at the head of the two-hundred-mile estuary of the Río de la Plata: "Buenos Aires deserves its name, for its air is clear as well as keen, there being no large manufacturing works to pollute it with coal smoke. The streets are well kept and everything is fresh and bright."[10] While his family stayed in Buenos Aires, d'Herelle went into the central regions, between Chaco in the north and the Pampa in the south, looking for locust swarms. A new system of railways provided access to these major agricultural areas.

His first step was to grow the bacteria in a series of locusts to enhance its virulence after a long period in laboratory culture. He made specific note of the local species of locust and made a point to adapt the coccobacillus to the strain of organism against which it was to be used. When he had a bacterial strain that could kill locusts within six to eight hours, he prepared large bouillon cultures for testing on groups of 250–300 locusts contained in large cages. The cages were infected with a handful of lucerne (*Medicago sativa,* a cloverlike legume) soaked with 20 ml of the culture. Within forty-eight hours the mortality was about 50 percent, and in five days all the locusts were dead. In similar experiments he tested the effect of using infected locusts to spread the disease with similar lethal results. Control cages had only a few dead locusts, which d'Herelle attributed to the trauma of their capture and transport.

On the basis of these demonstrations, the Argentine government decided to allow infections of patches of crickets (the immature forms of the locusts) and flocks of the mature locusts that were then in the Province of Santa Fé. D'Herelle described three limited field tests between 16 and 23 January 1912 and noted that "many other infestations have given identical results" (FdH: 14). These tests were on small plots, some enclosed, between one-half hectare and thirty-five hectares in area. Although the mortality of the land-bound crickets was noted to be between 98 and 100 percent, the exact mortality of the locusts could not be determined because they flew in and out of the test area. Even so, "one finds very many dead locusts everywhere on the ground." Even d'Herelle seemed astonished by the results: "The epizootic spreads with an unprecedented rapidity; a few days after the first infections, the illness was observed in a radius of about fifty kilometers around the first district infected; the specific coccobacillus was isolated from the intestinal contents of the collected cadavers" (FdH: 14). His note, presented to the Academy of Sciences by Roux on 26 February 1912, ended with his usual bravado: "Agriculture in the tropical and sub-tropical countries finds itself henceforth an advantageous measure, without any expense, in the struggle against an insect which has always been considered as a true plague."

In a longer summary of both the anti-locust campaigns of 1912 and 1913, published later in the *Annales de l'Institut Pasteur* (FdH: 16), d'Herelle described infections at four sites in the spring of 1912. These trials were rather limited in scope and generally were carried out in one or two days: the first infection was at Escalada in Santa Fé province on 16 January 1912, with the results described above; the second infection was on 22 January at the village of Matilde, also in Santa Fé; on 3 February, two Argentine workers used a culture supplied by d'Herelle from Buenos Aires at Nogoya in the Entre Ríos region and reported that all the locusts were destroyed within three days; the fourth trial was more extensive and took place in the region of Chamical in La Rioja province, which was heavily infested with crickets. Working by himself at Chamical between 23 March and 14 April 1912, d'Herelle infected sites more or less at random along the trails and roads, knowing that he could reach only a minority of the insects in the region. Nevertheless, when six inspectors went searching for locusts eight days later, they could find none in the area of Chamical.[11]

By mid-April 1912 the locust infestation was on the wane, so d'Herelle returned to some experiments already started in July 1911 to see if the coccobacillus could be adapted to kill other insects. While still in Paris he had repeatedly infected a species of small ant and found that it seemed to be susceptible to the bacterium. On a farm near Buenos Aires in January 1912 he tested it on a local species of ant, *Selenopsis gemminata*. In a field with many dispersed ant hills, he infected eight ant hills with a few milliliters of culture each. Within ten days, six treated ant hills were empty of ants. Two months later, all the ant hills within a hundred-meter radius of the first infected hills had no ants. Beyond this distance, the ant hills appeared normal and were full of active insects. It appeared that this species of ant was sensitive to the bacterium even without adaptation to this particular host insect. When this approach was tried with another species of ant, *Atta sexdens,* no such spectacular results were observed. D'Herelle started passages of the coccobacillus in *Atta,* an important scourge in many tropical and subtropical countries, in late April and early May, after the locust tests were over. Working in Tucumán with a local entomologist, Lynch Arribalzaga, he increased the virulence of the organism in one series of experiments and was cautiously optimistic about the eventual biological control of ants as well as locusts (FdH: 16, 325–326).

With the close of the locust campaign, the d'Herelles left Argentina in mid-May 1912 and returned to Paris, where Félix again took up his unsalaried position at the Pasteur Institute. That summer he worked on a curious project: the serologic diagnosis of pregnancy. The reasons for undertaking this work are unclear from both his memoirs and the note d'Herelle later published on this work (FdH: 19). After reading of some work published by the German scientist Emil Abderhalden, d'Herelle may have reasoned that the easily triggered anaphylactic reaction in guinea pigs might be used to assay for the serological reaction between sera from pregnant women and the antibodies raised against placental antigens in sensitized (i.e., immunized) animals. Although this work apparently had little further extensions, his careful approach gives additional insight into his experimental methods: "As I have the habit to be very prudent in experimental matters, with the objective to control my first observations, I requested Latapie who was on Wassermann's service to give me sera without indicating their origins, each tube simply numbered corresponding to a list which he gave me after the experiments were done." To his surprise, this test did not seem to be specific for pregnant women, but for female sera in general. "Every serum from a male failed to provoke anaphylaxis, but all the sera from females, even for three girls between ages eight and ten, provoked an intense shock reaction" (*PM,* 271 bis). This use of a double-blind testing technique—which was unusual for the period—may suggests a level of experimental sophistication and skepticism learned, not by careful apprenticeship with brilliant mentors, but by personal experience over the years.

By October 1912, he was ready to return to Argentina for the next anti-locust campaign. That year the invasions appeared to be less serious than in the previous infestation, and the eggs of the locusts were found in only three regions: Rafaela and Reconquista (two regions of Santa Fé) and Río Cuarto, a region in Córdoba. Again, taking the opportunity to experiment with the situation presented by nature, d'Herelle had different plans for each region. In Rafaela he would infect all the columns of the crickets; near Reconquista, he would infect the crickets just as they started their final metamorphosis to adult, flying locusts; near Río Cuarto, he planned no infections to see if the epizootic from the previous year had any carryover effect from year to year.

The results of this field experiment were reported in the *Annales de l'Institut Pasteur* and strongly confirmed d'Herelle's belief in the utility of his coccobacillus to control locust plagues (Figure 2). In Rafaela, "practically, the

Figure 2. Map of campaigns against locusts in Argentina. (FdH: 17, 389)

locusts disappeared from the region"; in Reconquista, "throughout the province, the agricultural inspectors estimated the total extent of the invasion to be
about 35 hectares, that is to say, the infestation was absent"; and near Río
Cuarto, "at the beginning of November I noted the presence of coccobacilli in
the cadavers of locusts found dead near the egg-laying sites. In the bands of
young crickets hatched in November, one showed the epizootic was present; the
mortality was about 60 percent" (FdH: 17, 391).

After a meandering tour into the western and northern parts of Argentina
in early 1913, d'Herelle returned to Buenos Aires and then back to France,
seemingly confident that his coccobacillus was the answer to future locust
invasions. Indeed, encouraging results had started to come in from other
regions: cultures sent out from the Pasteur Institute to Colombia, Cyprus,

and Algeria had been used to apparently good effect against locust infestations in those countries.

Two trials in Colombia were carried out in 1913. The locust was the same species as d'Herelle had infected in Argentina, but the utility of the bacteria in the tropical climate was uncertain. In each trial, however, the locust infestations appeared to be controlled by application of the coccobacillus (FdH: 17, 392–397). In the cases of Cyprus and Algeria, however, a different locust was involved, *Stauronotus maroccanus,* but laboratory tests showed that *C. acridiorum* was pathogenic for this locust, too. Cultures from Paris arrived in Cyprus in February 1913, were adapted to *S. maroccanus,* and then were applied to field trials. Not only did the mortality range between 40 and 100 percent, but the infection appeared to spread rapidly to great distances from the original sites of inoculation (397–398).

D'Herelle became increasingly confident in the effectiveness of biological control of insect diseases and spent the summer of 1913 investigating the biology of the coccobacillus. These studies involved tests of animal pathogenicity and appeared to help him refine his ideas about "natural" disease in contrast to "artificial" diseases. He noted that insect pathogens could provoke infections in rabbits, for example, although the rabbit usually was refractory to such infections in nature (*PM,* 285). What was the meaning of studies, d'Herelle wondered, where animals had infections that occurred only under exceptional laboratory conditions? Were results of such experiments relevant to the infections of the natural host with the same organism? Were these systems not just artifacts of the laboratory? This problem of experimental pathology came to dominate d'Herelle's thinking and became a point of contention in much of his future work.

As knowledge of his work spread, he began to receive inquiries about other possible insect diseases. One serious problem was a disease of honey bees known as *loque* or hive sickness. Beekeepers in the region of Paris started to send d'Herelle samples of dead bee larvae from diseased hives. He applied the same approaches to loque as he did to the diarrhea of locusts: by examining the contents of the bodies as well as the surface bacterial flora, he concluded that previous reports that loque was caused by *Bacillus subtilis* were incorrect and resulted from contamination when the larvae were removed from the hive without aseptic precautions. Instead, he isolated a facultative anaerobic bacterium that he believed caused the disease. Because this work was still incomplete by the time d'Herelle had agreed to return to Argentina, it was suspended and never completed. Later, a fellow Pastorian, Serge Métalnikov, became famous for the study of insect diseases and applying the same approaches as d'Herelle, exploited another organism, *Bacillus thuringiensis,* as a biological insect control.

In the fall of 1913 the locust plagues in Argentina appeared to be subsiding. Whether this was a consequence of the epizootic of the previous year or natural cyclic behavior was unclear. D'Herelle firmly believed that it was because of his work during the first two campaigns. "The invasion of locusts showed itself to be insignificant, but in contrast, the animosity toward me, on the part of a majority of the Agriculture Defense and the Ministry of Agriculture was singularly pervasive. As in this country [France], it came down to a question of politics, the adversaries of the government raised the question of why a foreigner was being hired in the campaign against the locusts when the invasion had become negligible? And furthermore, it was silly to claim a cause and effect relationship between the infections made during the previous two years and the diminution of the locusts: it was simple coincidence" (*PM,* 285–287).

D'Herelle requested the reports of the government inspectors that described the effects of the infestations, only to be told that they could not be found. Next, he asked quite bluntly if the Argentine government planned to employ him and his methods; if not, he would not have reason to remain in the country. The Minister of Agriculture requested that he make one final demonstration of the efficacy of his method, and "in a spirit of reconciliation" d'Herelle accepted the challenge. Having found a small patch of crickets in the north of the Santa Fé region, he proceeded to set up the field tests. The government observers who were to judge the test never arrived, however, and an irate d'Herelle returned to Buenos Aires and delivered his ultimatum: " 'Definitively adopt my procedure or consider my mission terminated.' The answer was evasive: as I have always aimed at clear situations, I postponed my resignation so that I could communicate to the press the motives for it so as to preclude the Minister from giving any false interpretations. And [then] I embarked on the next packet boat" (*PM,* 287).

The political and scientific consequences of d'Herelle's activities in Argentina appeared to provoke at least two interesting reactions. First was a scientific review of his work and his methods in general. The Minister of Agriculture appointed a commission of Argentine microbiologists to reevaluate d'Herelle's results. This commission was headed by Rudolf Kraus, director of the bacteriological institute of the Argentine National Public Health Department; the other members were Dr. Carlos F. Maggio, a bacteriologist from Kraus's institute, Fernando Lahille, chief of the section of general zoology of the Ministry of Agriculture, and Dr. Demetrio Morales, chief of the bacteriology section of the

Argentine Entomological Institute. Clearly, if d'Herelle was right in sensing xenophobia, this commission was suspect is several ways. The commission obtained a sample of *Coccobacillus acridiorum* not from d'Herelle, but from the Pasteur Institute. By 1918, however, it was recognized that many of the strains being used in laboratories around the world as *C. acridiorum* were not identical to d'Herelle's original isolate, and the characterization of the commission's strain was not reported in their summary publication.[12] After presenting the results of d'Herelle and others which had appeared in the literature, the commission described its own field tests near Tinogasta in Catamarca and concluded that the "results are completely negative." Furthermore, they stated their belief that the coccobacillus was a normal inhabitant of the insect intestine, possibly pathogenic when injected in pure culture. For whatever reason, the coccobacillus campaign had come to an end in Argentina.

A second interesting aspect came several years later when Arturo Cancela, a well-known Argentine writer, satirized this episode of science and politics in a novella, *El coccobacilo de Herrlin*. Published in Madrid in 1923 along with two other short works under the title *Tres relatos porteños* (Three stories of Buenos Aires), the novella fictionalized d'Herelle's work to mock both science and government. D'Herelle appears as a Scandinavian microbiologist named Herrlin, who comes to Argentina at the invitation of the government to rid the country of a plague of rabbits with his pathogenic coccobacillus. Through a bizarre series of mishaps, Herrlin suffers a blow to the head and takes leave of his senses. This loss of memory goes unnoticed, however, by the government bureaucrats who are interested only in the glamor of having a famous foreign scientist in their employ. After many rounds of parties, dinners, speeches, and general hoopla, the campaign against the rabbits appears to be a success: not a single rabbit can be found. Herrlin returns home in triumph, the government takes credit for timely action and wise planning, and the people have known all the while that there were never any rabbits. D'Herelle found this little story "very humorous" and quite accurate as to the political situation (*PM*, 288).

In the spring of 1913, after his return to Paris, d'Herelle again had the opportunity to extend his field trials, this time in Algeria. The Pasteur Institute in Paris was at the center of a rapidly expanding web of overseas Pasteur Institutes (Instituts Pasteur d'Outre-Mer), most directed by former Pastorians and many overtly related to French colonial interests.[13] These institutes carried out research on local diseases of human or agricultural importance, provided sera and vaccines produced in-house or at the Pasteur Institute in Paris, and often acted as hosts for scientific missions sent from Paris to study specific problems or to help with a local epidemic. In the early twentieth century, most of the missions seemed to be "study" missions, later missions undertook vaccination campaigns and other therapeutic trials, in what Dozon called "Les grandes campagnes d'éradication."[14] D'Herelle was clearly in the vanguard of these interventionist Pastorians. Because of the close administrative and political ties to France, the francophone countries of North Africa, including Tunisia, Algeria, and Morocco, had especially well-developed Pasteur Institutes. They carried on active research and some published their own scientific journals, for example, *Archives de l'Institut Pasteur de Tunis.*

In the spring of 1914 the Pasteur Institute in Algiers invited d'Herelle to visit and participate in their attempts to use his coccobacillus against a different species of locust, *Stauronotus maroccanus.* This North African locust differs from the American locust (*Schistocerca americana*) in that it is much less migratory and less cannibalistic. For several weeks d'Herelle worked with the staff of the Pasteur Institute in Algiers to inoculate regions infested with *Stauronotus* (Figure 3). He considered this trial successful, and apparently so did the Algerian Pastorians. In 1914 they published two accounts of their studies. The laboratory investigations by Sergent and Lhéritier showed that *C. acridiorum* could be adapted by repeated passage in *S. maroccanus* to give a highly pathogenic variant.[15] With Béguet, d'Herelle carried out field trials that Béguet later reported as quite promising.[16]

After his return from Algeria in early April 1914, the Turkish government invited d'Herelle to visit Smyrna to help plan for an anti-locust campaign during the next season, the summer of 1914. Always the vagabond, d'Herelle noted that on the way to Smyrna, he stopped for tourist visits in Greece, Constantinople, and Syria. By May he had returned to Paris, only to set off again in July for a visit to Corsica to consult on applications of his locust control method there. The onset of the Great War found him in Vizzavona, on Corsica. On 29 July 1914 he returned to Paris and again joined the Pasteur Institute as an unpaid volunteer, this time in the vaccine department as part of the war effort.

Even with the battle zone nearing Paris, in the spring of 1915 d'Herelle was able to leave his work at the Pasteur Institute and go to Tunisia from 10 April until 1 August. There he worked with the Pasteur Institute in Tunis in further attempts to control invasions of locusts of the species *Schistocerca peregrina.* For three years these locusts had devastated crops in Tunisia, and to avoid famine the government had resorted to loans of cereals to the population. The country was faced with economic disaster, and the government, on the advice of Charles Nicolle, director of the Pasteur Institute in Tunis, decided to augment the

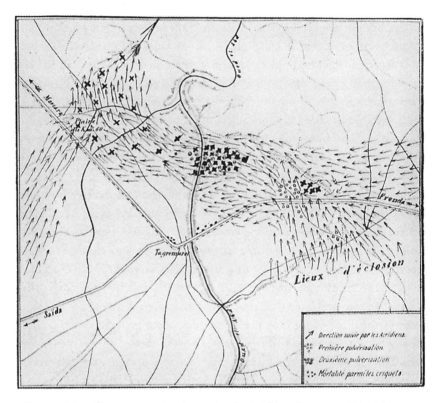

Figure 3. Map of campaign against locusts in North Africa. (Sergent and Lhéritier, 415)

attempts at mechanical control of the locusts with the biological control methods advocated by d'Herelle (FdH: 20; 21). His approach in Tunisia followed his previous pattern: select for in vivo virulence and then spray preparations of the bacteria in the path of the advancing columns of insects. In this campaign, he varied his method of application; instead of spraying liquid cultures, he used the powdered carcasses of locusts killed by laboratory infection with *Coccobacillus acridiorum*. Not only was this approach simpler, but it may have had the advantage of using the most virulent bacteria (FdH: 18).

The 1915 campaign in Tunisia was d'Herelle's last work with the coccobacillus and control of insects with epizootic infections. Not only were there conflicts surrounding the effectiveness of his method, but he soon discovered a much more exciting and potentially consequential phenomenon, the bacteriophage. Even though d'Herelle went on to other things, the controversies he started in his work on locusts and the ideas he so forcefully championed had a life of their own.

While the utility of *C. acridiorum* was hotly debated, the biological principles underlying its use had caught the imagination of the scientific community. Several scientists attributed to d'Herelle the first convincing and sustained effort at bacterial control of insect pests: in the 1930s, A. Paillot, a leading French insect pathologist, and Harvey L. Sweetman in the United States, and in the 1940s and 1950s another American, Edward Steinhaus. Although others had isolated pathogenic bacteria from insects before d'Herelle, Paillot and Steinhaus suggest that d'Herelle's results were sufficiently promising that others joined the field.[17] Serge Métalnikov in France and Rudolf Wilhelm Glaser in the United States both carried on extensive research programs based on d'Herelle's ideas. Metalnikov and his collaborators isolated numerous insect pathogens and in the late 1920s reported that a spore-forming organism, *Bacillus thuringiensis,* discovered in 1913, seemed particularly pathogenic for the corn borer and the gypsy moth, and in field trials they were able to show significant control of insect infestations. This research approach was actively pursued in the 1930s but was made seemingly obsolete by the discovery of insecticidal organic chemicals like DDT. By the late 1950s and 1960s, however, because of the increasing prevalence of pesticide-resistant insects and the concern over the environmental impact of the organic pesticides, research on biological control methods took on new interest. Since then, *B. thuringiensis* has become a major organism used in the biological control of numerous species of insects, and commercial preparations of its spores are readily available in neighborhood garden stores throughout the United States.

Steinhaus suggested that d'Herelle just had the bad luck to isolate a non-spore-forming bacterium:

> In light of the inadequate knowledge regarding host susceptibility and resistance, external conditions leading to epizootics, and principles of bacteriology at that time, it is not surprising that contradictory results and claims were made concerning the efficacy of *C. acridiorum*. Of course, this does not say that d'Herelle's successes were all that he claimed them to be. It has been shown (Glaser, 1918) that of the number of strains that existed as *Coccobacillus acridiorum,* not all were equally pathogenic, some were not even the same organisms d'Herelle claimed to have isolated, and pathogenicity was difficult to maintain on artificial media without frequent passage through susceptible locusts. Workers condemning the organism used it against locusts only distantly related to *Schistocerca* (which is cannibalistic and migratory). The case of *Coccobacillus acridiorum* was a clear example

of the great need for more basic research before the organism as a microbial agent could be adequately judged.[18]

While d'Herelle left insect pathology, he still maintained his interest in the problem of infectious diseases and their uses as biological control agents. Perhaps influenced by the needs of the war effort, he turned his attention to animal and human infections. Dysentery and other intestinal infections were a major focus of interest at the Pasteur Institute in the early years of the twentieth century, and d'Herelle decided to revisit a problem first discussed in 1900 by fellow Pastorian Jean Danysz: the possible use of dysentery organisms to control infestations of mice.[19] In a series of three related studies carried out between early 1916 and the fall of 1918, d'Herelle used Danysz's bacterium (*Salmonella typhimurium*) as a model for gastrointestinal infectious disease. The reasons he chose this animal model are not explicit in his papers, but his late memoirs described extensive field work and trials of this bacterium as a biological control for rat and mouse infestations during the winter of 1918–1919 (*PM,* 391 et seq.). This explanation is further supported by his subsequent interest in salmonella infections of chickens in 1919–1920.

While at first glance d'Herelle's research pathway appears to be haphazard and opportunistic, when examined in detail, a continuous path, albeit with changes in direction, can be discerned. His interest in locusts and their biological control can be seen to mesh with his wartime vaccine work on dysentery and the related applications of biological control of rodents. Furthermore, this approach was firmly sanctioned by the tradition of Pasteur, who had advocated the use of pathogenic organisms to control the rabbit population in Australia a generation earlier.[20] Further extension of d'Herelle's interests would soon lead to his study of epizootics involving avian typhosis and bovine epidemic hemorrhagic fever, this time with a new twist: control a bacterial pathogen by introduction of his newly discovered antibacterial agent, the bacteriophage.

Chapter 4 Bacteriophage
Discovered

In the early decades of the twentieth century, dysentery was a major research interest at the Pasteur Institute, and with the onset of World War I the urgency of this work took on even greater significance in Paris. This research program encompassed both fundamental laboratory investigations and their practical medical applications, which were carried forward in the newly established hospital of the Pasteur Institute. This hospital was devoted mainly to infectious diseases. D'Herelle's interests in gastrointestinal diseases of locusts and his work on *B. typhi murium,* the bacillus of mouse typhoid, thus fit well within this institutional program.

Between 20 July and 15 August 1915 ten mounted infantrymen in the French army along with two young civilian domestics were hospitalized with severe hemorrhagic dysentery. These patients, stationed at Maisons-Laffitte on the outskirts of Paris and only fifty miles from the stalemated French-German front, were cared for by Dr. Georges Bertillon. He was sufficiently impressed by the unusual severity of the disease in these patients to report the clinical features of this mini-epidemic in the *Annales de l'Institut Pasteur* (FdH: 22). The microbiological investigation of this outbreak at Maisons-Laffitte was assigned to Félix d'Herelle because of his interest in enteric bacteriology and extensive field experience.[1] The consequences of his investigation would bring d'Herelle worldwide fame and notoriety, raise hopes of specific antibacterial therapies, and eventually launch the "molecular revolution" in biology. In the course of studying the bacteria in fecal samples from these and subsequent dysentery patients, d'Herelle discovered an "invisible microbe antagonistic to the dysentery bacillus." This invisible microbe he named the "bacteriophage."[2] In subsequent studies in which he observed a correlation between the amount of bacteriophage in the stool samples and the stage of the disease, d'Herelle began to suspect a natural, biological role for the bacteriophages as agents contributing to the defense of the organism against bacterial infectious diseases.

Félix d'Herelle was forty-two years old at the time; he had been associated with the Pasteur Institute since 1911 and was anxious to make his mark in science. While d'Herelle enjoyed the backing of the director, Dr. Emile Roux, he received little in the way of concrete support at the Pasteur Institute. His first position was that of an assistant in the laboratory of Alessandro Taurelli Salimbeni; later d'Herelle was elevated to the position of laboratory chief. These titles seemed to convey status rather than real benefit because, even as a laboratory "chief," d'Herelle was forced, somewhat later, to work with very little space as a guest in the laboratory of his friend, the physiologist Edouard Alexandre Pozerski.[3]

The investigations at Maisons-Laffitte proved interesting, and d'Herelle seized the opportunity to demonstrate his investigative skill and bacteriological acumen to his colleagues at the Pasteur Institute. Bertillon was right in his clinical judgment: the epidemic was unusual in that the prevalent organism was not one of the expected dysentery bacilli. D'Herelle cultured the same organism from the five most serious cases and carried out the fermentation tests used for routine identification and characterization of the bacteria. These tests were inconsistent with the organism being one of the strains of the dysentery bacillus described by Shiga, Hiss, Flexner, Strong, or Gay. In confirmatory studies, polyvalent equine antisera against the Shiga and Flexner strains were tested for the ability to agglutinate (that is, cause to clump together by specifically cross-linking to bacteria to each other) the organisms, as were the sera of acute and convalescent patients. The new strain was not clumped by any of these sera except for the samples from the convalescent patients, as expected. This new isolate also was unusual in its virulence in rabbits: small doses killed rabbits within twelve hours when injected intravenously. These diagnostic tests led d'Herelle to conclude that he had identified a new, atypical dysentery bacillus, one he designated "sous le nom d'Herelle." The identification and characterization of this bacillus was published in the *Annales de l'Institut Pasteur* in March 1916, together with Bertillon's clinical report (FdH: 22).

During the next 18 months, d'Herelle continued his studies of dysentery in human beings in work he later saw as an extension of his prewar research on locust gastroenteritis. He examined filtrates of cultures of these dysentery bacilli and discovered that some of these filtrates, although free of viable bacteria, contained something that caused lysis, or dissolution, of other cultures of dysentery bacilli. During this period he devised new experimental approaches to study this antibacterial substance and elaborated theories about its nature and its role in pathogenesis of infectious diseases. This work, first published in September 1917 in the *Comptes Rendus de l'Académie des Sciences* (translation in appendix A) was entitled "Sur un microbe invisible antagoniste des bacilles dysentériques." This paper was the seed from which sprouted hopes for general antibacterial therapies on one hand, and the experimental system, *singularis,* of molecular biology, on the other. In little more than two pages d'Herelle set out, in remarkably concise form, the basic framework not only for the remainder of his career but for the entire field of twentieth-century bacteriophage research.

D'Herelle's other scientific activities at this time provide some clues to the circumstances surrounding the discovery of bacteriophage. From about 1914 d'Herelle had been involved in the effort at the Pasteur Institute to prepare bacterial vaccines for the Allied armies fighting in World War I;[4] indeed, at one point d'Herelle indicated that he was in charge of vaccine production and that his group was responsible for making more than twenty million doses of bacterial vaccines.

Bacterial vaccine therapy was, of course, a direct product of the scientific work of the Pasteur Institute. Since the time when Pasteur himself had started to make rabies vaccine the Pasteur Institute had been developing as a commercial source of biologics for the medical profession, which brought the institute fame and fortune. Roux was a strong advocate of this development as a stable source of support for the research activities of the institute, and his anti-diphtheria serum was a huge commercial success.[5] Killed bacteria or their products had been used as immunity-provoking substances in the prevention of diphtheria and anthrax as well as other bacterial diseases.[6] While many of the younger members of the Pasteur Institute and those older scientists with medical qualifications had been mobilized into the military, and the work on horse serum production had been relocated away from the front to the School of

Veterinary Medicine in Toulouse, a small group of older scientists and those who were not French stayed behind in Paris and practically lived in the laboratory where they prepared vaccines for the Allied armies. D'Herelle, as a Canadian, was in this latter group. He recalled later that the laboratory day routinely started at eight o'clock in the morning and usually ended after one o'clock the next morning (*PM*, 377–378).

Even while engaged in vaccine production and field investigations of dysentery outbreaks, d'Herelle managed to carry out some relevant investigative work. The methods for preparation of bacterial vaccines were not very reliable in 1915, and a procedure that worked for one organism might not work for another. D'Herelle decided to investigate vaccine preparation methods using a model system. With his usual acknowledgment to his patron, Dr. Roux, he decided to carry out a systematic study of a series of agents for killing a specific strain of bacteria and to assay the protective action of the resulting bacterial lysates upon injection into susceptible animals (FdH: 23).

The bacteria selected for this study was *Salmonella typhimurium* (*B. typhi murium* (Danysz)). This organism and its behavior were well known at the Pasteur Institute since Jean Danysz, its discoverer, was a member of the institute. In 1891 Roux had reported that active preparations of killed bacteria can be obtained by treatment of the bacteria with certain "essences," in particular the essence of mustard.[7] In what seems more like a lesson at the Cordon Bleu cooking school than research at the Pasteur Institute, d'Herelle proceeded to test "essences" of mustard, cinnamon (from both Ceylon and China), garlic, thyme, oregano, and cloves. In wartime Paris these materials may have been in better supply on the scale contemplated for vaccine production that were more exotic laboratory chemicals. All of these essences gave equally active vaccines, and perhaps out of deference to the precedent set by Roux in his early work, mustard was chosen as the standard treatment. The method of preparation was simple: a culture of a single bacterial type was grown on solid medium for about twenty hours. The thick layer of bacterial growth was then scraped off and the bacteria were suspended in 10 ml of physiologic saline which had been saturated with the essence in question; after three to four days the culture was sterile, that is, all the bacteria were dead. The suspension of dead bacterial bodies and their breakdown products in fresh culture medium could be used in the appropriate dilution as a protective vaccine.

Injection of these killed bacterial suspensions into mice was followed by feeding the mice cubes of bread on which were live, pathogenic bacteria. Doses of vaccine equivalent to 0.5–5 million bacteria gave immunity, whereas doses equivalent to 0.15 million bacteria did not, even when the challenge with live bacteria was reduced a hundredfold.

These experiments were carried out in late 1915 or early 1916 and were communicated to the Academy of Sciences by Roux on 3 April 1916 in a paper entitled: "Contribution à l'étude de l'immunité." They are of interest for three reasons. First, they involved investigation of methods for production of bacterial vaccines, a matter of direct relevance to the discovery of bacteriophage. Phage were found in filtered suspensions of cultures and stool samples. In this paper he specifically discusses the problem of avoiding strong denaturing conditions in order to achieve an active vaccine preparation. Mild treatments, however, might be expected not to kill all the bacteria, rendering subsequent filter sterilization necessary. The Chamberland filter, a porous earthenware device that retained bacteria, had been invented at the Pasteur Institute by Charles Edouard Chamberland and was in routine use there. It is quite reasonable to assume that as he worked on bacterial suspensions for vaccine use, d'Herelle would filter some of these suspensions in order to render them sterile, in case the "essence" treatment was incomplete. It would thus provide him the later opportunity to observe the phage in the filtered cultures of stool samples.

The second noteworthy feature of this paper is the specific choice of an animal model. In this 1916 paper, d'Herelle was already concerned about the relevance of the disease model being studied to the understanding of the pathogenic process. He believed that a pathogen should only be studied in its natural host. The first line of this paper reads: "The *Bacillus typhi murium* belonging to the paratyphoid group is *naturally pathogenic* [emphasis added] for murine species; the vaccination of the white mouse, a particularly sensitive animal, against the illness caused by this bacillus offers, then, real interest from a theoretical point of view" (FdH: 23). This emphasis on natural pathogens had become a major theme in d'Herelle's thinking even from his work on coffee blights and locust epizootics, and eventually it dominated his entire research career.

The third point to note in this paper is d'Herelle's complete acceptance of the contemporary models of immunity. His work was based on the notion that vaccination with preparations of killed organisms produced an immune status of long duration in the immunized animal. He noted that good vaccine preparations preserve the albuminoids and toxins, as well as all the properties of the living microbe, except life. Contemporary ideas of immunity held that bacterial lysis or dissolution by antibodies was the basis of induced immunity. This view derived from the experiments of the German bacteriologist Richard Pfeiffer, who showed that cholera bacteria are dissolved in the animal body (in vivo) when injected into immunized animals, and from the work of Jules Bordet, who showed that, under some conditions, these bacteria were lysed in the test tube (in vitro) by antibody and complement.[8] Thus, lysis of bacteria was central to models of immunity, and it is not surprising that d'Herelle's lytic activity from filtrates of dysentery bacilli should have been directly interpreted as relating to immune mechanisms. Unlike the constancy with which he held to his beliefs about natural pathogens, however, he soon modified his views about immunity, and in his 1923 monograph *Les défenses de l'organisme,* published a year later in English as *Immunity in Natural Infectious Disease,* declared them completely erroneous.[9]

It was in the midst of this work on wartime vaccine production and studies of experimental infection of mice with *S. typhimurium* that d'Herelle discovered his "invisible microbe, antagonistic to the dysentery bacillus." During the day he worked along with Salimbeni and Paul Jeantet to prepare vaccines; he pursued his microbiological research "during the rare moments of leisure, between two operations, or while timing sterilizations" (*PM,* 378).

In the course of the study of dysentery patients, d'Herelle made bacteria-free filtrates of the fecal samples that were then mixed with pure cultures of the dysentery organism isolated from the patients. These mixtures were inoculated into a variety of experimental animals. At the same time, portions of the mixture were spread on agar medium to observe the cultural growth of the bacteria (*BIB,* 3–4). These agar cultures exhibited the reproducible appearance of small, clear areas, initially called *taches,* then *taches vierges* and, later, *plaques.*[10]

Just why d'Herelle mixed bacterial filtrates and bacteria is explained by the contemporary findings on gastrointestinal diseases of pigs. An important agricultural problem in the late nineteenth century and the early twentieth century was epidemics of hog cholera. This rapidly fatal disease was studied by such notables as Theobald Smith, Friedrich Löffler, Elie Metchnikoff, and Louis Pasteur. Finally three diseases seem to have been described: hog cholera, swine plague, and swine erysipelas. In 1885 Daniel E. Salmon (honored in the genus name *Salmonella*) and Theobald Smith isolated and described a motile, Gram-negative bacillus (that is, one which was able to propel itself through the culture by some sort of active process, and one that failed to exhibit a characteristic deep violet color with Gram's staining method) from a number of cases of hog cholera. As they could reproduce the disease by feeding the organism, they concluded that they had isolated the hog cholera bacillus (*B. cholerae suis, B. suipestifer,* now *Salmonella cholerae suis*). Other workers, however, identified other organisms from cases of hog cholera.

What seemed most troubling was that some epidemics of hog cholera did not seem to be produced by either the hog cholera bacillus or the swine plague bacillus. In 1903, Emil A. de Schweinitz and Marion Dorset published a short report of their investigations of such outbreaks of hog cholera.[11] Their experiments showed that the disease could be transmitted not by the bacteria, but only by bacteria-free filtrates of body fluids from sick or recently dead animals. The conclusion, then, was that the bacteria were just associated with the disease rather than being the cause. De Schweinitz and Dorset suggest a cooperative interaction: "In *all* outbreaks of *acute* hog cholera there is some other agent besides the hog cholera bacillus at work, and that in those cases of acute disease where the hog cholera bacillus is found we have to do, not with a pure infection, but with a mixed infection by hog cholera bacilli and the organisms which are responsible for the disease we have just described."[12]

D'Herelle noted his debt to this early work on intestinal diseases in his monograph *Immunity in Natural Infectious Disease* (FdH: 73). He noted the general acceptance of the work of Salmon and Smith: "What more in the way of proof could be asked for? The famous trinity of experimentation [i.e., Koch's postulates] was accomplished, and with some to spare." He goes on:

> The work of de Schweinitz and Dorset can hardly be too greatly admired, and to my mind, form the point of view of its importance should be placed immediately after that of Pasteur and Koch. It has demolished the beautiful edifice of the etiology of hog cholera. They have shown that *B. suipestifer* is only an "associated" bacterium, according to the happy expression of Nicolle. The true pathogenic agent is a filterable virus. *B. suipestifer* multiplies in swine only through the favor of the infection caused by the filterable virus. (*INID,* 316–17)

In his monograph of 1926, *The Bacteriophage and Its Behavior,* he described the relevance of this work to his own thinking when he noted the cultural irregularities in his studies of *C. sauterelle:*

> These cultural irregularities were sufficiently pronounced to arouse my curiosity, and to explain them, and the phenomenon leading to their production, an hypothesis was advanced, one which proved to be entirely false.
>
> In accord with this hypothesis it seemed that the coccobacillus could only be an "associated" organism, the true pathologic agent necessarily being an ultramicroscopic organism, which, occasionally reaching the agar, inhibited the growth of the

associated bacterium. This hypothesis appeared the more natural in view of the admirable work of de Schweinitz and Dorset on hog cholera, but after having demonstrated that the filtrate by itself contained nothing virulent for the locust the hypothesis was modified in accordance with the concept that the disease required two agents, visible and invisible, be simultaneously present. (*BIB*, 3)[13]

These early observations of cultural abnormalities, however, were not mentioned in any form in his papers on the subject of bacteriophage in 1917, 1918, or 1919, nor in his monographs of 1921. Yet, in these publications d'Herelle was careful to describe the rationale and prior observations of others that presaged his discovery. By 1923, he added the work on hog cholera to his rationale, and by 1926 he included the early observations on *C. sauterelle*.[14] The frequent appearance of clear areas in solid medium cultures of *C. sauterelle* and failures of mixed cultures to grow that led him to try to extrapolate this procedure to the study of human enteritis, or dysentery. His 1948 account suggests that he had carried out this sort of experiment with samples from the 1915 Maisons-Laffitte epidemic but that the results were similar to those in the early studies of locusts: the samples were routinely studied at the height of the disease process and the results were irreproducible. He gives us his only glimpse of his shift in viewpoint in his 1926 book:

> It is true that this procedure occasionally revealed cultural irregularities, but the phenomenon was very inconstant and the fact prevented a solution of the question. One day, in re-examining my experimental data my attention was attracted to the fact that when such cultural irregularities appeared it was never at the beginning of the disease but always when filtrates were used which were prepared from fecal material collected during convalescence. I then resolved, and logically this is where I should have commenced, to examine the fecal discharges of individual patients systematically, from the onset of the disease up to the time when convalescence was established. (*BIB*, 3)

His first paper to describe bacteriophage, "Sur un microbe invisible antagoniste des bacilles dysentériques" (Phage I, FdH: 25; see appendix A), was presented at the meeting of the Academy on 3 September 1917 by Roux but appeared in the reports of the meeting of 10 September. Although this discordance of dates was not uncommon, it raises the question of whether the paper was actually presented to the weekly meeting of the Academy. It may have been submitted only for publication in the proceedings. This two-page note describes isolation of the invisible microbe from the stool samples of patients with bacillary dysentery.

Table 1. Chronology of First Bacteriophage Publications

10 Sept. 1917	First description of bacteriophage	FdH: 25. Acad. Sci. Paris
7 Dec. 1918	Technique paper; plaque method	FdH: 29. Soc. Biol. Paris
9 Dec. 1918	Role of phage in dysentery	FdH: 28. Acad. Sci. Paris
24 Mar. 1919	Role of phage in typhoid	FdH: 30. Acad. Sci. Paris
10 Nov. 1919	Role of phage in avian typhosis	FdH: 31. Acad. Sci. Paris

The microbe (a general term favored by Pasteur and his school) was isolated as active against the Shiga strain of *B. dysenteriae* (*Shigella dysenteriae*) but was tested against the Hiss and Flexner strains to study the specificity of action. Because the Shiga strain was the pathogen in the patients studied, it is unlikely that the bacteriophage was first isolated from the cavalry dragoons who were sick in August 1915 with atypical dysentery (strain "d'Herelle") and described by d'Herelle and Bertillon in 1916.[15]

Given later disputes over priority of discovery (see chapter 5) and more recent innuendos of possible misrepresentations as to the timing of d'Herelle's first work on phage,[16] it is relevant to read these first phage papers with attention to the exact timing of d'Herelle's observations (Table 1). From experiments described in the first two papers on bacteriophage, it is possible to determine, approximately, the date of the first isolation and propagation of bacteriophage. These estimates are consistent with his later accounts of the discovery of bacteriophage given in 1925.[17] The original 1917 paper describes d'Herelle's technique for passage of the microbe: a few drops of a lysate (either filtered through a Chamberland filter or unfiltered) are added to a fresh culture of Shiga bacteria, and in a few hours to a few days the culture clears; a few drops of this cleared culture will reproduce the lysis of yet another fresh culture (FdH: 25). In his paper of 1918 on "Technique de la recherche du microbe filtrant bacteriophage (*Bacteriophagum intestinale*)" (Phage II; FdH: 29), d'Herelle described his methods for isolation and propagation of bacteriophage. Here he indicated that he made daily passages of the lytic principle. The 1917 paper, dated 3 September 1917, stated that he had carried out fifty passages of the original isolate. If an average passage required one day, the latest possible date for the original isolate would be about late June 1917 (presuming it would take a week or two to write up results and schedule the paper for presentation to the Academy of Sciences). In his 1918 "Technique" paper, however, he stated that he made 935 daily passages of the first isolate. This paper is dated 7 December 1918, so the first isolation of bacteriophage might have been made as early as late April or early May 1916. In 1926 d'Herelle stated that he made his first isolate of bacteriophage in August 1916, a date entirely compatible with the range of May 1916–June 1917 based on his early statements, if some of the passages were made more frequently than once a day.

D'Herelle's paper of 1917 is remarkable for its clarity, conciseness, and self-confidence. In one straightforward paragraph he gave the detailed method to isolate bacteriophage, beginning "The isolation of the anti-Shiga microbe is simple." In the next paragraph he described the serial propagation of the microbe (inoculation of one culture with a tiny droplet, followed by growth and lysis, then inoculation of a second fresh culture with a tiny droplet from the first culture, and so on) and the plaque assay, which allowed enumeration of the microbes (mixing known, quantitative dilutions of the lysate with bacteria spread on culture plates gave countable numbers of plaques which allowed calculation of the number of phage in the original undiluted sample). In addition, he directly stated the crux of the problem—that the formation of plaques was inconsistent with the action of an enzyme (*ferment*), and demonstrated, instead, the particulate nature of the anti-Shiga agent.

The specificity of the bacteriophage was indicated by its activity against the Shiga strain and not against the Hiss and Flexner strains. However, some sort of adaptation to these strains was effected by serial propagation on them. Bacteria were needed to sustain the propagation of the bacteriophage, that is, they were obligatory for its growth. In his words, the anti-dysentery microbe is an "obligate bacteriophage."

As reported in d'Herelle's first paper, the isolation of bacteriophage from dysentery convalescents with residual enteritis was easy, but phage were not found in healthy individuals or in patients in the active phase of the disease. Although no serial studies on a single patient were mentioned in this paper, the correlation between recovery and the appearance of bacteriophage was emphasized. In a preview of his future work, and possibly in recognition of the importance of his discovery, d'Herelle wrote: "Ce microbe, *véritable microbe d'immunité* [emphasis added], est un bactériophage obligatoire; son parasitisme est strictement spécifique, mais s'il est limité à une espèce à un moment donné, il peut s'exercer tour à tour sur divers germes par accoutumance" (FdH: 25). From these basic microbiologic studies d'Herelle went on to animal models and then human diseases. While the bacteriophage-containing lysates were nonpathogenic for rabbits, he stated that lysates of phage-killed Shiga bacilli immunized rabbits against a dose of live bacteria that normally would kill a rabbit in five days.[18] These experiments exactly paralleled d'Herelle's work on bacteriotherapy with lysates made by essence of mustard. Indeed, he was still working on these vaccine experiments at this time and published some of these results in 1918 (FdH: 27).

Interestingly, this work on bacteriotherapy employed only the mustard-killed lysates, not any phage-lysates as bacterial vaccines. D'Herelle certainly thought of his experiments with phage lysates not as conventional bacterial vaccines, but as cultures of active anti-bacterial agents, in the nature of an endogenous epizootic infection. The possible use of phage lysates as vaccines, however, was being investigated by Tamezo Kabeshima, a recent visitor at the Pasteur Institute from Shiga's laboratory in Japan. Kabeshima, apparently d'Herelle's first collaborator on his phage, investigated the use of phage lysates as vaccines and published the results in 1919. In this paper Kabeshima said his work was "inspired by the work of d'Herelle" and noted that using lysates produced by the action of bacteriophage "he [d'Herelle] is able to achieve, with a little of this product [*bactériolysat*], immunization of small laboratory animals."[19] Kabeshima incorrectly cited d'Herelle's 1918 paper on the role of bacteriophage in dysentery as the reference for this result, and must have been referring to the "immunization" of rabbits against dysentery as mentioned in d'Herelle's first paper on bacteriophage in 1917.

While pursuing his study of the newly discovered bacteriophage, d'Herelle continued his work on vaccinotherapy and on murine typhoid. On 26 October 1918 he reported on a series of experiments spanning January and December 1917 (FdH: 27). This paper emphasized d'Herelle's interests involving immunity in species naturally subject to the disease in question, and he suggested *B. typhi murium* as a model for human infections by organisms of the paratyphi group. He added as another rationale for these studies the possible use of *B. typhi murium* as a biological control against infestations of mice. In this series of experiments, d'Herelle, again using mustard-treated bacteria as his vaccine, investigated the protection against the lethal effects of ingestion of *B. typhi murium* by injection of the killed bacteria at different times after the lethal dose of the live organism. The results of three experiments with thirty-two mice showed that optimal protection was obtained when the vaccine was administered eighteen to forty-eight hours after infection.

While he was completing his work on mouse typhoid during 1917 and 1918, d'Herelle's work on phage took two directions. First, he investigated some basic properties of the bacteriophage and perfected the plaque assay. In addition, in a short communication (Phage II; FdH: 29) he presented the first clear statements about the nature of phage and their quantitative assay. In this short paper d'Herelle made six key points:

1. The disappearance of bacteria correlated with the increase in the number of phages.
2. Filtration with various collodion membranes suggested that the microbe is about the same diameter as the albumin molecule.
3. The "principal property" is that the microbe is "an obligatory bacteriophage."
4. As to its structure and mode of reproduction, one can only propose hypotheses.
5. The microbe should be classified in a new genus, *Bacteriophagum*, e.g., *B. intestinale*.
6. Some of his original techniques were unsuitable to study all phases of the disease (dysentery), so modifications were proposed; "strong" or concentrated phage can be assayed by lysis of liquid cultures, but less abundant or less virulent phage can be best detected by the appearance of plaques on solid cultures on agar slants.

This last point signals a recurrent theme throughout d'Herelle's work on phage: the emphasis on the correct application of careful experimental technique. D'Herelle was concerned that even he found some of his results to be variable or irreproducible, and he set out to modify and improve his experimental techniques to overcome these difficulties. For example, in this paper he noted that his reliance on the liquid culture lysis assay was the reason he failed to find phages in all phases of dysenteric disease.

In this 1918 paper, he also introduced the term *taches* (spot) or "taches parfaitement circulaires" to describe phage plaques. Contrary to several standard histories, including d'Herelle's later recollections, he did not use the term *taches vierges* (virginal, blank spots) in the early papers on bacteriophages.

Having established a more sensitive and reproducible assay, d'Herelle was in a position to extend his original observations (Phage I) on patients with bacillary dysentery, and his next three papers (Phage III, IV, V) all dealt with his second preoccupation: the role of bacteriophages in the pathogenesis of gastrointestinal infections. In December 1918, the same month as he presented his work on phage techniques to the Society of Biology, he reported to the Academy of Sciences on his analysis of bacteriophages in thirty-four cases of bacillary dysentery. While in his first paper (Phage I) he suggested that the *appearance* of bacteriophages coincided with recovery, in this 1918 work (Phage III) his modified techniques, including plaque assays, enabled him to quantify the amount of phage present on a daily basis from the onset of illness to the end of convalescence. In this way he was able "to study in a more complete manner the mode of action of bacteriophage, and its precise role in the evolution of the illness" (FdH: 28). These quantitative studies, depicted in chart form in his later monographs, suggested to d'Herelle that the outcome of the illness was determined by a contest (*lutte*) between the pathogenic agent and the bacteriophage, "agent d'immunité."

The plaque assay allowed d'Herelle to make the important observation that phages active against *B. coli* (*Escherichia coli*) could be found in normal stool samples. This finding provided the key to the full development of his theory that these normal endogenous phages adapted themselves to become more virulent against the pathogenic invading organisms as the disease progressed. This somewhat Lamarckian change in phage specificity suggested that "immunity" was at once endogenous and extrinsic. He developed this theme more fully in his monograph of 1924, *Immunity in Natural Infectious Disease.*

The three-page note to the Academy of Sciences (Phage III), without data, was the prototype for many of d'Herelle's papers on his phage work. In these notes he summarized his results and stated his conclusions, always in clear and unambiguous terms. Experimental and clinical details, save for such essentials as the number of patients studied, were not included. These details were presented, however, often in florid completeness, in his monographs on bacteriophages. Although he did not indicate in the monographs which cases contributed to his preliminary reports to the Society of Biology and Academy of Sciences, it is possible on the basis of dates and other details to assign a some of these cases to specific reports.

By March 1919, d'Herelle had collected similar data on a group of twenty-eight patients with typhoid fever. His report (Phage IV; FdH: 30) to the Academy of Sciences followed the outlines of Phage III (FdH: 28). In addition to his conclusions, again, that the appearance of phages coincided with the recovery of the patient, this paper is noteworthy for three advances in d'Herelle's thinking about phages. He considered, for the first time, the problem of virulence of bacteriophages, the problem of host-range, and the relevance of an animal model to a human disease.

The biological nature of bacteriophage, its mode of action, and its interactions with the bacterial cell were issues he had dealt with to his satisfaction in his initial publication (Phage I; FdH: 25) and in his paper on the techniques of working with bacteriophage (Phage II; FdH: 29). He would return to these issues later, rather grudgingly, in his controversies with Frederick W. Twort and André Gratia over the nature of phage and its similarity to the agent discovered previously by Twort.

Chapter 5 Reaction and Controversy

When d'Herelle's first paper on phage was published in *Comptes Rendus de l'Académie des Sciences* in the fall of 1917, it was quickly abstracted in the French medical weekly, *La Presse Médicale.*[1] With the German army's increasing build-up on the Western Front, and with General Philippe Pétain's defensive posture for the French forces, however, activities at the Pasteur Institute in Paris were far from routine. The younger scientists had been mobilized, some of the departments had been relocated farther from the front, and the Institute responded to the needs of the Allied armies for vaccines. Before antibiotics, the only measures to be used against the horrors of wound infections were antisepsis, serotherapy, and vaccinotherapy, and the business of the Pasteur Institute was sera and vaccines.

Eugène Wollman, later to become a major phage researcher, was typical of the young French physician-scientists at the Pasteur Institute. He was thirty-one years old when he was mobilized and assigned as a regimental physician to a force of Senegalese troops sent to Salonika, Greece. Even at war, however, the research interests of these young Pastorians managed to surface now and then. Wollman noted the group immunity of his troops to influenza after most were exposed to a mild form of the disease.

Other centers of French science were even more disrupted. Microbiological research institutes both in France and in other countries had developed in association with the Pasteur Institute in Paris. Although they were named for Pasteur and had informal and formal links to the Pasteur Institute in Paris, they were, for the most part, independent, free-standing research organizations. These "affiliated" Pasteur Institutes in Lille and Belgium were under enemy control. Brussels had been in German hands since August 1914, the beginning of the war, and since then research work at the Pasteur Institute there all but ceased. Its director, Jules Bordet, was able to carry on some scholarly work and wrote his highly regarded work on immunology, *Traité de l'immunité dans les maladies infectieuses,* which was published after the war in 1919.

The key French scientific and medical publications were able to maintain a relatively normal schedule, but delivery to the occupied regions was problematic. These journals arrived in the United States, however, in a timely fashion throughout the war. Still, some German journals were held by the publishers for shipment abroad after the end of the war.

In light of the difficulties in scientific work and communications at the time, it is not surprising that the earliest scientists to take an interest in d'Herelle's reports were those closest to him geographically. Eight of his colleagues at the Pasteur Institute in Paris published eleven papers on bacteriophage in 1920, a rather intense level of interest considering that the Institute was in the process of recovering from the disruption of the war, the mobilized staff was just returning, and the nation was still suffering the effects of occupation. These eleven works, together with two by Bordet and Ciuca from the Brussels Pasteur Institute, six by d'Herelle, and papers by Twort in England and Puntoni in Italy brought to twenty-one the number of papers published on bacteriophage in 1920. This first wave of reaction to d'Herelle's initial reports on bacteriophage provides some insight into the way his contemporaries viewed his discovery.

The first publication to extend d'Herelle's own studies of bacteriophage was by Tamezo Kabeshima and appeared in December 1919. Kabeshima was an experienced microbiologist, trained in Kitasato's institute in Japan. He visited the Pasteur Institute during the two years, 1919–1920, and his interests in epidemic infectious diseases, immunity, and vaccine therapy fitted in well with the goals of the Institute.

Kabeshima's interest in preventative vaccinations and production of antitoxic sera for dysentery, a natural extension of his previous work in Japan on cholera and typhoid epidemics, led him to work in collaboration with d'Herelle.[2] In his first publication describing his work at the Pasteur Institute at the end of 1919, Kabeshima observed that it was very difficult to prepare antiserum against the Shiga dysentery bacillus in small laboratory animals, such as the rabbit, because the infections were so rapidly lethal. He noted that the recent results of d'Herelle might allow him to use bacteriophage to protect the animals from the lethal effects of the Shiga bacillus infections.

It is clear that he started his research by taking d'Herelle's results at face value and that he intended to apply them to his own work in a different way. Kabeshima seemed interested in phage only to the extent that phage treatment allowed his rabbits to survive a normally lethal infection and to make antisera. These antisera would be used both for agglutination studies (i.e., to identify a specific strain of dysentery organism) and for passive immunizations with hyperimmune serum.

In the course of this work, which was reported by Roux to the Academy of Sciences on 1 December 1919, Kabeshima apparently had formed some of his own ideas about the nature of phage, but he deferred presenting them to a future paper in a "promissory note" in this publication: "Inspired by the work of M. d'Herelle, I offer up the research on preventive vaccination against the Shiga bacillus in rabbits. However, the nature of the 'microbe bacteriophage' of d'Herelle is not considered in this note."[3] Indeed, Kabeshima found that d'Herelle's bacteriophage worked just as he said it would; the rabbits were protected from the lethal toxicity of the Shiga injections. Following up on these observations, Kabeshima reasoned that the bacteria in the chronic carrier states observed in some enteric infections might also be attacked by the bacteriophage. Five weeks later, on 5 January 1920, he presented a report to the Academy suggesting the feasibility of curing carrier states with phage.[4]

On 28 February 1920, Kabeshima's paper on "the nature of the so-called 'filterable bacteriophage microbe' of d'Herelle" was presented to the Society of Biology. In this paper he argued that the action of the bacteriophage "resembles, very much, that of an enzyme [*ferment*]: an extremely small quantity suffices to dissolve in a very short time a relatively large quantity of bacteria; this fact can be considered as a phenomenon of digestion."[5] He also observed that the bacteriophage was stable at room temperature without any change for at least four years, was stable upon heating to 70°C, and thus had the physical properties of an enzyme, not a living organism. The resistance of the bacteriophage to precipitation with acetone or with alcohol, and to extraction with ether, all suggested that it was akin to known enzymes rather than to known microorganisms. Kabeshima concluded: "In these conditions, one must conclude that the bacteriophage is not a living being, and that the evidence to the contrary is surprising; in summation, it is nothing but a sort of catalyzer."[6] He suggested that this catalyzer induced the bacteria to produce autolytic enzymes which, in turn, catalyze the next generation of bacteria. In this way he tried to account for the increase in amount of lytic agent with time and in the serial transmission experiments of d'Herelle. Kabeshima even added a corrigendum in a footnote to this paper to say that "the expression 'the microbe or principle of d'Herelle' employed in my previous reports should read thus: 'solution of bacteriolytic immune enzyme.'"

During this period (late 1919 to February 1920) d'Herelle was often traveling widely in rural France, already carrying out his field studies on phage therapy and prophylaxis of avian typhosis (see chapter 8).[7] Even though he was away from the Pasteur Institute much of this time, it was strange that he and Kabeshima apparently had no private discussions of their scientific differences. As one of d'Herelle's few colleagues at the Pasteur Institute who had taken up phage work, Kabeshima might have made his ideas known to d'Herelle prior to public presentation of his paper on 28 February 1920. Circumstantial evidence and a close reading of this paper, along with d'Herelle's hasty response of 6 March 1920, suggests otherwise, however. Either Kabeshima did not think this matter was important, as he gave publication priority to his paper on typhoid carrier states, presented on 2 January 1920, or he may have wanted to wait until d'Herelle was away from Paris for an extended period before presenting his objections.

Although Kabeshima had signaled in his 1 December 1919 paper that he had his own ideas on the nature of phage, he put off presenting them for three months. D'Herelle was scheduled to leave from Marseille on 6 March 1920 for a year's sojourn in Indochina.[8] In haste to reply to Kabeshima, d'Herelle dashed off a note which either deliberately, or because of lack of discussion with Kabeshima, failed to respond as clearly or as forcefully as he might have to the points raised by Kabeshima.

In his detailed analysis of the controversy over the nature of bacteriophage, Alan Varley has convincingly traced the origins of this protracted battle to these first exchanges between d'Herelle and Kabeshima.[9] Two pathways of research appear to diverge at this point. One has as its goal the understanding of the biological origin and the nature of the bacteriophage, and the other has as its goal the applications of bacteriophage in clinical and epidemiological studies of disease. These two paths were not unrelated, of course, and d'Herelle maintained an active and dominant position in both of them.

In 1920 phage research began to expand beyond a few marginal investigators at the Pasteur Institute.[10] In 1919, there had been four papers and one medical thesis published on phage, whereas in 1920 there were twenty-one papers on phage, and in 1921 seventy-three papers are known (Figure 4). In 1920 another school of phage research began to develop outside the small group in Paris when Jules Bordet, director of the Pasteur Institute in Brussels and a Nobel Prize winner in 1919 (for the theory of serological reactions), became interested in bacteriophage. As several authors have pointed out, Bordet's attention to phage is easy to explain: for a world authority on immune mechanisms in infectious disease, d'Herelle's claim in his first phage paper that "bacteriophage is the true agent of natural immunity" was at once a major challenge as well as an opportunity.[11]

Bordet apparently sent his colleague Mihai Ciuca from Brussels to Paris to obtain some cultures of *Bacillus coli* from d'Herelle.[12] This visit was most likely between March and September 1920, because d'Herelle noted that it occurred while he was in Indochina (*PM*, 497), and the first communication by Bordet and Ciuca was in October 1920. Bordet and Ciuca used this culture to study host immunity to infections using Pfeiffer's classical approach: they injected the culture into the abdominal cavity of a guinea pig and then examined the intraperitoneal exudate (that is, the fluid secreted into the abdominal cavity in response to the infection) for antibacterial activity.[13] Not only did they find lytic activity against the *B. coli* used to inoculate the guinea pig, but this lytic activity behaved exactly as d'Herelle claimed it did: it was serially transmissible.

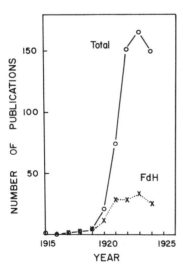

Figure 4. Growth in publications on the subject of bacteriophage for the 10 years immediately after the first paper in 1915 by Twort. The substantial contribution by d'Herelle to the total scientific literature on phage is shown by the dashed line.

In a second set of experiments, they examined so-called secondary cultures that grew up after the initial bacteriolysis had run its course. Bacterial colonies grown on agar plates from such cultures were morphologically changed, were more virulent for animals, and, most important, produced the lytic principle even when no longer in contact with the original material from the peritoneal exudate.

Bordet and Ciuca viewed their results in the context of Bordet's immunological theories. If d'Herelle had indeed found something related to immunity, Bordet tried to fit it into the known paradigms he had developed over his entire career. In Bordet's scheme, two components, a heat-stable sensitizer (i.e., antibody) and a heat-labile alexin (i.e., complement), are present in peritoneal fluid from inoculated animals. As first Pfeiffer and then Bordet had shown several decades earlier, the combined action of these two agents could cause the lysis of bacteria. Thus, d'Herelle's findings fit well into Bordet's scheme with the peculiar anomaly of the serial transmissibility of the lytic action. Bordet may have viewed his results as a fundamentally different discovery from d'Herelle's, but, as Alan Varley has argued,[14] it seems more likely that Bordet saw d'Herelle's phenomenon as an integral part of his own scheme; first, because the lytic principle was found in the peritoneal exudate, and second, because the principle was heat-stable, as were the sensitizer substances.

Bordet and Ciuca presented their first report as two back-to-back papers at a meeting of the Brussels affiliate of the Society of Biology on 20 October 1920.[15] The first paper described the experimental findings and the second paper gave their interpretation of the phenomenon of transmissible bacterial lysis. It was this second paper that was in direct conflict with d'Herelle's ideas and which initiated more than a decade of controversy.

Bordet's interpretation focused on two experimental observations: that the lytic activity appeared upon interaction of the bacteria with the infected host animal, and that thereafter, the bacterial colonies, even when isolated on agar plates, retained the property of giving rise to the lytic activity on serial cultures. Bordet termed these bacteria "lysogenic." The lytic activity was believed to be of bacterial origin, and its production was in some way provoked by an immune reaction in the infected animal. Thus, the bacteria, once exposed to the host immune system in the peritoneal space, were activated to produce the lytic agent. Once activated in this way, they could be subcultured and still produce the material. Further, to explain the transmissibility of the activity by cell-free filtrates, Bordet argued that the lytic agent provoked its own synthesis from susceptible bacterial strains. Bordet's model can be grouped with that of Kabeshima, as a "bacterial origin viewpoint"[16] or "endogenous theory,"[17] as opposed to d'Herelle's ultravirus viewpoint or "exogenous theory." Bordet and Ciuca proposed that the lytic principle arose when the peritoneal exudate (which contained white blood cells), through a "hereditary nutritive vitiation" of the bacteria, caused the bacteria to produce a bacteriolytic enzyme.[18] By this interpretation, physiological immune reactions of the animal altered the bacterial nutrition in such a way as to activate ("vitiate") the production of the lysin. This activation then became a stable, heritable property of the bacterial cell. Heritability was needed to account for the lysogenic strains observed in the secondary cultures.

As Van Helvoort has shown, Bordet approached d'Herelle's phenomenon from a physiological standpoint, in contrast to d'Herelle's bacteriological mode of thinking.[19] Bordet's interpretation was a challenge to d'Herelle in two ways. First, it subsumed bacteriophage into the conventional framework of endogenous immune reactions, and second, in doing so, it denied d'Herelle's claim to a major new discovery in bacteriology.

The two papers by Bordet and Ciuca were published while d'Herelle was still in Indochina carrying out his field work on bovine hemorrhagic septicemia (*barbone*). He returned to Paris sometime in December 1920 or January 1921 to find that he had no laboratory in which to work.[20] The next six months were especially difficult for d'Herelle. Not only was he involved in the defense of his ideas about phage; he was also embroiled in a confrontation with Calmette, the newly appointed deputy director of the Pasteur Institute. As he later recalled the situation:

> The reception which I had at the Pasteur Institute was very different than I had a right to expect. An occurrence took place in my absence: Calmette, who had been director of the Pasteur Institute in Lille, was designated deputy director of the Institute in Paris. Of him I will say nothing: he was my declared enemy, he pursued me with his enmity for the rest of his life; something I said about him enabled me to inspire this resentment. But I had the right, the duty, to put forth a judgement on his scientific work, and it is precisely this judgement of his scientific work which earned his wrath. Before I left for Indochina, there was talk of the famous BCG [*Bacillus Calmette-Guérin*] and the project of Calmette to use it to vaccinate children against tuberculosis. In the course of conversation with colleagues, I had said that I thought that the attenuated, but living bacteria which constituted BCG did not maintain their weakened state in the young organism, but recovered, little-by-little, their virulence, and did not prevent the formation of lesions by the time the child reached the critical age for tuberculosis, adolescence. . . .

I know, from Calmette himself, that my evaluation was repeated to him. Upon our first interview after my return from Indochina, he asked if it was true that I considered BCG as dangerous: I replied that was correct, I offered to give him my arguments, he refused all discussion.

Previously, he was very well-disposed toward me: in a talk which he gave in Strasbourg in 1920, he had even compared my work with that of Pasteur; but beginning at that moment, he swore toward me an implacable hatred. . . .

Roux, a weak character, had been subjugated by Calmette: he had finally accepted BCG which Calmette had imposed; it had been the subject of violent discussions whose echoes we heard, but Roux finally gave in. As my laboratory had been given to another during my absence, I requested Roux to assign me another; he responded that none were available at that moment, and that, besides, this was now Calmette's responsibility.

My salary as a laboratory chief was continued anyway, Calmette was not so bold as to monitor the gate, but he well knew that I was not late in coming to work: I have always been very persistent.

In spite of it all, I continued to work. A friend, Pozerski, had given me the use of a corner of a table in his minuscule laboratory. (*PM*, 485)

At this time d'Herelle started to work part-time in the mornings with Edouard Peyre at the Laboratory for Cancer in Villejuif, a suburb of Paris, under the leadership of Professor Gustave Roussy. This work on the relationship between cancer and infectious agents would, however, not be published for six years (FdH: 92; FdH: 93). During the spring of 1921 d'Herelle was also writing his first monograph on bacteriophage.

Upon returning from Indochina, d'Herelle published two short notes in February 1921. One seems to have been written to respond to the claim of his Institute colleague, Alessandro Salimbeni, who reported that bacteriophage preparations contained a slime-producing amoeba (myxamoeba or perhaps a slime mold, *Myxomycetes*) that was able to attack the bacteria and that accounted for the bacteriolysis (FdH: 29). In this note, d'Herelle described observations on phage preparations made with the ultramicroscope, a device that used scattered rather than transmitted light to observe very small objects. Not only did d'Herelle report that there were no amoebae in his preparations, but he described the morphological changes he observed during the course of infection and lysis by the bacteriophage. After adding phage to the bacteria, he first noted the increase in the number of bright microscopic "points" in the interior of the bacterial cell. After a while, when there are a great number of points, the bacterium becomes spherical; finally when the culture is totally lysed, the points are dispersed throughout the medium.

The second note described in some detail his analysis of the phenomenon of secondary cultures, that is, the growth of bacteria in a phage-lysed culture (FdH: 43). In particular, he investigated the origin of the bacteria which grew in the secondary cultures. His first thought was that they were derived from the bacteriophages. This notion was certainly reasonable, given his view that phage were microbes that could multiply and grow at the expense of the bacteria that were attacked. As he was unable to decide the issue on morphological grounds, he tested the biological and immunological properties of these secondary cultures. By the criteria of virulence for animals, specific serological agglutinations, and animal vaccination studies, d'Herelle concluded that these secondary cultures were survivors of the original Shiga dysentery culture. In becoming resistant to phage, they had acquired some new properties, but retained their identity as Shiga bacilli. "In the secondary cultures, one observes abnormal forms which represent forms of degeneration or resistance of the bacteria and result in an adaptation to the parasitism by the bacteriophage" (FdH: 43, 386). While he noted that the isolated colonies often produce filterable phage, he did not emphasize the point in this report.

Having described these two studies on some basic phenomena of bacteriophage biology, on 19 March 1921 d'Herelle published a brief summary of his work on *barbone* in Indochina, along with an account of his three clinical studies of phage supporting its role in immunity (FdH: 44). He emphasized that he was describing immunity in "natural diseases: dysentery, typhoid, paratyphoid, plague, *barbone,* avian typhosis, flacherie."

Up to this point, d'Herelle had answered Kabeshima's challenge to his interpretation of the nature of phage, and had responded to Salimbeni's identification of a myxamoeba as the lytic principle. He was clearly poised to follow his plan, as he had done with the *Coccobacillus,* to apply phage on a large scale against the major infectious scourges of the world. The monograph on which he was working at this time, entitled *Le bactériophage: Son rôle dans l'immunité,* emphasized the role of bacteriophages in the course of recovery from infectious disease and its potential for therapeutic use. There was only a very brief section dealing with the nature of the bacteriophage itself.

D'Herelle did not respond specifically to the papers by Bordet and Ciuca published in October 1920, perhaps because he saw their interpretation as so close to that of Kabeshima that his critique of Kabeshima's position was sufficient response to Bordet and Ciuca as well. With his position at the Pasteur

Institute in question and his work on the monograph in progress, d'Herelle's view of the future must have been anything but reassuring. Nonetheless, he took on a collaborator in Pozerski's lab, a young Georgian, Georgiy Eliava. On 23 April 1921 they published a note on production of antiserum against bacteriophage, and in it they directly challenged Bordet and Ciuca for the first time. The tone of this paper is one of respectful and scholarly disagreement: "It is evident that in the absence of other proof demonstrating the living nature of the lytic principle, proof that we have accumulated in course of numerous communications, the experiments of Bordet and Ciuca could constitute a presumption in favor of their hypothesis, because one does not expect a microbe to be destroyed in vitro by the contact with antiserum in the absence of alexin [complement]. It is precisely this that inspired doubts concerning the destruction of bacteriophage, and we have arranged to repeat these experiments" (FdH: 51, 720). D'Herelle and Eliava were able to confirm the inactivation of phage with antiserum alone, but in their study of this phenomenon, they also did a titration experiment in which a mixture of phage, antiserum, and bacteria, at a fixed ratio, was serially diluted into three tubes of sterile medium. After twenty-four hours of incubation, the bacteria had grown up to give a "normal" culture of Shiga bacilli in each tube. By forty-eight hours the first tube had lysed, and by seventy-two hours the second tube lysed, and sometime later, the third tube lysed. D'Herelle's interpretation was that the antiserum did not "destroy" the phage, it only "inhibited" it for a period of time. This interpretation was based on the then-current idea that both sensitizer (antibody) and alexin (complement) were required to kill (destroy) living bacteria. In his extrapolation to phage as a microbe, he argued that in the absence of alexin the bacteriophage was not really destroyed. Thus d'Herelle was able to preserve his hypothesis that phage was a living microbe as well as accept the hypothesis that both sensitizer and alexin were needed to kill living microbes. "The experiment of Bordet and Ciuca turns upon itself against their hypothesis" (FdH: 51, 721).

During the first half of 1921 d'Herelle was working on his monograph on bacteriophage, and in it he made no mention of the work of Bordet and Ciuca, nor did he discuss Kabeshima's interpretation of the nature of phage. He included one short section on the biological nature of phage that included his general arguments on why phage should be considered as a living microbe which parasitizes bacteria. He appeared to consider the point settled as he had responded to Kabeshima (and therefore Bordet) and Salimbeni in his publications. All the documentary evidence suggests that in early 1921 d'Herelle did not consider Bordet's view of phage as anything more than a minor scientific argument, one which would be swept away in the course of future research. He showed no hostility toward Bordet or his colleagues, and did not comment on their work in his monograph of that year.[21]

At the meeting of the Belgian Society of Biology (an affiliate of the Société Biologie de Paris) on 26 March 1921, there were three papers on phage by Bordet and Ciuca, four papers by André Gratia, and a final paper by Joseph H. Maisin. Gratia had been a student of Bordet's and reported (in papers read by Bordet) on work he was doing in Flexner's group at the Rockefeller Institute in New York. Maisin was a collaborator of Richard Bruynoghe from Louvain. The first paper, by Bordet and Ciuca, bore the title "Remarks on the history of research concerning transmissible microbial lysis." The authors observed: "In the interest of historical accuracy, we are calling attention to a prior work which d'Herelle did not know of, and which we, ourselves, have ignored, that in truth, contains all the findings which d'Herelle has reported. This remarkable work, by E. [*sic*] W. Twort appeared in Lancet, in 1915, that is to say, two years before the research of d'Herelle." After a description of the basic findings in Twort's paper, they concluded: "Without wishing to diminish the interest in the findings of d'Herelle, we believe it is necessary to recognize the incontestable priority of Twort in studies of this question."[22]

Who was Twort, and what did he do? Frederick William Twort was a medically trained bacteriologist who was superintendent of the Brown Animal Sanatory Institution in London.[23] This institution was founded by a bequest for an institution for study of diseases of "any quadrupeds or birds useful to man." Two other eminent British scientists had associations with the Brown Institution: John Burdon-Sanderson had held the superintendency prior to Twort, and Edward Mellanby had been a junior colleague of Twort there.

Twort had a long-term interest in trying to grow viruses on media in the absence of cells or tissues. He reasoned that nonpathogenic filter-passing viruses might be easier to grow in such media, and that the absence of pathological effects would make them hard to recognize when grown in animals. For several years he inoculated extracts of soil, dung, grass, hay, straw, and pond water into media based on agar, egg, or serum. Occasionally, he noted that "a few ordinary bacteria, especially sporing types, were often found to pass through the filter; but in no case was it possible to obtain a growth of a true filter-passing virus."[24]

The result that Twort did obtain—the subject of his paper that so intrigued Bordet—was described as follows:

Experiments were also conducted with vaccinia and with distemper of dogs, but with neither of these diseases was it found possible to isolate a bacterium which would reproduce the disease in animals. Some interesting results, however, were obtained with cultivations from glycerinated calf vaccinia. Inoculated agar tubes, after 24 hours at 37°C, often showed watery-looking areas, and in cultures that grew micrococci it was found that some of these colonies could not be subcultured, but if kept they became glassy and transparent. On examination of these glassy areas nothing but minute granules, staining reddish with Giemsa, could be seen.[25]

Twort described how this "glassy transformation" could be transferred to fresh colonies of micrococci and how they would become "infected" and undergo the glassy transformation. He found that the active material would pass through bacteriological filters, and that the action was serially transmissible.

Twort's paper was as restrained in its interpretation as d'Herelle's first report had been enthusiastic. Twort wrote:

From these results it is difficult to draw definite conclusions. In the first place we do not know for certain the nature of an ultra-microscopic virus. It may be a minute bacterium that will only grow on living material, or it may be a tiny amoeba which, like ordinary amoebae, thrives on living micro-organisms. . . . It [the lytic activity] may be living protoplasm that forms no definite individuals, or an enzyme with power of growth.

After lengthy consideration of alternatives, Twort tentatively concluded: "On the whole it seems probable, though by no means certain, that the active transparent material is produced by the micrococcus, and since it leads to its own destruction and can be transmitted to fresh healthy cultures, it might almost be considered as an acute infectious disease of micrococci." Twort ended this paper as follows: "I regret that financial considerations have prevented my carrying these researches to a definite conclusion, but I have indicated the lines along which others more fortunately situated can proceed." This parting shot was in reference to his lost battles with the Finance Committee of the University of London and the Medical Research Committee of the British Government.[26] This paper was published on 4 December 1915; Twort left England on 11 January 1916 in service as a bacteriologist in the British army bound for Salonika.[27]

In spite of Twort's circumspect discussion and his unwillingness to advocate a clear position on the nature of the "dissolving material," as he called it, it is clear why Bordet concluded that Twort and d'Herelle were talking about the same phenomenon. Why Bordet and Ciuca called attention to Twort's paper has been the subject of much speculation. Most of these conjectures appear to be anachronistic in the sense that the publication is explained in terms of the events that unfolded later, events that were contingent on d'Herelle's response to this paper. Thus, Twort's obituary biographer, Paul Fildes, suggested that "the opposing forces [i.e., Bordet] were responsible for the rediscovery of Twort as a tactical weapon."[28] Alan Varley has suggested that Bordet and Ciuca used Twort's views to support their endogenous origin interpretation of bacteriophage; Varley wrote of Bordet and Ciuca: "They threw down the gauntlet."[29] Likewise, Duckworth said of Bordet and Ciuca: "It was obviously a duty [i.e., calling attention to Twort's paper] they took delight in performing."[30]

The difficulty with these interpretations of Bordet and Ciuca's motivation is that they take it as given that a major controversy already existed, when in fact, it had yet to develop. D'Herelle had taken polite notice of Bordet's work in his paper with Eliava on antiphage serum and had not even included a rebuttal of Bordet's hypothesis in his monograph on phage. Bordet and Ciuca, when read without the context of the later controversy, seem to be measured and reasonable in their desire to bring Twort's work to the attention of the phage workers. Perhaps there is a bit of minor one-upsmanship here but nothing extraordinary. Twort's rather equivocal views on the nature of the dissolving substance seem hardly a major support for the already strongly articulated position of Bordet and Ciuca.

D'Herelle's reaction to the challenge to his priority in discovering bacteriophage may have reflected his besieged state of mind at that time. He answered Bordet and Ciuca in a note dealing with the history of bacteriophage published on 14 May 1921, and with another note dealing with the nature of bacteriophage on 21 May 1921 (FdH: 45; FdH: 46). He probably had little opportunity to seek advice and counsel: Roux was ill, and Calmette, his "sworn enemy," was effectively in control of the Pasteur Institute.

The strategy chosen by d'Herelle in dealing with this challenge to his priority was to claim (1) that he had done a complete survey of the literature and that an even earlier observation, that of the British bacteriologist Ernest Hanbury Hankin, was most likely the first description of bacteriophage phenomenon, and (2) that Twort's phenomenon was not related to bacteriophage. Neither claim was convincing. Hankin's observation of 1896 on the bacteriolytic activity of Ganges River water was vague and had not been followed up in any way, so it was easy to dismiss it as an irrelevant precedent. This is how d'Herelle saw it, too. His claim that Twort observed a different phenomenon was based entirely on the difference in thermal inactivation temperatures reported by Twort for the "dissolving material" (between 52 and 60°C) and d'Herelle for bacteriophage (over 65°C).

In his paper the following week, on the nature of bacteriophage, d'Herelle described his first direct test of the hypothesis of Bordet and Ciuca as elaborated by André Gratia. Gratia apparently realized, as none of d'Herelle's critics had, that the plaque formation by bacteriophage appeared to be a crucial point in favor of the ultra-virus hypothesis. Gratia, working in Flexner's lab at Rockefeller where microbic dissociation (i.e., mutation) was a topic of growing interest, devised an explanation for plaque formation which preserved Bordet's bacterial origin hypothesis.[31] Gratia argued that the bacteria in a given culture were heterogeneous and underwent spontaneous dissociation; only a few were in a sensitive state which could undergo the "nutritive vitiation" needed to induce lysogenic production of the lytic principle. These few would then produce the lysis locally, which in turn caused lysis in the region of the culture surrounding the "vitiated" cell when the lytic principle reached concentrations above the threshold for the majority of the cells.

D'Herelle, without reference to Gratia or his paper of 26 March 1921, described an experiment to test whether bacteria or bacteriophage was the determining factor in the number of plaques seen on confluent cultures of bacteria. He arranged ten tubes with different numbers of Shiga bacteria in each: one hundred million (1×10^8) up to one billion (10^9) per milliliter. To each tube was added the same volume of a highly diluted, filtered lysate of active phage. A constant volume of each tube was plated on agar, and the plaques that formed were counted. D'Herelle reasoned if the plaques came from some few "vitiated" bacteria, the number of such bacteria should vary depending on the number of bacteria plated on the agar. If, instead, the plaques were determined by the amount of phage lysate, the plaque count should be equal for all tubes, regardless of the number of bacteria. He observed this latter result and concluded:

These experiments show that the active element, the origin of plaques, is contained uniquely in the bacteriolysate: that this active element is composed of particles, which are disposed on the agar at definite points; that these particles are capable of self multiplication, independent of the action in series, and give birth to colonies. The active element can only be an ultramicrobe parasitic on the bacteria. This experiment suffices, by itself, to demonstrate the living nature of bacteriophage. (FdH: 46)

In July 1922, the British Medical Association invited d'Herelle, Twort, and Gratia to present "A discussion on the bacteriophage (bacteriolysin)" at its annual meeting in Glasgow. D'Herelle focused his talk on the evidence he believed supported his interpretation of phage as a living organism. It was implicitly directed at Bordet and Ciuca, but he also cited the interpretations of Kabeshima, Kuttner, Lisbonne and Carrère, Bail, Weinberg and Aznar, and Otto and Winkler.[32] D'Herelle's account was intended to be strictly logical: first, he stated the competing interpretations of the nature and origin of bacteriophage; second, he set up a series of presumably uncontested experimental observations; third, he discussed which hypotheses were consistent with each experimental observation. In his analysis of the competing hypotheses, d'Herelle's interpretations were listed:

> The [bacteriolytic] enzymes may be derived from the animal organism which is attacked by the given bacteria. The enzymes would then be the results of a defensive reaction on the part of the organism. This is the hypothesis of Kabeshima, Bordet and Ciuca, and Ann Kuttner. Kabeshima does not specify the particular tissue of the animal from which the enzymes originate; Bordet and Ciuca indicate the leukocytes; Ann Kuttner incriminates any tissue. 2. The enzymes may come from intestinal bacteria as the result of a microbial antagonism. For instance one knows the bacteriolytic action of filtrates of old cultures of *B. pyocyaneus*. This is the hypothesis of Lisbonne and Carrère, for whom the lytic enzymes are secreted by intestinal bacilli such as *B. coli, B. proteus*, etc. 3. The enzymes may be secreted by the bacterium itself which undergoes lysis. These enzymes would therefore be autolysins. This is the hypothesis of Weinberg and Aznar. Under the action of a cause x the bacteria would acquire the property of secreting autolytic enzymes. (FdH: 55, 290)

Hypothesis 4 was d'Herelle's own interpretation of phage as a living ultravirus.

D'Herelle's claim that the interpretation of Bordet and Ciuca belonged under hypothesis 1 was contradicted later in his paper, however, when he was considering how to explain the serial transmissibility of the lytic phenomenon. He stated: "It will be obvious, then, that this transmissibility in series eliminates hypotheses 1 and 2. . . . We come now to the third hypothesis. Only Bordet and Ciuca have attempted to give an explanation for this. For them the leukocytic principle would provoke in the bacteria a 'hereditary vitiation of nutritional nature.' I must say that I do not know how a filtered liquid can transmit a hereditary property. Besides, the whole theory of Bordet and Ciuca is based on an experience [experiment?] entitled 'leucocytic exudates' which I have elsewhere stated it is impossible to repeat—a statement which has not been challenged by Bordet. The result obtained by him in one experiment would appear to be purely accidental" (FdH: 55, 290). That d'Herelle really meant to assign Bordet and Ciuca to hypothesis 3 rather than 1 is indicated by d'Herelle's response to Bordet's note as published in the verbal responses to the papers (FdH: 55, 299).

Bordet had obtained an advance copy of d'Herelle's paper from André Gratia and through him submitted a short commentary on d'Herelle's understanding of the Bordet and Ciuca interpretation. Bordet seemed truly vexed at d'Herelle's apparent mixup: "I was not a little surprised to find that Dr. d'Herelle in this paper attributes to my co-worker and myself, as regards the intimate nature of the phenomenon, an opinion which is wholly different from what we felt entitled to uphold from the very beginning of our studies on the subject. . . . I wonder how Dr. d'Herelle could give such an erroneous account of our work as in his paper. . . . I think there is no need to dwell longer on the subject. But one must agree that I could not refrain from correcting d'Herelle as regards our views, nor from presenting them again as they are expressed in all our papers."[33] Bordet made no arguments to support his position, made no response to d'Herelle's claim that the Bordet and Ciuca experiment was not reproducible, and made no mention of the Twort-d'Herelle priority issue.

In his paper, after his analysis of the nature of the bacteriophage, d'Herelle turned to the work of Twort. His strategy was to argue that bacteriophage action and Twort's bacteriolysis were two fundamentally different microbiological processes. D'Herelle spoke of "the plurality of the serial phenomena." He noted, "According to this description of Twort, it is not a question of real bacterial dissolution, but of a transformation of a normal culture on agar into a glassy and transparent one. This phenomenon is totally different from that produced by *Bacteriophagum intestinale.*" He concluded on a conciliatory tone: "This conclusion, however, does not detract in any way from the interest attaching to the important researches of Twort. One can already see that the phenomenon observed by this author may play an important role in the etiology of the so-called filterable virus diseases, as he indeed seems to have foreseen. On the other hand, the bacteriophage undoubtedly plays a part in the defense of the organism in the course of infectious diseases, as I have shown elsewhere" (FdH: 55, 292).

In his paper at this same meeting, Twort outlined again his original observations, as he had little new to report. He had been forced to work on other topics because of his funding difficulties at the Brown Institution. In his explanation for the nature of the lytic principle, Twort was cautious in his conclusions. He thought d'Herelle's emphasis on plaque formation was not proof of the particulate nature of the phage, and he suggested an alternative explanation based on bacterial variation, as had Gratia. Twort also took issue with Bordet and Ciuca:

his experiments on spontaneous production of lytic activity from apparently normal bacteria "appear to me to be evidence against the view that the lytic material is a definite living organism, but also against the view of Bordet and Ciuca that the lytic agent arises from an association of the bacterium with cells from the animal body."[34] Twort was not dogmatic and seemed open to several possibilities:

> I repeat my original opinion regarding the lytic agent of the micrococcus—namely, that "the possibility of its being an ultramicroscopic virus has not been definitely disproved," and that "it seems probable, though by no means certain, that the active transparent material is produced by the micrococcus"; and I hold the same view regarding the lytic agent which various workers and myself have found associated with the dysentery-typhoid-coli group of bacilli. However, as I have already pointed out, it is just possible that an ultramicroscopic virus may be of the nature of an enzyme, and if so, the original source of such a virus might be the cell it infects.[35]

The issue of priority was not explicit in Twort's paper, but by including the term bacteriophage in its title and by extending his interpretation to the very organisms d'Herelle worked on, it seemed clear that Twort saw the two phenomena as identical.

Gratia, who had already published a note in the fall of 1921 with D. Jaumain under the title "Identité du phénomène de Twort et du phénomène de d'Herelle," started his paper at the Glasgow meeting with the sentence: "The Twort phenomenon and the d'Herelle phenomenon are identical."[36] Gratia apparently accompanied his talk with some laboratory demonstrations of the phenomena he was describing.[37] Although Gratia did mention the conflicting interpretation of some recent immunological data on antigenic specificity of phage, he devoted the bulk of this paper to arguing against phage as a living organism. He noted that the major facts relating to the lytic phenomenon "are easily explained by the virus theory, yet both facts are not unquestionable proofs of the living nature of the bacteriophage, because they are by no means exclusive features of living things."[38] He invoked analogies such as fire, which is serially transmissible but not living, and formation of gas bubbles in soda water, which occur at specific points without being alive.

Twort and d'Herelle were again on the program together the following year when the Royal Institute of Public Health held its annual meeting in Scarborough 16–21 May 1923. D'Herelle's approach at this meeting was to attack the relationship between autolysis and bacteriophage production. In a passing reference to Twort's work he wrote: "If in the bacterioclasis phenomenon of

Twort, there is indeed fragmentation of the bacterial body, 'breaking down of the bacteria' in the words of Twort, the bacterial body transforming itself into 'minute grains staining reddish with Giemsa,' in bacteriophagis there is a *total* dissolution of the bacteria, without residue of any kind, colorable or visible with the microscope" (FdH: 69). The rest of the paper was descriptions of d'Herelle's attempts to reproduce the production of phage under the conditions that led to autolysis as reported by Jaumain, a collaborator of Gratia.[39] In no case, however, could d'Herelle induce phage production by inducing autolysis.

Twort used this opportunity to elaborate his theories on the nature and origin of ultramicroscopic viruses. In a general discussion of the field, Twort devoted only three paragraphs to the alternative interpretations of d'Herelle and Bordet and Ciuca; he remained "unprepared to consider the question proved one way or the other."[40] With no mention of the priority dispute or additional comments on phage, Twort concluded with his position on viruses: "an ultramicroscopic virus belongs to one or more of those forms of life which in the scale of evolution are situated between the simple enzymes and bacteria."[41]

For the next seven years d'Herelle's peregrinations led him to the Middle East, India, and the United States. The priority dispute ceased to be something d'Herelle had to confront constantly. Many workers had accepted the independent discovery of the same phenomenon and simply called it the "Twort-d'Herelle phenomenon," which gradually gave way to the simpler term "bacteriophage phenomenon" or "bacteriophage." D'Herelle had, in a sense, won by virtue of giving the phenomenon a name that caught on. By whatever name it went, interest in phage was increasing fast. From 73 papers on phage published in the world literature in 1921, phage publications appeared at the rate of more than 150 each year for the next two decades.[42] Twort continued to do some work on phage, as did Gratia. By his nature Twort was reticent about the dispute, and Gratia, while disagreeing with d'Herelle on the biological nature of phage, nevertheless was committed to its utility as an antibacterial agent to treat infections. D'Herelle was content to leave the priority issue alone because he was becoming the dominant authority simply by virtue of his output of publications and because of the widespread acceptance of his terminology.

The final and most acrimonious phase of the dispute between d'Herelle and Gratia apparently started in February 1930 with a presentation by Gratia to the National Society of French Surgeons. He had been invited to speak on the use of bacteriophage to treat staphylococcal infections, one of the common surgical wound infections. At the time d'Herelle was working in the United States at

Yale and preparing for an extended lecture trip to Montreal.[43] D'Herelle's close friend, André Raiga-Clemenceau, was the likely source of information about Gratia's talk. Raiga-Clemenceau was a surgeon in Paris who had developed a keen interest in the use of phages in surgical infections and was an unabashed partisan of d'Herelle.[44] In his talk to this group of d'Herelle's supporters, Gratia again raised the issue of the identity of Twort's discovery with that of d'Herelle. While this was not the main topic of Gratia's paper, it provoked d'Herelle to send a comment to the *Bulletin et Mémoires de la Société Nationale de Chirurgie* that was presented at their meeting on 7 May (FdH: 104). He was still in the United States, but would be in Paris for the summer, and d'Herelle arranged an invitation to speak in response to Gratia at the 9 July 1930 meeting of the surgeons.[45] Apparently, too, d'Herelle had suggested that "the First International Congress [of Microbiology] where the question of bacteriophage would be amply discussed would be an excellent occasion to elucidate this question."[46] Thus, the old battle was renewed.

D'Herelle had been invited by Bordet to participate in a session at the First International Congress of Microbiology to be held in Paris, also in July 1930. Bordet was the president of the congress, and he convened the opening session on "Microbial Variation and Lytic Phenomena," which included Bordet, d'Herelle, Arkwright, Ledingham, and Neisser as the main speakers. There were also twenty-two brief communications on this topic. Gratia, d'Herelle, Manoussakis, and Marbais contributed short "discussions." Bordet talked on "Transmissible Lysis" and summarized his ideas about the bacterial origin of the lytic agent. He related this physiological change in the bacteria to the other topic of the session, the changes between the rough and smooth phenotypes and the interpretation of the meaning of these changes. D'Herelle, for his part, began with a general consideration of lytic phenomena and took the occasion to again assert that bacteriophage and Twort's phenomenon were not the same, probably responding to Gratia's revival of the issue. He devoted most of his paper to the meaning of plaques, the nature of ultramicroscopic organisms, and the problem of symbiosis in cultures of phage and bacteria. Like Bordet, d'Herelle gave a review paper and presented no new unpublished data. Both authors wrote in polite and civil language and barely mentioned the other by name. From the written material, at least, it seems that d'Herelle and Bordet were involved in a scientific dispute and that there was little personal animus between them.

For Gratia, however, the statement by d'Herelle that Twort had described something different than bacteriophage was too much to bear in silence. He spoke up in the discussion session and reopened the debate from the Glasgow meeting of eight years earlier. According to the published record, Gratia said: "In 1922 at the Congress of the British Medical Association, in Glasgow, in the presence of both Twort and d'Herelle, I exhibited two series of tubes, one with the characteristics of d'Herelle's phenomenon, the other with the phenomenon of Twort. These two series were prepared with the same filtrate and were interchangeable and indistinguishable, as one is able to change water to snow and snow to water. D'Herelle has never responded to this crucial demonstration."[47] Gratia also then reviewed his discovery of Twort's priority and summarized briefly the tortuous history of d'Herelle's attempts to differentiate bacteriophage from the "Twort phenomenon."

D'Herelle briefly responded by stating that Twort's phenomenon was one in which granules were the end product of bacterial breakdown, whereas in bacteriophage action no such material was visible in the microscope. He called the Twort phenomenon a "granular transformation," and this had become for d'Herelle the definition. He claimed that Gratia's 1922 cultures did not show the granules, so he had not exhibited the phenomenon of Twort, only two examples of bacteriophage. "The cultures presented by M. Gratia did not reproduce either macroscopically or microscopically the phenomenon described by Twort" (FdH: 113).

Gratia was apparently incensed by d'Herelle's failure to acknowledge that Twort had, indeed, described the action of a staphylococcal bacteriophage in his 1915 note to *Lancet*. Gratia was one of the few who kept the priority issue alive. Even Bordet, who has been portrayed (somewhat unfairly) as d'Herelle's archrival, thought that Gratia was wasting his time. In January 1931 Gratia wrote to Twort, "Two days ago, I had an argument with Doctor Bordet, who considered my recent work on the identity of your phenomenon and the bacteriophage as amounting to nothing."[48] Gratia embarked on a campaign to settle the matter. He submitted an extensive review of his position to the *Annales de l'Institut Pasteur* that was published in the first issue of January 1931. In this article he elaborated on the discovery of Twort's forgotten paper. In December 1920, it was Peter Olitsky, one of Gratia's colleagues at the Rockefeller Institute, who pointed it out to him, and Gratia, in turn, provided the information to Bordet and Ciuca.[49] He again complained that d'Herelle did not accept his experimental demonstrations presented at the International Congress the previous summer. D'Herelle objected to some of the techniques used and to the fact that while Twort reported that complete lysis of a colony could be observed starting at the site of inoculation with the lytic agent at the edge of the colony, Gratia's examples did not. Gratia countered with the argument that it was just a matter of the virulence of the lysin and that he did not have as strong a stock as Twort.

In two more pairs of articles by d'Herelle and Gratia, each pair printed together in the *Annales de l'Institut Pasteur,* this polemical exchange continued. What seemed to be in dispute was the nature and origin of granular material that Gratia said he observed in cases of phage lysis. D'Herelle simply called them artifacts. When d'Herelle asked for Gratia to send him some of the material for his own examination, Gratia did so, but said that it did not survive the travel well, which accounted for d'Herelle's negative findings. In turn, Gratia invited d'Herelle to come to his laboratory to repeat the experiments. In a gesture reminiscent of the days of chivalry and duels, d'Herelle suggested, instead, an investigation of the specific point related to the "Twort granules" by two independent phage workers. D'Herelle proposed Paul Flu from Leiden, and asked Gratia to find a "responsible bacteriologist, a university professor, who is familiar with the techniques" to represent him in the independent test of the d'Herelle-Gratia controversy. When Gratia apparently did not respond to this challenge, d'Herelle forced the issue. In a short note in the *Annales,* he again proposed to Gratia that Flu and someone nominated by Gratia meet to adjudicate the argument. "If M. Gratia persists in ignoring this proposition, I will meet him at the next Congress of Microbiology. I expect, that as I said before, that the experimental conditions involved in transporting the material to Berlin will result in tubes that resemble those exhibited in Paris. We will certainly obtain the nomination of a Commission which will verify the question related to the glassy transformation of Twort" (FdH: 118). The confrontational nature of the dispute was becoming apparent to the editors of the *Annales,* and for this last communication d'Herelle took the apparently unprecedented action of obtaining a judicial order to publish his note. Whether the editors refused to publish it initially or d'Herelle anticipated its rejection is unclear from the documentary evidence. The note in the *Annales* is preceded by a statement from the editor: "The following note was not addressed to the Editorial Committee of this publication. It was received by Masson and Company, managers of these Annales, and at the same time M. Perrin, a bailiff for the Civil Tribunal of the Seine, presented a legal order to publish it 'in three days without delay, or in the next number of the *Annales de l'Institut Pasteur.*' This is the first time that such a process has been employed in regard to this publication, and we are notifying the scholarly community." Gratia seemed eager to take up the challenge and secured Ernest Renaux, a protégé of Bordet and a colleague of Gratia's on the Faculty of Medicine of the University of Brussels.[50]

The Flu-Renaux study, which was carried out in Flu's laboratory in the Institute of Tropical Medicine in Leiden, focused narrowly on the issues as d'Herelle specified: Is it possible to produce, with an authentic staphylococcal phage, the glassy transformation of Twort, including fine granules which stain reddish with Giemsa, with the properties of sterility, propagation, transmissibility, and not only from secondary resistant cultures? In early 1932, Flu and Renaux described the conditions of their experiments and concluded ten years of dramatic and acrimonious debate with the following: "In summary: in work with bacteriophage BLS on staphylococcus 4a, we have found that the phenomenon of Twort consists in the appearance in the colonies of the staphylococcus, of a glassy substance composed of fine granules colored red with Giemsa. This substance is characterized by its sterility, its propagation and its transmissibility."[51] The drama was over. Gratia soon moved to a professorship at Liège, where he developed another pathway of research on lysins involving bacteriocins.[52] D'Herelle seemed anxious to expand his work on the clinical application of phages and the role of phage infection in phenotypic changes in bacteria.

Chapter 6 The Nature of
Phage: Microbe or Enzyme?

When d'Herelle first made his observation of bacteriophage lysis, the obvious question was, what "causes" the phenomenon? For a bacteriologist of the Pasteur-Koch tradition like d'Herelle, causation should be specific, as Carter has noted, a *necessary* cause, and perhaps a *sufficient* cause as well.[1] That is, d'Herelle was not satisfied with vague notions of "growth conditions" or "vitiation" of endogenous lysins. He sought a specific agent, chemical or biological, that "caused" the lysis in the same way it was believed that Shiga's bacillus "caused" dysentery. How d'Herelle conceived of bacteriophage reflected his own biases, or, as Van Helvoort has termed it, his "bacteriological research style."[2]

Between his discovery of phage in 1915 and his first formal report in 1917, in which he concluded that bacteriophages were biological entities, "ultramicrobes," there is no contemporary evidence with which we can reconstruct with certainty his initial ideas and their subsequent elaborations and modifications. Specific clues, however, can help us understand his reasoning and the development of his conception of the bacteriophage phenomenon.

In his earliest experiments d'Herelle had two results that appeared to him to exclude simple chemical agents or toxins as the cause of the lysis. First was the serial propagation of the lytic agent at high dilutions, and second was the appearance of plaques, the number of which correlated with the lytic activity. He argued that although a "simple" chemical substance might lyse a culture, the serial propagation, in some cases for hundreds of transfers at high dilution, required the substance to retain equal potency even though it had been diluted many trillions of times. To d'Herelle, the obvious alternative was that the active substance in some way was regenerated, or grew each time a culture lysed after being exposed to phage. By the time he wrote his first paper on phage in 1917, d'Herelle had concluded that bacteriophages were ultramicrobes that multiplied in the course of the lysis of the bacteria.

A second piece of evidence that supported his ultramicrobe hypothesis was his observation that the solution with the active lytic agent could produce focal lysis of bacterial cultures growing on solid medium. These small, round clear areas, later called plaques or *taches vierges,* were interpreted by d'Herelle as colonies of the ultramicrobe in the same way that Koch had interpreted bacterial colonies that appeared on solid medium. D'Herelle saw no way that a soluble enzyme (called *ferment* in French, recalling the earlier belief that fermentation represented the basic chemical process of living beings) could give rise to discrete colonies. He argued that the plaques required phage to be of a particulate nature:

> The following experiment gives, moreover, the visible evidence that the antagonistic action is produced by a living germ: if one adds to a culture of Shiga a dilution of approximately one to a million of an already lysed culture, and if, immediately after, one spreads out on an agar slant a droplet of this culture, one obtains, after incubation, a coat of dysentery bacilli showing a certain number of circles about 1 mm in diameter, where the culture is void; these points can only represent the colonies of the antagonistic microbe: a chemical substance would not be able to concentrate at defined points. In working with measured quantities, I have seen that a lysed culture of Shiga contains five to six million of these filterable germs per cubic centimeter. One three-millionth of a cubic centimeter of the preceding culture from Shiga, or a single germ, introduced into a tube of broth, inhibits the culture of Shiga even when liberally inoculated; the same quantity added to a 10 cm³ culture of Shiga sterilizes it and lyses it in five or six days. (FdH: 25)

In this first paper d'Herelle clearly associated the lytic action in liquid culture with the agent producing the focal growth inhibition or killing on the surface cultures on agar slants. He used the plaque count to estimate the concentration of the germs in the lysate, and then calculated that one germ was sufficient to produce the subsequent lysis of an entire culture. He did not state that in order to make this calculation he had to assume that one microbe gave rise to one plaque. If the plaques required some sort of cooperative behavior—for example, if ten phages had to infect one cell to produce lysis—this calculation would fail. It is possible, however, that he considered this issue unimportant for two reasons: first, if such cooperativity was involved, he would have noted that the titer of plaque-forming units would not be proportional to the dilutions of the lysate, and second, even if some sort of cooperative infection was needed, this would not challenge the particulate nature of phage.

By 1925 he had refined and made explicit many of his arguments supporting the particulate nature of bacteriophage. D'Herelle's efforts in this direction were motivated by his need to defend his ideas against those of Bordet, whose more physiological research approach led him to conceive of bacteriophage as emanating from physiological processes within the bacterial cell, rather in the nature of a lytic enzyme.[3] In *The Bacteriophage and Its Behavior,* published in 1926, d'Herelle wrote: "The small amount of bacteriophage present appears, then, to *concentrate* its action at particular points (d'Herelle, [310]) [reference to Fdh 25]. Can the physical state of the bacteriophage be 'discontinuous'? Can the principle exist, in what up to this time we have called a bacteriophage liquid or a bacteriophage filtrate, in particulate form, as corpuscles in suspension? . . . The hypothesis which I have formulated in answer to the above questions is easy to verify" (*BIB,* 81–82).

D'Herelle's hypothesis and its verification depended on the following experimental observations: first, a suspension of bacteriophage was active in transmission of the phenomenon at a dilution of one to ten billion (10^{-10}) but was completely inactive at a dilution of one to 100 billion (10^{-11}). Second, if one ml of the one to ten billion dilution was added to ten identical broth cultures, each with 9 ml of sensitive bacteria, he observed total lysis of some cultures and normal growth in the rest. In fact, in six such experiments he found that the lysis occurred in 30 percent of the cultures (FdH: 37). D'Herelle was satisfied by the result:

> This experiment settles the question. If the bacteriophage was to be found in a state of solution [i.e., in continuous form] in the 10^{-10} dilution, it is obvious that each [1 cc., or ml] of the 10 cc. of this dilution would have contained a tenth part of it, that is, none of the [individual 1 cc. portions of the] 10 cc. would have been favored. Each would have contained a like quantity, and all of the 10 suspensions, each receiving one of these 10 [individual] cc., would have behaved in the same manner; they would

have been the seat of a comparable phenomenon. But this is not the case, as shown by the fact that 3 suspensions undergo bacteriophagy, while 7 do not. There is, then, among the 10 cc. distributed in equal amounts among the ten suspensions, 3 portions of 1 cc. each which contained the bacteriophage principle. In the other 7 it was lacking. This is absolute proof that the bacteriophage exists in discontinuous form, that is to say, in corpuscular form. (*BIB*, 83)

This statistical explanation, which d'Herelle argued intuitively, is based on the properties of sampling that can be described by the mathematical expression known as the Poisson distribution. This powerful statistical argument was to appeal much later to another physicist and would be the first experimental question Max Delbrück studied when he turned to phage research in the late 1930s.[4] D'Herelle bolstered not only this argument but also his own stature with his well-known footnote giving Einstein's opinion of this experiment: "In discussing this question with my colleague, Professor Einstein, he told me, as a physicist, he would consider this experiment as demonstrating the discontinuity of the bacteriophage. I was very glad to see how this deservedly-famous mathematician evaluated my experimental demonstration, for I do not believe that there are a great many biological experiments whose nature satisfies a mathematician" (*BIB*, 83).

D'Herelle realized that the particulate nature of the bacteriophage was central to his view of the phenomenon. In *The Bacteriophage and Its Behavior* he included additional experimental support for this view, because "the concept of the corpuscular nature of the bacteriophage dominates entirely the study of this principle" (*BIB*, 83). After his several arguments as to the corpuscular nature of phage, he wrote, "Since we have now presented the evidence proving the corpuscular nature of the bacteriophage we will no longer make use of such vague expressions as bacteriophage 'liquid,' 'fluid,' or 'filtrate,' but will employ the more precise term 'suspension of bacteriophage corpuscles,' or even more simply, 'bacteriophage suspension'" (*BIB*, 96).

Although it now seems a comparatively simple conceptual step to go from quantifying bacteria by counting the number of colonies that grow on solid medium to quantifying the number of phage corpuscles by counting the number of plaques formed on a film of bacteria spread on solid medium, this way of determining the "amount" of bacteriophage required, of course, the assumption of the corpuscular nature of phage. The validity of the plaque-counting assay and the corpuscular nature of phage, however, would remain controversial and divide phage workers into two camps until the early 1940s. D'Herelle's test of this method was to compare the estimate of the phage concentration by "plaque-former" assay with that obtained by limiting dilution of the ability to lyse a sensitive culture.[5] In one experiment he found that there were 478 plaque-formers in 1 ml of a one to ten million (10^{-7}) dilution of a phage suspension, which indicated that the initial suspension had 4.78 billion (i.e., 4.78×10^9) plaque-formers per milliliter. In his dilution experiment, he found that in a series of tenfold dilutions of the suspension, 10 ml of the one to ten billion (10^{-10}) dilution was the most diluted one which caused lysis of a liquid culture of sensitive bacteria. He then divided the 10 ml into 1 ml aliquots and tested each aliquot for its ability to cause lysis. When he found that five of ten cultures lysed, he concluded that five aliquots had the minimal number of corpuscles needed to cause lysis. As he believed that a single corpuscle was needed, he could calculate that there were five culture-lysing units in 10 ml of a one to ten billion (10^{-10}) dilution, or 5 billion phage per milliliter (*BIB*, 97–98). The agreement between these two approaches to assay the concentration of active lytic principle was again taken as strong evidence not only that the plaque assay was accurate and meaningful, but that bacteriophage, the "lytic principle," was particulate.

In addition to his conception of phage as corpuscular, d'Herelle believed that "these corpuscles multiply during the course of their action, solely at the expense of living bacteria" (*BIB*, 309). The mechanism of bacteriophagy—the dissolution of a bacterial culture by exposure to bacteriophage—was another controversial issue until the early 1940s. D'Herelle's views, which were clearly bacteriological as opposed to physiological, held that phage were ultra-microbes, that is, living organisms invisible even under the microscope. Sometimes he used the term "living ultravirus" and placed bacteriophage with other known "filterable agents" such as smallpox, plant mosaic, and rabies (*INID*, 314). As Van Helvoort has shown, d'Herelle adopted the traditional Pasteurian notion of virus and microbe as living agents of infectious disease, in this case, a disease of bacteria.[6]

Although he did many experiments to convince himself and others that phage were "living," d'Herelle considered crucial an experiment that Emory Ellis and Max Delbrück repeated later as one of their tests of d'Herelle's conception of phage.[7] D'Herelle stated his model for phage "growth" in succinct form in his early publications: "Bacteriophagy always takes place in the same manner; the sequence of events is always the same. The bacteriophage particle must invariably become fixed to the bacterium to exercise its action [attachment]. Destruction of the bacterium is always accomplished by bursting [lysis]. The bacteriophage corpuscles always multiply within the bacterial cell and are always liberated with the rupture of this cell [intracellular replication and maturation]" (*BIB*, 115). He described the course of multiplication of a typical phage growth experiment:

> After 30 minutes of contact at 37°C. the bacteriophage corpuscles have almost entirely disappeared from the liquid.
> After 60 minutes the situation is the same.
> After 90 minutes the corpuscles have *suddenly* reappeared in the liquid, and their number is 18 times greater than was that of the inoculated corpuscles. In other words, each inoculated corpuscle has yielded 18. (*BIB*, 116)

The data for another such growth experiment, presented in this same text, are recast in graph form (Figure 5), making the stepwise increase in phage concentration more apparent and supporting d'Herelle's contention that "the increase in the number of corpuscles does not take place in a continuous progressive fashion, but by successive liberations" (*BIB*, 117).

This model for phage growth follows a conception of bacteriophage as cellular parasites, and as such D'Herelle and others were concerned to find out whether only living bacteria were suitable hosts.[8] Bacteria that were killed by heat, chemical agents, or aging of the culture all failed to support the growth of the bacteriophage and were not lysed. Eugène Wollman, one of d'Herelle's colleagues at the Pasteur Institute, devised an experiment to see if actual contact between bacterium and phage was necessary by sequestering the bacterial culture inside dialysis sacks of differing porosities immersed in suspensions of phage.[9] The phage content of the cultures seemed to increase with time in all cases except where the porosity was the most restrictive, a result corroborated by

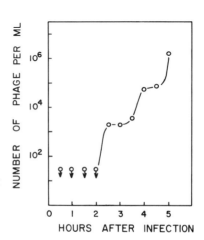

Figure 5. Bacteriophage growth curve showing step-wise production of extracellular phage in a culture of bacteria initially infected with a single phage particle. Data from *BIB*, 116–117.

Igor Asheshov working in Dubrovnik (*BIB*, 102–103). D'Herelle seemed at a loss to explain these findings but he apparently accepted them as valid, perhaps because of his friendship for, and confidence in, Wollman.[10] While not abandoning his belief that living bacteria were necessary for normal phage growth, he equivocated: "It is necessary, then, to conclude that the multiplication of bacteriophage corpuscles can take place, at least to a certain degree, in the absence of the bacterial cell, and that for this development the corpuscles utilizes [*sic*] certain diffusible products present in the culture of susceptible bacteria" (*BIB*, 103). The construction of the bacteriophage as an ultravirus which is an obligatory intracellular parasite still left unsettled the nature of its biological and chemical organization. D'Herelle devoted substantial attention to these issues, which he appeared to take seriously in his program to understand and explain the phenomenon of the bacteriophage.

The living nature of the bacteriophage was attested, first, by its power of "assimilation of a heterologous medium" and, second, by its "power of adaptation" (*pouvoir d'adaptation*) (*BIB*, 331). It is not easy to understand these terms in the way d'Herelle applied them. He realized that for an ultramicroscopic entity there was an experimental problem: "For in no case do we see the actual assimilation; we observe only the effects of the process. The being increases in size or it multiplies in the heterologous medium, and that is sufficient to justify the conclusion that it possesses the power of assimilation" (*BIB*, 331). The problem, then, is to determine if bacterial substance is converted into bacteriophage substance or if the phage grows by accretion of bacterial substance in the same way a crystal grows by "homologous assimilation." D'Herelle attempted to redefine this question into one of the "autonomy" of the bacteriophage, that is, whether or not "the bacteriophage corpuscle is an *autonomous being*, independent of the bacterium which undergoes its action" (*BIB*, 333). Logically, this redefinition transferred the explanatory burden to the phrase "independent of the bacterium." He then argued that the diversity of bacteriophage strains, which can be isolated using a single bacterial host strain, means that the bacteriophages are independent of the bacterium in which they have multiplied. Likewise, the fact that there are natural and acquired bacterial resistances to phage implies that the phage is independent of the nature of the host bacterium. Asheshov found that two phages that made plaques of very different sizes were stable, even though they were repeatedly passed on the same culture of host bacteria, a result that again suggested to d'Herelle that the bacteriophage were independent of the host bacterium.[11] In an argument that owes more to sophistry than to logic, he noted that Bordet and Ciuca could eliminate phages from a lysogenic culture of bacteria with antibacteriophage serum and concluded: "If a bacterium infected by a bacteriophage can be 'cured' by serum therapy it is evident that the bacteriophage must be a parasite, foreign to the bacterium" (*BIB,* 340). The point of all these arguments was that "the characters of the corpuscle belong to itself and are not determined by the characters of the bacteria which undergo its action. The bacteriophage corpuscle is, therefore, an autonomous being" (*BIB,* 341). In most of his later discussions of this issue he simply equates phage multiplication with assimilation of a heterologous medium (*CMP,* 95).

The second property d'Herelle asserted for the bacteriophage was adaptation, a notion that has its roots in eighteenth- and nineteenth-century French biology. D'Herelle firmly aligned himself with Lamarck: "Since the time of Lamarck many theories have been brought forth to explain evolution, but analysis of these diverse theories immediately shows that, despite all care taken by their authors to avoid it, they are all still dominated by the conception of Lamarck—adaptation to the environment. Natural selection, mutation, are only corollaries to the principle of adaptation" (*INID,* 74). Although d'Herelle's position took into account the widespread and dominant neo-Lamarckian views of French biology at the time, he was a confirmed materialist and did not accept the dogma of Lamarck and later, Bergson, of "an original impetus," an *élan vital,* as the force driving adaptation.[12] D'Herelle's discussion of adaptation in 1926 gives a sense of his interpretation of neo-Lamarckianism:

> But adaptation is accompanied by another phenomenon. Living matter, protoplasm, retains the impression of the reaction effected, an imprint whose mark in the substance is engraved more deeply as the reaction is the more intense. Obviously, it is unnecessary to attach to the word "impression" any psychic meaning. As used here it implies simply that living matter which has reacted to a given stimulus reacts again more quickly, and in general more intensely when subjected to a second stimulus of the same nature as the first. That reaction of living matter is specific, we have said. The "recollection" is likewise specific, for it modifies in no way the response to a different excitation.
>
> This "reactional memory" is transmitted hereditarily, but if a stimulus of the same nature as the first fails to occur until after the lapse of a long time the "recollection" of the reaction effected is progressively lost. (*BIB,* 350–351)

Following "hereditarily" in the last paragraph was a footnote in which d'Herelle qualified his statement: "Here, of course, we are not considering the case, still very obscure, of the transmission of characters to descendants through the intermediary of gametes. The only transmission of characters with which we are concerned here is that which takes place when a cell becomes two cells through division. Here, the transmission of *acquired* characters is beyond doubt. All immunity demonstrates this, as do the facts of all types of adaptation which can be experimentally effected with bacteria." D'Herelle was greatly influenced by the current work on immunization with specific antigens, and he thought of the phage-bacterium interaction as similar to the interaction between an antigen and the antibody-producing cells in the body. The "imprint" of the antigen is "engraved" ever more deeply on the immune system by repeated exposure to the antigen. Immunological memory was long term, but the recollection often faded with time.

A correlate of adaptation is variability: the greater the adaptability, the greater also is the variability (*BIB,* 354). This notion led d'Herelle to nearly a decade of experiments aimed at the study of the range of possible variations in the properties of bacteriophage. Just as the variability of bacteria had posed problems fifty years earlier in the classification and understanding of these simple organisms, the variability in phage isolates raised anew the question of monomorphism versus polymorphism and the proper classification of this newly discovered microbe.

Although d'Herelle firmly held to the monomorphic conception of bacteria (according to which a given form of bacteria was fixed and associated with a definite strain, species, or "biotype"),[13] when it came to phage, he advocated the equivalent of polymorphism (a hypothesis which held that morphological characters varied for a given species of organism, depending on life cycles, culture conditions, and other environmental influences). If one followed the polymorphism view, morphology was an unreliable guide to identification and classification. Indeed, in its extreme form, the polymorphic approach held that all microbes were of one "species" or "biotype," which could be found in nature in a wide variety of forms. From 1915 to about 1930, several influential bacteriologists, such as Felix Löhnis and Philip Hadley, seriously advocated a variant of the polymorphism hypothesis for bacteria. This notion was termed "cyclogeny" and related the morphology of cells and of colonies to stages in the supposed life cycles of the bacteria.[14] D'Herelle applied this same notion to phage under the concept of "unicity"—that is, there is but one "kind" of bacteriophage, and it is capable of wide variation based on its adaptive powers. This idea was controversial for phage, just as it was controversial for bacteria. In the case of phage, d'Herelle exploited the phenomenon of variation as evidence of adaptation and hence the living nature of phage. Why he held so firmly to the concept of unicity is unclear. It was not supported by any critical experimental data and had no epistemological utility except to emphasize the variations seen among phage isolates.

D'Herelle's interest in variation in bacteriophage started with his examination of adaptation as one criterion for living beings, but it developed into the study of the basic heritability of characteristics of phage, then the study of the phage-host virulence and resistance, and eventually to the use of phage to study bacterial mutations. He began this research program in the mid-1920s, and it continued intermittently until he joined the faculty at Yale University in 1928, when he concentrated his full-time efforts on phage and bacterial mutations (see chapter 10). Not only could he and others isolate phage stocks from the same sources with widely varying properties—for example, plaque size, lysis time, and heat sensitivity—but it was also possible, given a "pure" stock of phage, to isolate variants that were resistant to certain chemical agents: they had "adapted." Likewise, variants specific to new bacterial hosts could be found by "adapting" the phage to the new hosts. This process was in the Pastorian tradition by which microbial variants with altered pathogenicity were isolated by "adapting" them through repeated passage in different species.

The concept of a bacterial virus, which seemed so obvious to d'Herelle, was to prove profoundly unsettling to many microbiologists. As Van Helvoort has argued, the apparently continuous evolution of the concept of "virus" from Beijerinck's notion of *contagium vivum fluidum* in the late 1890s to "filterable viruses" in the 1920s to the modern concept of a virus in the 1950s was punctuated by acrimonious debates; consensus formed and dissolved several times.[15] A key node in this development involved the debates over the nature of bacteriophage and precisely what was meant by a "virus." Van Helvoort accurately characterizes d'Herelle's position as being within the bacteriological paradigm and deriving from the Pastorian notion that viruses—filterable or not, visible or not—are organized, living microbes that may be agents of disease.

Questions about the organization of biological substance were not limited to viruses. The size and physical nature of genes were key problems confronting the leading American geneticist Thomas Hunt Morgan, who leaned toward a particulate concept of the gene, as opposed to a more continuous concept of the gene as a given quantity of a substance. He considered it likely that the gene was an organic molecule or possibly a collection of organic molecules, but "If, on the other hand the gene is regarded as merely a quantity of so much material, we can give no satisfactory answer as to why it remains so constant through all the vicissitudes of outcrossing, unless we appeal to mysterious powers of organization outside the genes that keep them constant."[16] A very different approach to genetics was represented by the German zoologist Richard Goldschmidt, who argued for the gene as a specific quantity of a catalyst and viewed a mutation as "change in the quantity of the gene, i.e., from x to y molecules."[17] Well into the late 1930s Goldschmidt still drew parallels between the action of phage and gene mutational changes, both envisioned as continuous, non-discrete entities.[18] Muller's well-known comment that phages might be "naked genes" also emphasizes the extent to which interest in biological organization in one field influenced that of another.[19]

In the case of phage, d'Herelle conceived of them as microbes, capable of causing infectious diseases in their hosts, the bacteria, in the same way the cholera vibrio causes an infectious disease in its human host. He noted, with some exasperation it seemed, that: "As has often been said, history is forever repeating itself, and the history of science appears to be particularly subject to such repetitions. Dead theories must be killed anew. That the struggle of Pasteur should have to be repeated will doubtless prove astonishing to students of the future. Against the principle formulated by those opposed to the living nature of the ultraviruses, namely, that 'all cells in a state of disorganization transmit very readily this state to a cell free from change' (for this is indeed their postulate) it is necessary to prove once more that the law announced by the clear genius of Claude Bernard, by Pasteur, and by Koch, is always true, that "all disease reproducing in series arises from a living germ capable of multiplying in the body" (*INID*, 339). By citing such historical authorities as well as identifying his opponents with discredited ideas about spontaneous generation such as those of Georg Stahl and Justus Liebig, d'Herelle appeared to be covering his inability to persuade his critics with experimental evidence in a cloud of rhetoric.

Even upon close study of his writings on the living nature of phage, often it is difficult to get a precise and clear idea of his intended meaning. Trying to understand his explanations in the context of microbiology in the 1920s is even more difficult. There are two major points on which his arguments turn. The first is the notion of microbe, and the second is the meaning and implication of the concept of the obligate intracellular parasite.

"Microbe" was adopted in 1878 in France as a compromise in a search for a rather general term to encompass "germs." Thus, brewers yeast, bacteria, and rabies, all could be called microbes. At a time when the exact nature and specific characteristics of various "germs" were unknown or unknowable, such a vague term was quite useful. The concept did, however have two requirements: some sort of organization and the characteristic of being living. These features applied because the very defining type of microbe was that group of entities which caused fermentations; they were "living, organized ferments." It was not clear whether the organization was strictly structural or functional or both. Indeed, this distinction is probably a modern one; the cell theory gave a structural cast to the matter, but since many of the defining properties of microbes were functional, such as the ability to cause disease or promote alcoholic fermentation, physiological organization was also important. Operationally, the distinction appears to have been one of solubility. Soluble ferments were not "organized." To be "organized" meant to be in some sort of particle, corpuscle, or cell. The importance of this characteristic can be seen in the role filtration tests and filter technology had in early microbiology. The Chamberland filter and the Berkefeld filter were two of the most widely used eponymous filtration devices for microbiological studies.[20] The agents that could transmit disease yet could pass though filters, the so-called filterable viruses, presented an anomaly that was important in focusing attention on the nature of a large group of infectious agents that had eluded bacteriological characterization.[21]

The filterability of bacteriophage meant that d'Herelle had to provide additional arguments for its particulate nature. His detailed and carefully described studies on the relationship between plaque-formers and the lytic agent made a powerful case for the particulate nature of phage. Other aspects of the organized nature of phage were less clearly put forward. The particles were made of *something,* of course, which was called "bacteriophage substance" to distinguish it from "bacterial substance." This phage substance could be distinguished from bacterial substance by immunological criteria. D'Herelle and others were able to produce antisera in animals injected with phage suspensions which showed relatively specific agglutination reaction with phages of the type used in the immunizations. The chemical study of phage substance, however, did not interest d'Herelle and was not taken up by others until the 1930s.

The structure of the bacteriophage proposed by d'Herelle in 1924 was derived from his "micellar theory of life" as presented in his monograph *Immunity in Natural Infectious Disease.* In this book he argued for the existence of individual colloidal micellae that have the properties of assimilation and adaptation and that cells are built up of aggregates of these micellar units (this theory will be expanded in Chapter 7). In this view with clear nineteenth-century origins,[22] a single colloidal micella is the fundamental unit of life, and bacteriophage, and indeed all ultraviruses (filterable viruses), are specific types of colloidal micellae. The microbe bacteriophage, then, is viewed as a colloidal aggregate of various molecules and the properties of this aggregate are determined by the composition and organization of the molecules that make up the micella. What were the properties which d'Herelle assigned to this ultraviral micella? Assimilation and adaptation to be sure, but these terms implied something more: multiplication and metabolism.

His explanations about ultraviruses as obligate intracellular parasites clarify his notions about ultravirus multiplication and metabolism. First, he repeatedly used the idea of parasitism in its macroscopic form: the parasite attacks the host, enters the host, utilizes host material to grow and multiply, then the host dies or is ruptured with release of more parasites. The zoospore of *Nucleophaga amoeba* which penetrates to the nucleus of *Amoeba verrucosa,* Ehr. is used as an analogy to bacteriophage both in name and in action (*BIB,* 355). Parasitism was central to his concept of ultraviruses, and he frequently wrote that the virus multiplied "at the expense" of the host organism, for example, by heterologous assimilation of bacterial substance into bacteriophage substance. The capacity to carry out this assimilation resided in the organization of the ultravirus corpuscle.

D'Herelle had little interest in the growing field of physiological chemistry, and his attempts to account for the obligate nature of the intracellular parasitism of viruses in chemical terms were unclear and imprecise. He recognized that enzymes could account for the digestion of bacterial substance, and with his colleague Georgiy Eliava he searched in bacteriophage lysates for activities that could cause the lysis of bacteria (FdH: 51). These *lysines* were interpreted as the *ferment soluble* secreted by the bacteriophage that led to the internal digestion and eventual lysis of the bacterial host cells. Since the lysines could be separated from the bacteriophage, d'Herelle and Eliava concluded that they were secreted substances rather than material contained in the organized viral micella. In another of his seemingly hair-splitting arguments, d'Herelle wrote: "I do not employ the term 'enzyme' for these lysines, since there are two kinds of ferments with one essential difference: enzymes do not attack living material. . . . It is evidently not the same for the lysines which exert their action on living bacteria" (*LPG,* 182 footnote).

The interwar period was one of great progress in understanding and clarifying metabolic processes generally and microbial metabolism specifically. D'Herelle and his colleague Vladimir Sertic intensified their investigations of the lysines produced during the course of bacteriophage growth, and in a series of papers from 1929 to 1937 they examined these lysines in more detail but without clarifying their role or specificity. By 1937, however, d'Herelle had started to come to grips with the details, in metabolic terms, of what it meant for the phage to be an obligate intracellular parasite. After reviewing his work on the lysines, and the popular view of phage as being "on the borderline of life" (an idea he found absurd), he emphasized that metabolism specifically was no longer the older, vague notion of assimilation, but rather "the power to exercise metabolism (1) which confers on a being the living state and the moment when that power ceases to manifest itself, even though all the conditions are favorable for its exercise, the being ceases to be alive, it is dead." The important expansion on this text is in footnote 1: "I say 'the power to exercise' and not 'the exercise' since in certain beings of simple constitution (among others a number of bacterial species, the bacteriophages and a certain few protozoans) are able to enter into a state of dormant life [*vie ralentie*] when the exercise of metabolism is impossible because of the paucity of nutrients; in such conditions the being continues to be 'alive' so that much later when proper conditions for the exercise of metabolism return, exercise of metabolism is recommenced" (*LPG*, 183). In this note he groups phages and spores together as dormant forms which can be activated upon exposure to the proper environment. For viruses, the obligate intracellular parasite, the interior of the cell is the appropriate environment for the exercise of phage metabolism. Just as the bacterial spore is unable to grow without the support of the proper growth medium, the phage is unable to grow without the proper support of the bacterial cell: "Everything indicates that the ultraviruses are intracellular parasites; probably they can assimilate nothing but living protoplasm" (*BIB*, 328).

A close examination of d'Herelle's conception of bacteriophage, then, suggests that he viewed phage as organized molecular aggregates, a colloidal micella, capable of entering a host cell, digesting the cellular protoplasm, and utilizing the digested products for growth and multiplication. There is no evidence to indicate that he believed the host cells offered any more than the appropriate nutrients, in analogy to bacterial culture medium, needed by the phage. The phage appeared to be activated, in analogy to spore germination, upon entry into the susceptible cell. It then carried out its own specific reactions, directed by its own characteristic micellar structure and composition. The process that ensured stability of phage properties was believed to be similar to the poorly understood process by which characteristics were passed from parental cell to the daughter cells during cell division. As the notion of genes and heredity in bacteria were not yet of major concern to bacteriologists, they did not see the need to explain the mechanisms behind the processes of phage multiplication and type variation and stability.

For d'Herelle, then, bacteriophages were ultramicrobes, obligate intracellular parasites with a limited autonomy to subvert the biological processes of the host cell. He unambiguously classified bacteriophages among the ultraviruses, that group of agents that cause a variety of specific animal and plant diseases. They were not, however, just miniature bacteria, too small to be seen with the light microscope. Instead, they were fundamentally different in form and structure. What was this form and structure? In his second monograph, *Les défenses de l'organisme,* published in 1923, he tackled the problem head-on. In this grand overview, he argued that bacteriophages were the building blocks of all other life forms, the most primitive kind of living being. An understanding of the nature of phage, d'Herelle claimed, would explain the nature of host defenses against disease, the structure of cells, and even the origin of life itself.

Félix and Daniel Hoerens d'Herelle, Paris about 1880. (Source: dHFP)

Félix and Marie Caire d'Herelle, about 1898. (Source: dHFP)

Félix d'Herelle with expedition to Labrador, 1899. (Source: dHFP)

Laboratory in Pasteur Institute, about 1919. (Source: dHFP)

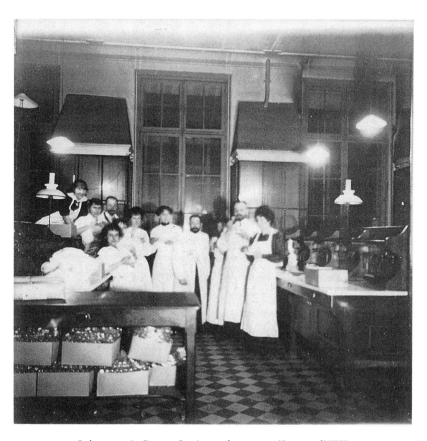

Laboratory in Pasteur Institute, about 1919. (Source: dHFP)

Formal portrait of d'Herelle, about 1927. (Source: dHFP)

Chapter 7 The Origin of Life:
Colloids and Protobes

D'Herelle was a dedicated materialist and a believer in Baconian science as the way to know the natural world.[1] His earliest writings—for example "How Will the World End?"[2] and his paper on the global balance of carbon (FdH: 1)—indicate his concern with the large questions and deep problems of rational thought. It is not surprising, then, that he should undertake a complete synthesis of his ideas on immunity. While it seems that this project was initiated to clarify and promulgate his ideas about the role of phage in the defenses against infectious disease, d'Herelle subsequently extended his ideas to encompass even more of natural knowledge—the nature of living matter and the origin of life, itself.

Immediately upon completion of his first monograph, *Le Bactériophage: Son rôle dans l'immunité,* d'Herelle was at work on his second book, *Les Défenses de l'organisme.* This work was a unified theory to explain the ways organisms defend themselves against natural invaders, both animate and inanimate. The unifying principle was that of colloid chemistry, a field of active experimentation and theorizing at that time. The results of studies of the diffusion of solutes through membranes led Thomas Graham to propose in 1861 that matter can exist in solution in either a diffusible, crystalloid state or a non-diffusible, colloidal state. Graham suggested that the colloidal state represented a form of the aggregated state of normally diffusible substances. Because many substances with colloidal properties came from living organisms and the substances such as albumins behaved as colloids, for many late nineteenth- and early twentieth-century scientists interested in the nature of life processes, colloids and their behavior became central problems. From 1910 to 1930 there was intense interest in and research on biocolloids, and, as Neil Morgan has demonstrated, linked the older, microscopic study of the chemistry of life with the more recent structural study of proteins.[3] Biocolloidology emphasized the application of the new physical chemistry to the problems of biology and was central to the thinking of biologists including Jacques Loeb and biochemists including The Svedberg.[4] Immunological reactions represented a strand of this research, concerned as they were with a major class of biocolloids, blood serum substances. Thus, flocculations (formation of fluffy, tiny particulate precipitates) and coagulations (formation of large clot-like precipitates) were taken as important biological examples of the gel-sol transitions of colloid chemistry.

D'Herelle saw the structure of antigens, the reactions of antigen and antibody, and the specificity of immune processes as each reflecting various aspects of the known properties of colloids. The preface of his second monograph carries the date 25 April 1922, indicating that it was written while he was still working at the Pasteur Institute. Of the book's 294 pages, however, only the final 44 pages were devoted to the role of bacteriophages in "exogenous immunity," that is, host defense provided by the commensal bacteriophages living in the animal body.

By the time *Les Défenses de l'organisme* was published, d'Herelle had left the Pasteur Institute to join the staff of the Institute for Tropical Medicine at the University of Leiden. In his work in Leiden from 1922 to 1924, as it turned out, he did not extend his immunological ideas so much as fortify his responses to Gratia's challenges about the nature of bacteriophage, its microbial status, and its living nature. There he revised this monograph for translation into English by George H. Smith, the translator of his first book. This revision, *Immunity in Natural Infectious Disease,* published in 1925, retained the theme of the French edition in the title and not only included the material on colloids and immunity from the original work, but also was extensively modified so that more than half the book was now devoted to d'Herelle's colloidal theory of life. In thinking about colloids and immunity, he saw the utility of these ideas in relation to his concept of phages as living microbes. The bacteriophage characters of non-diffusibility, reaction with immune sera, and intracellular invisibility were all colloidal properties. In a most logical and natural way he combined contemporary thinking about colloids with his view of phages as ultramicrobes, and synthesized a concept of phages as the ultimate building blocks of life.

D'Herelle's view of phage as a living being was important in his controversy with Jules Bordet and André Gratia over the nature and origin of phage. Bordet's view was that the lytic principle was a cellular enzyme, the synthesis of which was activated ("vitiated" was his term) by the interaction of that enzyme and susceptible cells. Interestingly, the term "vitiated" has connotations of "coming alive." D'Herelle's understanding of Bordet's position was that the lytic principle was not alive, that is, the bacteriophage is an enzymelike substance. If d'Herelle could show that bacteriophages were "living beings," he thought that Bordet's argument would be demolished.

Not only could he use this theory to defend the nature of phage as living beings, but he could use it to explain the origin of life as well. These ideas soon caught the imagination of such speculative biologists as J. B. S. Haldane, H. J. Muller, and A. I. Oparin, who readily employed them in their own writings on this problem.

To examine d'Herelle's work in some detail, it will be useful to consider his theory of the origin of life, on one hand, and his notions of life and matter, on the other. For d'Herelle's ideas on the origin of life, we can go back to Lamarck and his influence in French biology. Without some notion that organisms evolve in a progressive way, that is, change from simple to complex, the problem of the origin of life is more or less stuck with creation stories of one kind or another, where the origin of each life form requires its own explanation. Once an evolutionary scheme had been introduced, however, it became possible to think of the origin-of-life problem in much simpler ways. It seems intuitive that it would be easier to understand the origin of a supposedly simple microbe than a complex organism such as a monkey. Indeed, the interest in the question of spontaneous generation was driven by the origin-of-life problem. The work of Needham, Buffon, Spallanzani, Pouchet, and finally Pasteur on spontaneous generation was predicated on the assumption that it was sufficient to study the case of microorganisms because that was where the origin of life was likely to be.

While it appeared that Pasteur laid to rest the idea that microbes arise de novo in laboratory flasks as an everyday occurrence, the origin-of-life problem remained. By the late nineteenth century, small, primitive organisms were generally believed to be the earliest forms in the evolution of life on Earth.

Some circumspect writers used cautiously vague terminology, but others claimed that contemporary bacteria were, indeed, the early life forms.[5] Some scientists, including Kelvin, Rutherford, and Arrhenius, argued that life on Earth originated from germs driven down from interstellar space and that life has always existed—just as has matter and energy—so that no explanation of origins was required. While this hypothesis, called "panspermia," solved the problem of the origin of life on Earth, it did not satisfy scientists for long. E. A. Schäfer in his presidential address to the British Association for the Advancement of Science in 1912 noted that the emperor had no clothes: "But the acceptance of such theories of the arrival of life on earth does not bring us any nearer to a conception of its actual mode of origin; on the contrary, it serves to banish the investigation of the question to some conveniently inaccessible corner of the universe, and leaves us in the unsatisfactory position of affirming not only that we have no knowledge as to the mode of the origin of life—which is unfortunately true—but that we never can acquire such knowledge, which, it is to be hoped, is not true."[6] Benjamin Moore in his book of 1913 credited Schäfer with refocusing attention and clarity on the problem of the origin of life with a new optimism. Moore himself outlined an explanation based on evolution of colloidal aggregates that eventually became complex enough and exhibited the properties of living organisms.

Henry Fairfield Osborn summarized the situation in 1917 in his book *The Origin and Evolution of Life:* assemblages of chemical elements "were gradually bound up by a new form of mutual attraction whereby the action and reactions of a group of life elements established a new form of unity in the cosmos, an organic unity, an individual or organism quite distinct from the larger and smaller aggregations of inorganic matter previously held or brought together by the forces of gravity. This grouping occurred in the gelatinous state described as 'colloidal' by Graham."[7]

Two currents of thought run through the literature of this early part of the twentieth century: first, the earliest life forms must be sub-microscopic, that is, smaller than the known bacteria, and second, the colloidal state of matter was probably involved in the origin of these first life forms.

Both these notions shared the great heuristic value of maximal imprecision. Unobservable sub-microscopic life forms could have whatever properties were needed to fit a given hypothesis. Likewise, the colloidal states of matter were sufficiently vague and poorly understood as to be useful in almost any explanatory scheme. With these two dominant notions in force, it was quite natural that the numerous viruses, discovered and characterized in the early decades of the twentieth century, should fill the explanatory niche waiting for them. As Farley has documented, this formulation of the problem as involving colloidal states and sub-microscopic organisms dates from 1907–1908.[8]

During this time researchers discovered the viruses that were pathogenic to plants and animals, including tobacco mosaic virus, the agents of vaccinia, herpes simplex, poliomyelitis, rabies, and hog cholera, to name a few. These agents were characterized by two properties: their small size (ability to pass through filters that retained known bacteria) and their specific pathogenic effect on host organisms. Various attempts at further characterization, including cell-free cultivation, heat inactivation, and ultramicroscopic observations, suggested that such filterable viruses formed a group of organisms perhaps as diverse as the bacteria. Bacteriophages, on the other hand, were thought, at least initially, to be uniform and homogeneous.

D'Herelle's writings on phage as a primitive living organism—a *protobe,* to use his term—had wide appeal. Haldane cited them in his widely quoted article of 1928 on the origin of life.[9] Likewise, in 1922 H. J. Muller thought that phage might be the way to study pure genes themselves, in his view, the important stuff of life.[10] Oparin, in his most influential book, *The Origin of Life,* regarded as noteworthy the views of Kozo-Poljanski, who believed bacteriophages to be remnants of the basic living units from which cells arose.[11] D'Herelle's views would become institutionally recognized in his appointment in 1928 to the Chair of Protobiology at Yale University, probably the only such chair ever to have existed.

Although bacteriophage may be the "missing link" in evolution, the usually studied phages were likely not of the most primitive sort, as they had lived for untold years adapting to their specific hosts. Instead, d'Herelle reasoned, the place to look for such primordial phages was where prebiotic conditions might still prevail. He agreed with Buchanan that the most primitive bacteria were probably the sulfur-using thiobacteria, and that the protomicellae of early life probably coalesced to form this group of organisms (*INID,* 344). Thus, he undertook a study of sulfur spring waters at a French spa, Challes-les-Bains. Not only did he find that the water contained ultra-filterable forms of thiobacilli as well as phages active on thiobacilli, but some samples of bacteriologically sterile, sulfur-containing water showed reduction of sulfide to colloidal sulfur upon standing. He concluded: "The reduction of the sulfur could have only been produced by an ultravirus; this is the only hypothesis possible. This ultravirus may possibly be a common ancestor for all living things, and might be designated *Protobios protobios*" (*INID*, 345). Figure 6 shows d'Herelle's basic evolutionary scheme for the origin of life from *P. protobios*.

In *Immunity in Natural Infectious Disease* he set forth his ideas about the physico-chemical nature of phages and their role in the origin and evolution of life. In contrast to prior writing on the role of viruses in the origin of life (e.g., Moore, Osborn, Troland, and Minchin), d'Herelle provided a detailed, fully formed theory for the role of bacteriophages and then went on to extrapolate his theory to the whole of biology, developing what he called the "micellar concept of life" as a replacement for the cellular theory of life. His goal was to give a materialistic account of the nature of life in general, and of the living nature of the bacteriophage in particular. He cited Herbert Spencer and suggested that the various "micromerist" theories of living substance—for instance, the gemmules of Darwin, the micellae of Naegli, and the idants of Weismann—"are all derived from that suggested by Spencer. It may well be, however, that had this philosopher known of the colloidal state (which even now can hardly be comprehended) his hypothesis would have followed exactly the form that I have given" (*INID*, 51–52).[12] This position was not so old-fashioned as might be thought. The "old conception of the cell as an assemblage or colony of elementary organisms or primary vital units," that is, a

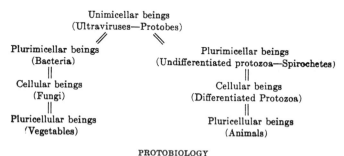

To express the relationship, the successive development of living beings may be schematically represented in the following manner:

Unimicellar beings
(Ultraviruses—Protobes)

Plurimicellar beings   Plurimicellar beings
(Bacteria)   (Undifferentiated protozoa—Spirochetes)
‖   ‖
Cellular beings   Cellular beings
(Fungi)   (Differentiated Protozoa)
‖   ‖
Pluricellular beings   Pluricellular beings
(Vegetables)   (Animals)

PROTOBIOLOGY

The ultravirus, or Protobe, which represents the most rudimentary being possessing elementary life, is nevertheless endowed with the same "powers" as beings much higher in the scale of organization.

Figure 6. D'Herelle's proposal for bacteriophage (*Protobios protobios*) as the evolutionary ancestor to both plants and animals. (*INID*, 347)

fundamentally micromerist view, was not ruled out by such mainstream cell biologists as E. B. Wilson, who wrote in this regard in 1923, "perhaps it is such, perhaps not—nor am I able to see how the possibilities here considered [i.e., questions of the replication of various granules of the protoplasm] are in any manner out of harmony with the conception of the cell as a colloidal system."[13]

In elaboration of his theory, d'Herelle first reviewed the current ideas about colloidal states of matter. Like many scientists during this period, he was unconvinced that proteins were large molecules in the conventional sense. As Fruton has noted, "It was clear, therefore, that in 1916 the verdict of the leading organic chemists working on proteins was that values above 5000 for their molecular weights were not acceptable."[14] From the diversity of analyses of various albumins, for example, d'Herelle wrote:

> The assumed molecule of albumin can be decomposed into its constituent amino acids, and each albumin, in accord with the living being from which it was derived, contains a different mosaic of these acidic amines. Each animal species, each individual it might be said, possesses special proteins as can be demonstrated by serological reactions.
>
> What can we conclude? Simply that the protein molecule does not exist. . . .
>
> The smallest possible particle of protein matter is in reality a micella, formed of an assemblage of polymerized molecules of amino acids, and that which chemists subject to elementary analysis are the residues of the micellae.
>
> . . . The secret of life, knowledge of the physico-chemical property which confers upon protein matter the powers of assimilation and of adaptation, is still far from being known, but we do know where the secret resides—and that is indeed something. It resides in the micella. (*INID,* 25)

From rather vague speculation about the colloidal state of cellular protoplasm and its likely relevance to the origin of life, d'Herelle focused his arguments on specific aspects of colloid theory, namely the structure of the micelle.

Micellae, he argued, were specialized structures with individual properties and functions. The cellular protoplasm was composed of a collection of such micellae, aggregated in ways that permitted the cell to function:

> A protoplasmic micella should be a micellar system formed by the union of what might be termed protomicellae. The granule of each protomicella should be a polymerized molecule of some substance such as an acid amine, a cyclic base, a lipoid, or a carbohydrate. The union into a micellar system of a number of protomicellae of different amino acids, of different cyclic bases, of different lipoids, and of different carbohydrates, each with its adsorbed ions and its liquid atmosphere, should form the protoplasmic micella. The general architecture of the protoplasmic

micella should always be of the same type, whether it forms by itself an ultravirus or whether it enters into the cell of a man, but they should differ from each other through the nature of the protomicellae assembled. In view of the number of acid amines and cyclic bases the number of possible combinations is almost infinite. The behavior of each cell physiologically and morphologically should be determined by a micellar type, possibly by two types, one being cytoplasmic and the other nuclear. (*INID*, 50–51)

From such an all-encompassing physico-chemical description of the micellar concept of life, d'Herelle went on to claim that bacteriophages, being particulate and small (of the dimensions of an albumin molecule as measured by filtration experiments), are colloidal micellae.

As bacteriophages are living beings and are physico-chemically identical to the micellae that are in turn the basis for all cell structure and function, d'Herelle argued that phages are, without doubt, the lowest life forms, intermediate between inanimate organic substances and living protoplasm. "The view that all vital behavior is the outcome of the properties of some single, protein-like substance was replaced by a perspective in which different vital functions were attributed to different metabolic reaction sequences, catalyzed by sets of specific enzymes."[15] With bacteriophage, however, d'Herelle had a new solution to the problem: phages were living, metabolizing, organized particles the size of colloids. Somehow, they could carry out all the reactions needed for life, yet were small enough to be the "basic" stuff of life.

Although he devoted a substantial part of his monograph to his theory of micellae, he could find very little to say about the living nature of bacteriophage. Because the phage was invisible, the usual criterion of visible—that is, microscopic—multiplication did not apply. Thus, d'Herelle relied on *properties* or *characteristics* that could define living beings. He repeatedly used two characteristics that for him were necessary and sufficient to define life: *assimilation* and *adaptation.*

Assimilation meant the ability of an organism to extract nutrients from its environment for its own use.[16] Heterotrophic organisms require organic matter, while autotrophic organisms can subsist on inorganic materials and carbon dioxide. Assimilation as a property of living things is closely linked to metabolism, that is, the conversion of the environmental nutrients into different substances as required by the organism. A second quality that was believed to be an essential, defining feature of life was the ability to "adapt," that is, to survive in the face of altered and unfavorable conditions. This notion of adaptation was, of course, linked to the concept of variation, a concept which was central to contemporary ideas of evolution.[17]

The increase in number of phage during growth was taken as evidence that the phage assimilated some of the substance of the bacteria (and possibly the culture medium as well) and incorporated this substance into newly made phages. For such a demonstration, the assumptions of the *autonomy* and of the *particulate nature* of phage were critical. The observations that phages were apparently the same, independent of the specific host they were grown on, suggested to d'Herelle that they possessed their own ability to assimilate nutrients and convert "bacterial substance" into "bacteriophage substance" (*INID*, 19–20; 340–342). Although oxidative metabolism was not absolutely required as a consequence of such assimilation, its occurrence would be strong evidence for such independent metabolism by phages. In a determined effort to look for respiration in phages, Jacques Bronfenbrenner at the Rockefeller Institute spent two years carrying out precise measurements of the oxidations in preparations of bacteria and bacteriophage. In the end, Bronfenbrenner had to conclude that phages do not respire at a rate greater than about 1 percent that of the host bacteria.[18]

Adaptation, a rather vague concept in d'Herelle's writings, was taken to mean some sort of purposeful response to changed environmental conditions. Initially, he grew phage sequentially on different hosts and observed alterations in virulence. He cited work of others who were able to "adapt" phage to grow in acid medium[19] or in the presence of inhibitory antiseptics.[20] Much later, he recognized that this adaptation was a result of an intrinsic variability in the phage which he thought of as deVriesian mutations.

D'Herelle's forcefully presented arguments and elegant experiments caught the imagination of many leading scientists of his day. After d'Herelle, the extension of the biocolloid theories from micellae to the coacervates of Bungenberg de Jong attracted the attention of Oparin; d'Herelle's contributions were influential in his thinking.[21]

Even in 1931 the nature of the entire group of "ultraviruses" was still unclear and a subject of debate. The physiologist Henry Dale, in his presidential address to the British Association for the Advancement of Science entitled "The Biological Nature of the Viruses," asked: "Are organization, differentiation, separation from the surrounding medium by a boundary membrane of special properties, necessary of the endowment of matter with any form or life? Or is it possible to conceive of a material complex, retaining in endless propagation its physiological character, as revealed by the closely specific reactions to it of the cells which it infects, though it is not organized into units, but uniformly dispersed in a watery medium?"[22] In 1927, C. E. Simon had suggested that vaccinia virus was a living organism because it was reported to be cultivatable, but he found the idea of the inanimate nature of tobacco mosaic virus "perhaps not so repellant."[23]

In 1935, however, Wendell Stanley reported that he had obtained the virus of tobacco mosaic in crystalline form.[24] For the first time, it appeared that a biological "organism" had been reduced to the realm of organic chemistry. In the popular press as well as in scientific circles, this work was interpreted as demonstrating a kind of "missing link" in the evolution of living forms from inanimate substances. Thus, *Scientific American* referred to viruses as part of "the smooth slide up to life" and offered this editorial comment on an article with that title: "Many men of science believe the revelations concerning the nature of life—the same ones described so ably in the accompanying survey— are destined to make the present time famous or classic in the future annals of science. Few scientists had been so optimistic to predict, for our times, the solution of the major mystery and problem of all science—what is life—yet many signs seem now to point toward success. Better still, they point toward the simultaneous solution of several other baffling mysteries. The reader is urged to ponder well the solid content of this article.— *The Editor.*"[25]

Clearly the prevalent view by the 1930s was materialistic and antivitalistic, and one took for granted that small, simple organisms were where to look for answers to two age-old questions: what characteristics or properties are neces- sary and sufficient to define life? and how did life begin? In a similar flush of optimism in 1937 Max Delbrück wrote a short essay entitled "The Riddle of Life" based on the possibilities of research on viruses.[26]

While the crystallization of tobacco mosaic virus by Stanley was recognized immediately as relevant to the role of viruses as "living" molecules, the concept of a bacteriophage as simply another virus with a different host organism was still a minority view. Most textbooks of the 1930s adopted the Bordet-Northrop view of phage as some sort of lytic enzyme. Until the mid-1940s the status of bacteriophage among the viruses was in constant flux. As described in some detail by Van Helvoort, the nature of phage was the subject of heated debates: Was it ultramicrobe, gene, or autocatalytic protein?[27]

With the application of the electron microscope to the study of phage in the early 1940s, the particulate nature of phage could no longer be denied. In a review of the first electron microscope studies of animal, plant and bacterial viruses, Levaditi and Bonét-Maury noted that the particulate and definite organized structure of bacteriophage vindicated d'Herelle's view in his long debates with opponents.[28] In a strange rebuttal of sorts several months later, d'Herelle objected to the criterion of "organization" being applied to phage. He again argued for a functional rather than a structural definition of phage, thus preserving the living nature of his beloved microbe. Even as d'Herelle's concept of bacteriophage was being confirmed over the competing concepts of the Nobel Prize winners, Bordet and Northrop, he could not fully accept the demise of the pleasantly ambiguous nature of phage (FdH: 140).

Chapter 8 The Hope of Phage Therapy

D'Herelle's concern with the biological nature of bacteriophage, even in his first paper, seems to have been secondary to his interest in the practical use to be made of phage in understanding and attacking infectious diseases. In the Pastorian tradition, he was impatient to try out his laboratory science in the hospital and in the community—in Van Helvoort's words, to take bacteriophage "from the lab-bench to the bedside."[1] That his first observations of bacteriophage were made in the study of dysentery suggested a natural transition from the theory to practice in the case of enteric infections.

Although the observations that the presence of phage in the stools of dysentery and typhoid patients seemed to correlate with their recovery, d'Herelle was concerned that these findings might be overinterpreted. This claim may appear to be at odds with his reputation for dogmatism and strongly held beliefs in the importance of bacteriophage in the recovery from infectious diseases; however, he was careful in his written work to recognize the limitations of some of his early work. This recognition spurred him on to additional studies of both human and animal diseases. In July 1921 he commented on the choices of diseases to study: "From the point of view of the study of immunity human infection offers an inconvenience. Man is not available for experimentation; observation alone is permitted. On the other hand the study of a human infection, such as typhoid fever or cholera, for example, in a refractory animal—and they are all so—can only lead to illusory results. Study of disease in the animal, on the contrary, permits of confirmatory experimentation upon the susceptible animal itself where error is no longer unavoidable. However, this method of procedure is very complicated; the disease does not come to us, we must go to it" (FdH: 56, 173).[2] At this point, d'Herelle had made observational studies of both dysentery and typhoid in humans, but these observations appear to have been sporadic, preliminary investigations. The samples were analyzed as they became available and concerted, continuous study of individual patients had not been done. In the summer of 1919, however, d'Herelle carried out two hospital-based studies of intestinal diseases to test more rigorously his conclusions about the relationships between the pathogenic bacteria and the bacteriophage.

In the Pasteur Hospital he followed at least six patients with bacillary dysentery (*BIRI*, 176–185) from mid-July until the end of September 1919, as judged from the dates given in the clinical descriptions of these patients. In a parallel study, d'Herelle examined about one hundred pediatric patients with diarrhea in the Hôpital des Enfants-malades (*BIB*, 245). These patients were followed closely, often with several bacteriological examinations each day, a fact that prompted d'Herelle to give special acknowledgment to the nursing staff. These observational studies only confirmed his previous ideas about the role of bacteriophages in the recovery from such infections; given his past work with epizootics among locusts and mice, he was on the lookout for some ways to "field-test" his conclusions.

By this time, as noted in his clear statement in 1921, d'Herelle had decided that animal models of human disease were suspect and that the study of "natural" infections was the only valid way to study immunity. By "natural" infections he meant the study of diseases to which the animal, in nature, was susceptible. Thus, the study of the reaction of rabbits to injections of cholera vibrios, for instance, would necessarily result in misleading information, at least with regard to understanding human reactions to cholera, because rabbits do not get cholera.

Having concluded that phages play a major role in natural immunity and recovery, d'Herelle proposed that the artificial spread of bacteriophage, in essence the creation of a kind of bacteriophage epizootic among the infected populace, could be used to control epidemics. Soon he had a chance to test this idea in a natural setting. In the spring of 1919 Eduard Vulquin, a chemist at the Pasteur Institute, mentioned to d'Herelle that he noted a serious outbreak of a highly contagious, lethal disease among the chickens in the village where Vulquin's parents lived. D'Herelle soon obtained several dead animals from the farmers at Pougy (near Arcis-sur-Aube, about 125 kilometers east of Paris) and was able to isolate an organism he identified as *Salmonella gallinarum*. This organism was known in the United States as "fowl typhoid," but it had never been found in France. When d'Herelle notified the veterinary authorities, he was informed that the disease was not fowl typhoid, but the well-known and endemic chicken cholera. Shortly thereafter, however, d'Herelle was proven correct and as usual, he almost gleefully noted: "In reality, as they found out a little later, this supposed chicken cholera was fowl typhoid: it was a error of diagnostic bacteriology" (*PM*, 398). He christened this new European affliction *typhose aviaire*, avian typhosis.

This outbreak gave d'Herelle an almost ideal opportunity to test his ideas about the role of phage in controlling the spread of epidemic bacterial disease. Avian typhosis was in domestic animals which were generally localized to farmyards, it was caused by an organism related to those with which he had a lot of experience, and there was no alternative treatment to compete with his program. In addition, chickens were relatively cheap, so controlled experiments could be done on adequate numbers of animals. His research on avian typhosis began in early 1919, when he first started to collect blood samples from various sources, and concluded in February 1920, when he left France to extend his research to another bacterial disease, hemorrhagic septicemia of buffalo, this time in French Indochina.

By now d'Herelle seemed to have developed a standard approach to a new research problem. His first paper described his bacteriological studies on the basic features of the organism, its distribution, and its pathogenicity (FdH: 31). He received sixty-seven blood samples from dead or dying chickens from many areas of France. From fifty-six samples he isolated *B. sanguinarum* Moore (*S. gallinarum*), eleven were sterile, and in only one sample did he find the bacterium of fowl cholera. Although he found that the disease had been observed in France since at least 1916, he traced this particular outbreak to an apparent initial case in December 1918 in the village of Chainq, located about four kilometers outside of St. Florentin in the Yonne region. The disease had become endemic and d'Herelle was pessimistic about measures to contain its spread because of the great mobility of domestic farm animals. He concluded his paper with a rather sardonic comment: "The purchase of chickens from these regions should be made with discernment" (FdH: 31, 819).

This paper, written at the time when d'Herelle was immersed in his observational studies at the Pasteur Hospital and the Hôpital des Enfants-malades, was communicated to the Academy of Sciences on 3 November 1919. Two weeks later, on 17 November, he communicated his observations on the bacteriophages isolated from the chickens in the Department of the Aube. Again, he followed his standard approach: this report described the bacteriophages in the intestines of normal, healthy chickens as well as those found in chickens suffering from avian typhosis. The specificity, that is, the virulence, of the phage for the pathogenic bacteria, *B. sanguinarum* (*S. gallinarum*), was demonstrable only in phages isolated from sick chickens or chickens infected with the pathogen. In the case of one flock studied, d'Herelle noted that the appearance of phages active against the pathogen preceded the recovery of the infected individuals, just as he had observed in human diseases. In this note, then, he went on to generalize his belief that the study of epidemics is the study of the contest between two agents, the invading bacterium and the bacteriophage that is specific for that organism. Just as the pathogen is contagious, he repeated, "immunity is transmissible between individuals of the same species." He concluded this paper, as usual, with a tantalizing and provocative statement: "This result proclaims that the ingestion of a culture of bacteriophage, appropriately selected for high virulence to the pathogenic bacillus, can confer natural immunity. Immunization experiments based on this principle are actually in progress in avian typhosis, through the courtesy of various veterinarians; the results obtained so far: the abrupt cessation of the enzootic on the same day as the administration of the bacteriophage confirms in an indisputable manner the role of this microbe as the agent of immunity" (FdH: 32). With this final sentence, d'Herelle set off a twenty-year campaign to stamp out epidemics as well as local infections by means of the bacteriocidal action of bacteriophages. Only with the discovery and development of specific antibacterial chemotherapy and antibiotics in the 1940s did interest in phages as agents in the battle against infectious diseases begin to wane.

D'Herelle's full account of his work with avian typhosis and his first trials with phage therapy appeared in his first book, *Le Bactériophage: Son rôle dans l'immunité,* published as a "monograph of the Pasteur Institute" in 1921. Not only did he give a detailed description of the natural history of avian typhosis, but he included an account of controlled infections and laboratory tests of bacteriophage prophylaxis. Field reports from trials in various regions of France were also described.

After his observations on the prevalence and virulence of phages in fowl with avian typhosis, d'Herelle carried out an experimental trial of bacteriophage in Paris, far from the area of endemicity:

> Six chickens, procured from a region free of infection, were placed under observation. Their excreta were examined daily for ten days for the purpose of establishing the complete absence of a bacteriophage active for *B. gallinarum.*
>
> Chicken no. 1 then received, *per os,* 1 cc. of a culture of a strain of bacteriophage very active for *B. gallinarum* (+ + + +).
>
> Chicken no. 2 received 0.5 cc. of the same culture by subcutaneous injection.
>
> The next day examination of the feces of these two animals showed the presence of a bacteriophage strongly virulent for *B. gallinarum.* Therefore, the bacteriophage passed into the intestine, whether ingested or injected. This same fact has since been verified with man and with different animals.
>
> Chicken no. 1 next received *per os* daily for twenty-five days 2 cc. of a bouillon culture of *B. gallinarum.* The active bacteriophage persisted in the intestine with its primary virulence (+ + + +) and maintained itself up to nine days after the last dose of the pathogenic organism.
>
> Chicken no. 2 which had received nothing after the inoculation of the active bacteriophage ceased to show an active strain for *B. gallinarum* within three days after the injection. In other words, chicken no. 1, subjected to repeated reinfections, retained an intestinal bacteriophage active for *B. gallinarum* for thirty-four days, while chicken no. 2, not infected, for only three days.
>
> It follows that the intestinal bacteriophage remains active only if it is able to develop in the intestine at the expense of this bacterium, but in such a case it remains active just so long as this condition in fulfilled. Inversely, the presence in the intestine of a bacteriophage possessing virulence for a given bacterium indicated that this bacterium was a short time previously in the intestine.
>
> In the course of the preceding experiment chickens nos. 3 and 4 were placed in contact with chicken no. 1. They all ate and drank from the same containers, the more so since they were changed about in pens in such a manner as to simulate conditions of life analogous to those of the chicken-yard. Two days after the first contact, in the case of chicken no. 3 and three days with chicken no. 4, their excreta contained a bacteriophage very virulent for *B. gallinarum* (+ + + +). From this time on they each received each day for twenty-one days, 2 cc. of a bouillon culture of *B. gallinarum.* At no time did they appear sick. The intestinal bacteriophage remained active for the bacillus throughout the entire period of the administration of the pathogenic bacillus, and even longer—seven days in no. 4 and ten days in no. 3. The

intestinal bacteriophage did not then disappear, for as in the case of chickens nos. 1 and 2, it remained active for one or several members of the colo-typhoid-dysentery group. But the virulence for *B. gallinarum* did not persist when the ingestion of the cultures of this last bacillus was stopped. The experiment with chickens nos. 3 and 4 shows clearly that the bacteriophagous ultramicrobe is infectious in exactly the same sense as is the pathogenic bacillus itself, since these birds were "contaminated" by contact with chicken no. 1. (*BIRI*, 211–215)

D'Herelle went on to show that two more chickens, nos. 5 and 6, which were bacteriophage-free, rapidly succumbed to the lethal effects of a single dose of *B. gallinarum*. After birds 1–4 had stopped excreting active phage, he again gave them *B. gallinarum*. Not only did they remain healthy, but bacteriophage with virulence for the pathogen reappeared in a phenomenon he dubbed "latent virulence."

While this controlled study of experimental infection and phage prophylaxis utilized only six animals, the outcome so strongly supported his view of the role of phage in natural immunity that major field trials started immediately. For these trials, which he called "immunization experiments," he prepared filtrates of a culture of *B. gallinarum* lysed by a highly virulent phage isolate. These bacteriophage lysates were packaged in sealed ampules of 0.5 ml and provided to veterinarians with instructions for subcutaneous injection into the birds to be "immunized."

Between 2 October 1919 and the end of February 1920 d'Herelle visited "village after village" in rural France, wherever he could find an outbreak of avian typhosis. These travels took him to Agen, Pully-en-Auxois, Provins, Rouillac-en-Charente (*BIRI*, 243–245). He carried out microbiological examinations of the sick birds, as well as providing phage preparations for "immunizations" by various routes of administration. By the end of this period, he claimed that the results fully supported his theories of natural recovery from epidemic infectious diseases. First, bacteriophages active against *B. gallinarum* were never found in well birds. Second, the introduction of virulent anti-gallinarum phages into flocks, either by direct inoculation of each bird or by putting a chicken containing the virulent phage in its intestine into the same barnyard, always resulted in the cessation of the epidemic and the recovery of most of the sick birds. Third, he found four birds which recovered spontaneously (out of one hundred examined in detail), and each of these four had phages virulent for *B. gallinarum*. He concluded: "I had, then, absolute proof of the fact that the recovery from and cessation of epidemics depends entirely on the behavior of the bacteriophage, and furthermore, I had a general method which allowed me to experimentally reproduce these two phenomena" (*PM*, 404). On the basis of this belief, in the summer of 1919, d'Herelle sought wider applications for his "general method," especially a human application.

Dysentery seemed like a promising condition to which to apply his ideas, first because he was accumulating information about dysentery phages in the laboratory, and second, dysentery was a major cause of epidemic morbidity and mortality and had been a focus of interest at the Pasteur Institute for some time.[3] D'Herelle sought out Professor Victor-Henri Hutinel, chief of a large pediatric service at the Hôpital des Enfants-malades in Paris and the doyen of French pediatricians. After d'Herelle explained his proposal to Hutinel, "he agreed to let me treat the young patients on the condition that I first demonstrate that ingestion of the cultures of bacteriophage were themselves harmless" (*PM*, 404). Although d'Herelle and members of his family had repeatedly ingested large quantities of bacteriophage cultures, he proposed another trial on himself of a dose one hundred times greater than that proposed for use in the sick children. Several hospital interns who were present also requested a "small glass" of phage. On 1 August 1919 a large flask was "shared all around," and even Professor Hutinel tasted the culture: "Opinion was unanimous, the flavor, if not delicious, was not too disagreeable." The next morning all who had ingested the phage reported no ill effects, and Hutinel allowed d'Herelle to proceed to his clinical trials (*PM*, 405). Precisely at that time, the first patient appeared in the hospital: a twelve-year-old with rather severe dysentery, ten to twelve bloody stools per day. After taking a pretreatment sample for microbiological analysis, d'Herelle injected him on the morning of 2 August with 2 ml of the most virulent anti-dysentery phage he had in his collection. That afternoon the patient had three more bloody stools, and during the night one non-bloody stool, but "The next morning all the symptoms had disappeared." Although this case was certainly remarkable, it was not until early September 1919 that several more dysentery patients appeared so the first result could be tested. Three brothers, aged three, seven, and twelve, were admitted in grave condition, their sister having died at home after only several hours of illness. Each patient received one dose of the virulent anti-dysentery phage preparation and all three started to recover within twenty-four hours. For some reason, however, these dramatic results were not extended for several years and they were never published.

Toward the end of 1919, Alexandre Yersin, the director of the Pasteur Institute in Indochina, was visiting Paris. D'Herelle decided to approach Yersin about working in Indochina, which was, in his words, "the land of my dreams:

one meets cholera, plague, and various epizootics such as the terrible *barbone* [bovine hemorrhagic septicemia] which a few years before had killed all the buffalos in Java, over a million animals in just a few months" (*PM,* 409). D'Herelle asked to see Yersin on the pretext of asking him some epidemiologic questions, and when Yersin, in general conversation, mentioned that the shortage of bacteriologists in Indochina prevented study of even such economically important diseases as *barbone,* d'Herelle seized this opening to propose that he spend 1920 in Indochina with the commission to study *barbone* (*PM,* 410).

D'Herelle left Paris in early 1920 and slowly made his way to Saigon in French Indochina via Suez, Djibouti, Colombo, and Singapore. Saigon in the 1920s was one of the great cosmopolitan cities of Asia. D'Herelle thought it was rivaled only by Kuala Lumpur as a center of international opulence and modernity. The city of about 100,000 inhabitants was the largest city in Cochinchina. As a French colony it boasted of its own overseas Pasteur Institute, located in two buildings not far from the center of town. Yersin, who discovered the plague bacillus during the Hong Kong epidemic of 1895, was director of the Institute in Saigon, but was a rather misanthropic man who lived in Nha-trang, a coastal town two hundred miles north in Annam, the other part of French Indochina, where there was another Pasteur Institute. The Institute in Saigon had a small apartment for Yersin's annual visit of a few days, and Yersin turned it over to d'Herelle for the duration of his visit.

A clear motivation for d'Herelle's desire to spend a year in Indochina is not apparent in his personal recollections nor in his published work. Rather, it seems that he was seeking a place where there were opportunities to study several serious epidemic diseases, where he would be free of establishment interference, and where he could indulge his taste for exotic environments. Although he alluded to a proposal to Yersin made during their meeting in Paris, when he arrived in Saigon, he seemed to cast about for leads as to what might be interesting to follow up. He did not immediately, for example, set out to organize a bacteriophage trial with some local disease, as he had done in the case of avian typhosis.

At first cholera and plague attracted his attention. He made friends with the chief of the Public Health Service in Cochinchina, a Dr. Lecompte, who invited him to study all the cases on his service (*PM,* 434). It was there that d'Herelle saw his first case of cholera, a disease that held his attention for the rest of his life. The patient was comatose and appeared moribund; after obtaining his bacteriological samples, d'Herelle went to the patient's home to obtain samples from the family members. There he saw the filth and squalor which contributed to the spread of the cholera. Twenty years later he wrote: "This was my first encounter with cholera, it was a spectacle which one does not forget" (*PM*, 434).

All in all, he studied about one hundred cases of cholera, searching, of course, for anti-cholera phages. D'Herelle was puzzled by the fact that while the overall death rate from cholera in Indochina was about 60–70 percent, he found only one survivor in his sample. He was unable to find any anti-cholera phages in the patients who died, and from the one survivor he managed to isolate only one rather avirulent strain of anti-vibrio phage (*BIB*, 261).

About this time, he started to collaborate with Dr. LeLouet, the chief of the veterinary service at the Pasteur Institute, on the vaccination of water buffaloes against *barbone*. The pathogenesis of this disease was rather well known; a bacillus classified as a species of *Pasteurella* was responsible. The disease seemed to behave like fowl plague, made famous by the early research of Louis Pasteur himself. This cattle disease could decimate the cattle population very quickly; in one outbreak, about 30 percent of the 30,000 water buffaloes in the two French regions of Indochina died within a month. The government was under strong pressure to find some way to stop this economically devastating plague.

D'Herelle and LeLouet embarked on a program to devise a vaccine for this disease. Their first approach was exactly analogous to Pasteur's original work on the *Pasteurella* infection in fowl plague. They carried out repeated passages of the organism in rabbits in the hope of selecting an attenuated strain which was still immunizing. In spite of d'Herelle's long experience during the war when he made killed organism vaccines, again he seemed to follow in the footsteps of Pasteur and sought an attenuated live organism vaccine. The model of Pasteur had such a powerful hold on d'Herelle that he did not even try his own invention, bacteriophage therapy, until the end of the attenuated vaccine trials.

The rabbit-attenuated strain of *barbone* was non-lethal to the buffalo and protected the animals from a subsequent challenge of virulent bacilli. Still, however, there were some failures. Sometimes the vaccine was insufficiently attenuated and the buffaloes got sick. At this point d'Herelle started on his second approach to *barbone* involving bacteriophage. First he studied a small outbreak of *barbone* in its natural setting to see if the presence of phages which were active against the organism of *barbone* could be correlated with the clinical outcome. In May 1920 he went to the village of Bac Lieu and found that in four sick buffaloes, which died shortly after he examined them, there were only the usual coliphages (that is, phages specific for the *E. coli* bacterium) in the intestines. The ten healthy buffaloes in the village all had virulent anti-Pasteurella phages as well as the usual coliphages, while in a neighboring village, untouched by the outbreak, the healthy animals lacked the anti-Pasteurella phages. These findings supported his model and even extended it from strictly intestinal diseases to septicemias as well (*PM,* 445). A second field study of another outbreak confirmed these observations, and d'Herelle noted: "It was exactly as I had shown in the course of the epizootic of avian typhosis: the epidemic ceases when all the surviving animals are refractory to the illness because of the fact that present in their intestines is a bacteriophage virulent for the pathogenic bacterium" (*PM,* 448).

D'Herelle and LeLouet then carried out two trials of bacteriophage as prophylaxis for *barbone.* These trials used seventeen animals in all, an expensive undertaking that was supported by the Governor-General of French Indochina. The basic plan involved injection of a single dose of anti-*barbone* phage and subsequent challenge, two to six weeks later, with virulent organisms. The first series of such "immunizations" failed: both the phage-treated and the unimmunized control animals died rapidly. As part of the second series of immunizations, four buffaloes received not one but two injections of the bacteriophage lysate. These animals, alone, resisted repeated challenges with virulent *barbone* bacilli. As part of these experiments d'Herelle and LeLouet monitored the stools of the animals for the presence of both coliphages and anti-Pasteurella phages. They found that right after the injection of the phage lysate into the jugular vein the *barbone*-specific phages could be recovered from the intestinal track, but by several days later they had disappeared. D'Herelle interpreted these findings in a way which "saved the phenomenon" and yet explained their results. He noted that the host bacteria for the anti-Pasteurella phages were not normally found in the gut so that there existed no long-term natural reservoir for the maintenance of the phage in the inoculated animals. The effective immunity that was elicited by two, but not one, injections, he suggested, resulted from the antibodies raised against the breakdown products of the *barbone* bacteria present in the phage lysates. Thus, he interpreted the immunity in more classical terms such as that produced by killed bacterial vaccines as used for typhoid and gangrene.

Not only did d'Herelle study cholera and *barbone,* but he had a go at bubonic plague in Indochina as well. Perhaps this interest was to please Yersin, the discoverer of the plague bacillus, but more likely it was another expression of d'Herelle's quest for wide application of his ideas about exogenous immunity and bacteriophage. In September 1920 there was a small outbreak of bubonic plague in Bac Lieu village, where he had previously studied *barbone:* all twelve died. Since human convalescent patients were rare, he reasoned that because the epidemic is spread by rodents, they may be more resistant and may have some natural immunity. In apparent confirmation of his speculation, he was able to isolate phages extremely active against the plague bacillus from rat feces found in four places in Bac Lieu. In his usual grandiose conclusion to his two-page note, he stated: "I propose to study the degree of immunity conferred by these cultures, and to study the conditions of their application as a vaccine in the prophylaxis against human plague" (FdH: 40). It would be five years before he got the chance to make good on this proposal, but his claim of successful cures of the plague with these Bac Lieu phages set the stage not only for major changes in his own career, but also it became the stuff of the romantic novel *Arrowsmith*.[4]

In the spring of 1921 d'Herelle returned to France to begin work on his first monograph on bacteriophage under the cloud of deputy director Calmette's hostility to d'Herelle's presence at the Institut Pasteur. At the same time he worked mornings with Dr. Edouard Peyre at the Institute for Cancer Research at Villejuif on a project aimed at better understanding the role of viruses and cancer (FdH: 92; FdH: 93).

By the middle of July 1921 he had finished his draft of *Le Bactériophage: Son rôle dans l'immunité,* and presented it to Emile Roux, his patron and director of the Pasteur Institute, while Calmette was away on vacation. Roux agreed to sponsor it for publication as a monograph of the Pasteur Institute, and d'Herelle quickly proceeded to a meeting with the publisher before Calmette's return. The book was published in October 1921 with a press run of 1500 copies (FdH: 48).

Sometime during the fall of 1921, a delegation of three professors from the University of Leiden came to Paris to ask d'Herelle about moving to their university and joining the newly formed Institute of Tropical Medicine under the directorship of Paul Christian Flu.[5] Flu, a native of Indonesia, was intrigued by the possibility that phages might be used to purify water supplies by specifi-cally killing the pathogens which often contaminated public water supplies in the tropics. Given his unhappy situation at the Pasteur Institute in Paris, d'Herelle immediately accepted this offer, which included adequate laboratory space and research support. His appointment at Leiden as conservator in the Institute of Tropical Medicine ran from 18 July 1922 through 30 June 1923. Later he was reappointed from 1 October 1923 through 30 September 1924.[6]

The two years at Leiden were devoted to work on the "nature" of bacte-riophage. This work appears to have been driven by d'Herelle's need to respond to Gratia's challenges (see chapter 5). While this research program must have been stressful, with the public debates and acrimonious polemics, he later recalled his time in Leiden with considerable happiness. In his autobiographical memoir, he initially entitled the chapter on his stay in Leiden: "Il est inerte. . . . Non. Il vit" [It is dead. . . . No. It is alive]. in reference to his research program there on the biological nature of phage (*PM*, 488). He later crossed out this title and substituted: "Au pays de l'hospitalité" [In the land of hospitality]. He viewed Leiden as a refuge for international scholars who were persecuted elsewhere: in the case of Albert Einstein, for being Jewish, in his own case, for being outspoken.

His position at Leiden as conservator was probably the only one available to Flu at a time of increasing economic difficulties. Although this position as conservator was apparently a minor one, later biographers have aggrandized it somewhat.[7] He and his family lived in Noordwijk, a small village on the North Sea, and d'Herelle traveled the fifteen kilometers to Leiden each day. Because his mother was Dutch, he knew enough of the language to get along and felt quite comfortable in this new environment (*PM*, 488–510).

While at Leiden d'Herelle assisted Flu in his work on bacteriophage, as well as pursuing his own research program on the biological nature of bacteriophage. It was during the period, also, that he wrote his second monograph, *Les Défenses de l'organisme*. In contrast to his first book on phage, this tract was much more theoretically oriented.

This approach, however, seems at odds with d'Herelle's fundamental goal of practical application of science to epidemic diseases. In this second book he carefully worked out a theory of physiological reactions of organisms to foreign colloids and developed his "micellar theory of life" which he contrasted to the "cellular theory of life."

At Leiden d'Herelle met some of the luminaries of his time: Lorentz, Einstein, and Einthoven, and he became a close friend of the immunologist Willem Storm van Leeuwen.[8] D'Herelle was apparently well-received into Dutch scientific circles, perhaps because he spoke Dutch, and perhaps because he had the support of two highly respected patrons in the persons of Flu and Storm van Leeuwen. And although d'Herelle was only a conservator in the Institute for Tropical Medicine, Flu proposed him for an honorary medical degree, which he received on 25 January 1924.[9] This award seems to have been somewhat controversial, according to the discussions in the faculty meetings prior to this degree.[10] The therapeutic value of bacteriophage was beginning to be questioned even at that time. D'Herelle was quite proud of this award, apparently the first official recognition of his status as a world-class scientist. He was fond of noting later that among the very few British subjects who had ever received an honorary doctorate from Leiden was Winston Churchill.[11] Recognition from another corner came when the Royal Academy of Sciences of Amsterdam awarded d'Herelle the Leeuwenhoek Medal in 1925 for his discovery of bacteriophages. This prestigious award has been given at ten-year intervals to persons who have made distinguished contribution to microbiology. The medal recipients before d'Herelle were Christian Gottfried Ehrenberg (1875), Ferdinand Cohn (1885), Louis Pasteur (1895), Martinus Willem Beijerinck (1905), and David Bruce (1915).[12] D'Herelle was especially proud to note that he was in the company of his model, Pasteur, the only other French scientist to be so honored.[13]

Even these tokens of professional honor were unable to protect him from the larger problems in Holland in the early 1920s. The financial condition of the government was worsening each year, and when Flu arrived as professor in 1922 he found that one of his lecturer positions had already been eliminated which forced him into additional teaching.[14] Even at the beginning of his second appointment in October 1923, d'Herelle realized that the financial situation was precarious: in a letter to Roux he wrote: "The project of which I am in charge at the University of Leiden expires next July and I believe it will not be possible to prolong it; considering the state of finances, the Council of Ministers have taken two decisions: all the salaries are to be reduced by 20 percent, and the vacancies which are produced henceforth (same for Professorial chairs) will not be filled, until the present situation is ameliorated. When will that be?" He then went on to ask for Roux's support in his application for a position as a bacteriologist for the Quarantine Service in Egypt. In this letter he also inquired, probably without much realistic hope, about the possibility of returning to the Pasteur Institute.[15]

The opportunity to go to Alexandria came about because of the retirement of the incumbent bacteriologist, and d'Herelle had heard of the vacancy from a friend in Cairo. This laboratory, controlled by the Conseil Sanitaire, Maritime et Quarantenaire d'Egypte, was under the direction of the League of Nations through its health organization, the Office International d'Hygiène Publique (OIHP). This laboratory, along with a hospital and quarantine lazaretto, was set up in 1878 as a result of the International Sanitary Conferences held periodically since 1851 and was part of the international effort to monitor and prevent epidemic diseases, especially plague and cholera, from passing from Asia to Europe through the Suez Canal. There were special concerns about the problems of epidemic diseases thought to be associated with the hajj, the annual Muslim pilgrimage to Mecca. In addition to the work with the pilgrims, the Conseil Sanitaire, Maritime et Quarantenaire d'Egypte also checked the ships that passed through the Suez Canal.

The Conseil was made up of representatives of the European powers as well as representatives of the Egyptian government. D'Herelle had influential support for his application to the Conseil; Roux had been a French delegate to the two previous International Sanitary Conferences, and Thorvald Madsen of Copenhagen, who had a personal interest in bacteriophages and was the president of OIHP, may have had some role in the selection.[16]

One of the requirements for the position as chief of the bacteriological laboratory was a medical degree, and d'Herelle apparently offered his newly awarded M.D. from Leiden as proof: he recalled later, "I sent my dossier, but it was necessary to be a doctor of medicine according to the international regulations, it was the very first time in my life that the diploma served for anything" (*PM,* 510). Later, after he left the position, his successor, E. Lagrange, wrote to his former teacher, Calmette: "But as to the knowledge that d'Herelle is not a physician, it is widespread." In the same letter Lagrange stated, "If d'Herelle is not a physician he has committed fraud—" and then described d'Herelle's medical practice on patients in India.[17] The question of d'Herelle's medical training is still unresolved, but that he received at least two and possibly three honorary M.D. degrees is attested to by the archival records. His family recollection is that he disclaimed being a physician and preferred the title "Professor," which derived from his time at Yale University (*HM*). Apparently his credentials satisfied the Conseil which offered him the appointment in Alexandria which he took up in May 1924, just in time to arrive in Tor at the tip of the Sinai peninsula for the hajj that year.[18]

At Tor was an encampment for the sanitary quarantine of pilgrims which operated for about forty days each year. The officials examined the ships which brought loads of pilgrims for evidence of illness and then disinfected the ships with formaldehyde solution. Pilgrims returning from Mecca and Medina were held for three days quarantine to see if any illness developed. Any sick individuals were held further in quarantine for a specified number of days determined by their diagnosis. The facility could take 3,000 pilgrims per day and had a capacity to hold 10,000 people in quarantine at one time. The medical care was apparently minimal, the intent of the quarantine being preventive rather than therapeutic. D'Herelle carried out the bacteriological studies in a temporary laboratory set up in the encampment. This first year he stayed for the entire period of the pilgrimage, but in subsequent years he went for a few days at the beginning and after insuring that the first few boats were "clean," he left the routine work to one of his assistants. In the four years that he was responsible for the surveillance at Tor there were no cases of cholera or plague detected among the pilgrims, and no outbreaks occurred during the pilgrimage inland to Mecca. In the more than fifty years that the camp had been operating, no case of cholera had passed beyond its gates, although many cases had arrived.

One of d'Herelle's first duties in Alexandria was to reorganize the bacteriological service of the Conseil (*PM*, 531–532). As there were laboratories at Port Said and Suez, as well as at Alexandria, these had to be staffed. Because of the national representations on the Conseil, there was considerable political maneuvering to advance the cause of various candidates. Finally, a bacteriologist was appointed to the post at Port Said: an Italian "professor" with "titles and decorations." Within the first two weeks he had diagnosed bubonic plague on a ship, resulting in the detention and quarantine of the entire ship. Eight days later he diagnosed plague again and another ship was quarantined. At this point d'Herelle began to suspect an error and went to Port Said himself. "One glance at the cultures was sufficient" to convince him that the organisms were not plague, and subsequent tests confirmed these initial impressions.[19] The shipping companies lodged a protest with the Conseil and demanded compensation for damages plus interest. The inexperienced Italian bacteriologist, fearing repercussions from his government which had pushed for his appointment, accepted d'Herelle's offer to move to Bombay and spend some time in the Haffkine Institute studying plague in India. This debacle convinced the Conseil that competence and experience rather than nationality should be used to pick the next bacteriologist. D'Herelle was then able to appoint two bacteriologists with experience in tropical medicine as his deputies.

Although d'Herelle apparently carried out his official duties easily and to the satisfaction of the Conseil, he felt that his research program was not going well (*PM*, 532). He saw no cases of plague or cholera, as the few cases that did occur were invariably treated in the local hospitals by Egyptian practitioners. He managed, however, to popularize his anti-dysentery phage as a treatment for bacillary dysentery, a common affliction in the region. An old friend from the Pasteur Institute, Dr. Arthur Compton, was chief of the municipal bacteriological laboratory of Alexandria and carried out several clinical studies on dysentery.[20] According to d'Herelle, his phage became the standard treatment in Alexandria for this condition (*PM*, 533). He also noted that he sent "thousands of ampules" to the director of the medical service in the Sudan (*PM*, 533).

D'Herelle still had time on his hands. "For want of infectious diseases, I utilized my considerable leisure to study cancer and tuberculosis" (*PM,* 532). He again took up the problem he had started with Peyre at the Institute for Cancer Research in Villejuif, namely the role of ultraviruses in the origins of Rous sarcomas in chickens and of plant tumors associated with *B. tumorifaciens* infections. This work was published in two notes in 1927 with Peyre as co-author (FdH: 92; FdH: 93). His work on tuberculosis was "too fragmentary to publish" but focused on the symbiosis between the bacillus, bacteriophage, and the host. He noted that when he infected tubercle bacilli with phage that he obtained "mutations brusque." This early observation on the use of phage to study and induce mutations in bacteria would be his main interest when he moved to Yale in 1928.

A somewhat different view of d'Herelle's situation in Alexandria was given by Edwin W. Schultz, a sabbatical visitor from Stanford University. Schultz had received one of the first Guggenheim Foundation fellowships in 1925 and used it to go to Alexandria to work with d'Herelle in January 1926. His project, negotiated in advance with d'Herelle, was entitled "A comparative study of the antigenic properties of bacteriophages and ultraviruses" and had the goal of testing the similarity of bacteriophages and vaccinia virus as antigens in rabbits. This project was in line with Schultz's interest in the question of the nature of bacteriophages. Unfortunately, the stocks of vaccinia available in Egypt as well as from the Pasteur Institute in Algeria were all inactive and so this aspect of the project was abandoned. After being injected with phage preparations, all the rabbits except one died of some epidemic infection in the animal quarters. Schultz summed up the situation: "The unsuitable conditions (particularly the sunless room) under which the animals are housed makes the situation appear rather unpromising, so far as it concerns me in these particular experiments. I might add at this point that the general equipment of the laboratory, especially for research work, is rather primitive. Dr. d'Herelle has ordered a large quantity of equipment and supplies from Europe, but the shipment will probably not reach Alexandria until later in the season."[21] Schultz did note that in the course of this work he had made some interesting observations relevant to his interest in the nature of bacteriophage. He was using trypsin to digest the soluble bacterial protein in the phage lysates to try to render these proteins non-antigenic; he had assumed that the phage were trypsin-resistant, as reported in the literature. He found, however, that some strains of bacteriophage were trypsin-sensitive and proceeded to use this property to determine if the phage could adapt to more prolonged trypsin digestion. By such serial selection he obtained evidence that phages "adapt" to their environment, a key point in d'Herelle's conception of the living nature of bacteriophage.[22] When d'Herelle left for Tor about the first of June 1926, Schultz felt that he had accomplished what he had come for and proceeded to Berlin to spend some time with Rudolf Otto, director of the Robert Koch Institute, and a critic of d'Herelle in the controversy over the nature of bacteriophage. While Schultz appeared to agree with d'Herelle on this issue, he seemed open-minded enough to want to learn first-hand what the other side had to offer.

By 1927, after three years in Alexandria, d'Herelle was getting restless: although he could hardly complain about his living conditions, his work load, or his annual three-month leave in Paris, "I was not satisfied: I was a sentinel on the barricades of epidemics, but there were no epidemics which came by, it was necessary that I go find elsewhere, this cholera which above all had taken my heart after the unexpected little defeat in Indochina. . . . Life presents a series of singularities. I have already noted that I sent one of my bacteriologists to Bombay to stay for awhile in the Plague Institute; for this purpose I had corresponded with the director of this institute, Lt. Col. Dr. Morison of the Indian Medical Service: very kindly he invited me to spend a few days with him to get acquainted with his institute" (*PM*, 538). The background to this invitation was related to d'Herelle's report in the fall of 1925 on the use of bacteriophage to treat four cases of plague in Alexandria. The consequences of this invitation were d'Herelle's departure from Egypt and the initiation of field trials of bacteriophage in India on a scale so massive that even d'Herelle himself was no doubt astonished.

Chapter 9 Fighting Cholera
and Plague in India

In the summer of 1925, d'Herelle finally found the opportunity to test the phage active against a strain of the plague bacillus that he had isolated while in Indochina in 1920. In July 1925 three individuals were diagnosed with bubonic plague on one ship in port in Alexandria, and shortly thereafter a fourth patient was discovered on another ship. These four patients were taken to the quarantine station hospital; d'Herelle described his treatment of these patients with his anti-plague phage from Indochina:

> In each of the four cases the sole method of treatment was with injection of the bacteriophage, given directly into to the bubo. The results are presented here in some detail:
>
> Case 1. Georges Cap. . . . 18 years old. On July 10, 1925 he complained of fever, lassitude, vertigo, headache, and examination showed a bilateral tonsillitis. On the following day his condition became worse. During the night of the 11th and the 12th the crural gland on each side swelled. He was brought to the hospital on July 12th.

A diagnosis of *B. pestis* was made on material aspirated from one of the swellings by specific antiserum agglutination and guinea pig inoculation.

On July 13th, at 2 P.M., the patient had a temperature of 40.3°C., the pulse was 130, the face was congested, the eyes were injected and drooping, and prostration was extreme. The two buboes were the size of nuts, and painful when pressed. I gave an injection of 0.5 cc. of Pestis-bacteriophage into each of the two buboes, the needle being introduced about the center of the bubo. Apparently the injection caused no pain, since the patient showed no reactions of defense.

At 8 P.M., of this same day there was some sweating of the axilla and the forearms.

On the morning of the 14th the condition of the patient was completely changed. He stated that he felt weak, but that he was not in pain and felt well. The buboes were somewhat painful and had slightly increased in volume.

On the 15th he sat up in bed; and on the 16th he begged for food.

On the 16th the buboes had increased in size to that of a small hen's egg, but they were not painful. Puncture of the left bubo with a syringe permitted the withdrawal of a few drops of bloody fluid. Direct examination showed nothing in the way of organisms, and the culture made from it failed to yield growth. Some of it was inoculated into a guinea pig and the guinea pig was still alive 10 days later. The aspirated material, examined for bacteriophage, showed that it was present, with a very high virulence for *B. pestis* ($++++$).

On the 25th both of the buboes were incised very freely. Both contained some purulent material. By August 8th healing was complete. (*BIB,* 567–576)

The temperature profile for this patient indicates the course since receiving the single, bilateral injection of bacteriophage (Figure 7). D'Herelle's descriptions of the treatment and clinical courses of the other three plague patients are equally dramatic. These cases were first presented in the lead article in *La Presse Médicale* on 21 October 1925 (FdH: 84).

D'Herelle gave a copy of this report to Dr. A. Morison, the British representative on the Conseil Sanitaire, Maritime et Quarantenaire d'Egypte in Egypt, who immediately wrote to C. E. Heathcote-Smith, the British Consul General in Alexandria, as follows: "To my mind the article is very interesting and of intense importance, offering (as it appears to me to do) an almost certain cure for bubonic plague. . . . I see every reason to hope for a favorable result by this method of treatment even in pneumonic plague. If so, then the dread of plague is conjured [conquered?]. Anti-plague serum is useless as a preventative. *The only true prophylaxis is deratization, and the only true treatment is bacteriophage.* Dr. d'Herelle has supplied already the Sanitary Administration of Egypt with the necessary bacteriophage. I think India ought to arm itself. Also all countries where plague prevails. All honour to D'Herelle. I am proud of having introduced him to Egypt."[1] This enthusiastic letter, together with the copy of

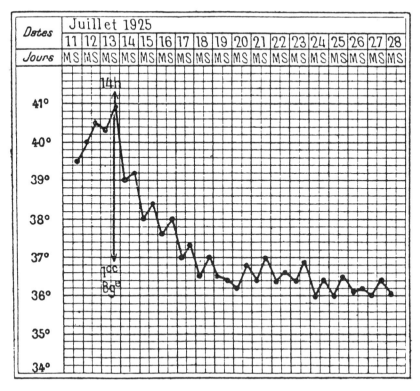

Figure 7. Temperature chart for the patient Georges Cap, who was treated on 13 July 1925 for bubonic plague by injection of antiplague bacteriophage by d'Herelle. (FdH: 84; reprinted with permission of the publisher.)

d'Herelle's article, was forwarded by Heathcote-Smith that same day to London, addressed to His Majesty's Principal Secretary for Foreign Affairs, Sir Austen Chamberlain. The matter found its way to the India Office where the *Presse Médicale* article was sent on to India to the Secretary of the Department of Education, Health and Lands. In an internal memo, however, J. H. Smith, the medical adviser at the India Office, expressed caution. In a note dated 24 December 1925, he first pointed out that the only copy of d'Herelle's article had been dispatched to India, so he could not express an opinion without seeing the paper. Second, he was skeptical of Morison's reaction to d'Herelle's article: "Dr. Morison appears to have allowed his enthusiasm to run away with his judgement when he made, on the basis of only 4 consecutive cases of recovery, the assertion that 'the only true treatment is bacteriophage.'" The medical adviser went on to suggest that a study of fifty cases with controls be carried out by a "laboratory of standing," for example, the Haffkine Institute in Bombay.[2]

On 6 January 1926, the Secretary of State for India, Frederick Edwin Smith, Lord Birkenhead, sent a coded telegram to the soon-to-depart Viceroy in India, Rufus Isaacs, Lord Reading, directed to the Department of Education, Health and Lands in India, offering to act as intermediary in obtaining "a supply of remedy for trial in India under laboratory control."[3]

Not surprisingly, the Viceroy responded promptly with the request that the phage go directly to the Director of the Haffkine Institute in Bombay. The bureaucratic chain of communication then seemed to be as follows: The medical adviser to the India Office wrote to the Undersecretary of State for India, who in turn wrote to the Foreign Secretary, Sir Austen Chamberlain, whose deputy then wrote to Heathcote-Smith in Alexandria who, in turn, conveyed the request to d'Herelle that a supply of antiplague phage be dispatched to the Haffkine Institute for trial in India.[4] Finally, on 20 February 1926, Heathcote-Smith notified the Foreign Office that d'Herelle had agreed to provide the phage "at an early date."[5]

The phages arrived in March 1926 and very soon thereafter d'Herelle received word in Alexandria that the Haffkine Institute was having trouble with them.[6] Apparently, the phage grew very poorly at the Haffkine Institute and took twenty-four hours to lyse the cultures. Upon hearing this, d'Herelle immediately applied for an unpaid leave from the Conseil in Egypt and went to Bombay, at his own expense, to straighten things out.

He arrived in Bombay on 23 April 1926 and soon found the source of the problem in growing the phage. It seemed that the standard bacteriologic medium used for enteric organisms, as well as plague bacillus, was Martin's medium, developed for this purpose at the Pasteur Institute in Paris. This medium included a digest of macerated pig stomach and beef muscle. In India, however, this medium could not be used because it offended both Muslims and Hindus. The Haffkine Institute, therefore, routinely used a modified Martin's medium based on a hydrochloric acid digest of goat tissue. D'Herelle found that this medium was very poor for producing bacteriophages and developed a modification whereby the goat tissue was digested not by HCl, but by papaya juice (the commercially available source of papain). With this modification, as well as improved filtration to eliminate their prevalent contamination problems, d'Herelle managed to produce active anti-plague phage stocks in India.[7]

While d'Herelle was engaged in the laboratory study of plague bacilli, clinical studies were being attempted at Hyderabad and Agra. The protocol for these trials involved, first, the establishment of a definite diagnosis of plague and then, treatment of alternate cases with bacteriophage.[8]

D'Herelle returned to Alexandria in the first week of June 1926, in time for the annual pilgrimage to Mecca and the possibility of a cholera or plague epidemic.[9] In India, the acting director of the Haffkine Institute, Lt. Col. J. Morison, had become a convert to bacteriophage therapy.[10] His report to Major General A. Hooten, the Surgeon General with the government of Bombay, noted that the trial had been unsuccessful, apparently because the phage isolated in Indochina did not work in India. Morison was nevertheless enthusiastic: "The possibilities are so great that I would urge the Government of India to invite Dr. F. d'Herelle to return to India to study further the bacteriophage in relation to plague and also to cholera for at least six months." In this report, too, was the mention of the first isolation of cholera phages from clinical cases, one of which was considered "very active." Morison concluded his letter with the description of d'Herelle as "a consummate technician, and a most inspiring worker."[11]

Both d'Herelle and Morison seemed to attach significance to the isolation of cholera phages directly from patients. Previously d'Herelle had isolated such phages, but only from animal sources. Given his deeply held beliefs about the importance of the study of disease in its natural hosts, these new findings substantiated and reinforced his general view of the role of bacteriophages in natural immunity. From this point onward, the Bacteriophage Inquiry (as d'Herelle's project was called) focused more and more on cholera and less and less on plague, and by the time it was published it had become known as the Cholera Study.

Even in 1926, more than two decades before India's formal independence from Great Britain, the governing bureaucracy was under severe strain and was developing faults and fissures. The linkages between London, British India (those Indian states under British control, in contrast with the independent "princely states"), and the Indian populace, never very certain, were loosening daily. In 1917 Edwin Montague, Secretary of State for India, set out British policy toward India as aiming toward "the increasing association of Indians in every branch of the administration and the gradual development of self-governing institutions with a view to the progressive realisation of responsible government of India as an integral part of the British Empire."[12]

This policy was realized in the Government of India Act of 1919. Under increasing pressure from Indian nationalists, both Hindu and Muslim, Britain agreed to divide the provincial government into "transferred" and "reserved" designations. They would turn over to local (Indian) control certain administrative departments in the provincial governments. "Transferred" departments included those dealing with education, public works, and public health. The "reserved" subjects included justice, police, and land-revenue functions. This partial concession was inadequate for the nationalists of the Congress party such as Gandhi and Jinnah, but in a spirit of pragmatic compromise they agreed to this system of "dyarchy" as a way to expedite full government by Indians.

One consequence of this arrangement was to politicize the transferred departments. Willingly or not, they were drawn into Indian political struggles as the dominant Congress party launched repeated campaigns of non-cooperation to put further pressure on their British rulers. As a result of a Congress boycott between 1920 and 1937 the transferred departments were staffed almost entirely by Indians belonging to minor communal (religious and ethnic) organizations rather than to the secular Congress party, which represented the majority of Indians.[13]

At the same time, communal tensions were on the increase, often encouraged by one group or another for political advantage. Both the secular Congress party, with Hindu and Muslim supporters, and the Muslim League seemed in basic agreement that the goal of Indian independence rested on cooperation. The minor communal organizations, however, were frequently involved in civil strife and rioting.[14] Provincial administration in the transferred departments, such as public health, thus became even more disconnected from the central government in British India and the policy makers at the India Office in far away London.

Against this background of political instability in provincial governments and administration, British medicine and medical research seemed oblivious to the turmoil in the streets. The Indian Medical Service (IMS) was open, de facto, only to British-trained physicians and was limited to serving the needs of the British Army and the Europeans and their families in the Indian Civil Service. Morale was declining and recruitment to the IMS was becoming difficult.[15] The main source of support for medical research, the Indian Research Fund Association, was firmly under the control of the British establishment in India. The Bacteriophage Inquiry would operate under these circumstances of communal unrest in the populace with a politicized provincial administration, together with a conservative, entrenched British medical establishment.

In response to Lt. Col. Morison's enthusiasm and Major General Hooton's support in early summer, by mid-September 1926 the Government of Bombay approached the Secretary of Education, Health and Lands of the Indian Government. By December 1926 the Indian Research Fund Association had committed funds to support the project so the Government of India requested the India Office to contact the Secretary to the Ministry of Health (Sir Neville Chamberlain) to ask the Foreign Secretary (Sir Austen Chamberlain, Neville's half-brother) to approach the Conseil Quarantenaire in Egypt to ask for a "loan of d'Herelle's services."

The British Consul-General in Alexandria, Heathcote-Smith, approached the Conseil in Egypt. While the Conseil agreed to grant d'Herelle unpaid leave, there was yet another snag: the government of Egypt still had to approve the plan; when they were approached, they raised the problem of credit for discoveries or publicity that might come out of d'Herelle's work in India. Finally, the India Office mediated an acceptable solution: simultaneous publication in India and in Egypt of the report of d'Herelle's study yet to be even started in India (FdH: 103; FdH: 111). By this time the correspondence mentioned only cholera as an object of study.

By the time d'Herelle arrived in India in late February or early March 1927, the effect of nearly a decade of nationalist agitation was being felt. Gandhi's policy of *satyagraha* ("holding fast to the truth") translated into a policy of non-cooperation and boycott of British goods, activities, and institutions. The Indian economy was suffering from depressed agricultural prices, increased rural poverty, and accelerating urbanization. In the wake of strikes, protests, and boycotts, the British had responded with repression and retaliation. In such a social and political climate, the success of any broadly based population study would have been unlikely, yet d'Herelle seemed undaunted. He immediately embarked on two studies; one aimed at treatment of individual cases of cholera, and the second aimed at study of phage and cholera in natural populations. For the former he arranged to work at the Campbell Hospital in Calcutta, a large public hospital which had a rather low mortality rate for cholera. D'Herelle may have thought that his chances of finding cholera phages would be higher in an environment with more recovering patients. For the field studies he selected two regions in the Punjab where cholera was endemic.

By this time the entire project was focused on cholera, but d'Herelle still exploited plague for its publicity value: thus, he discussed plague at length, together with cholera, in an interview published in the *Times of India* of 21 May 1927 under the headline: "Treatment of Plague: Results of Research Work."[16]

D'Herelle was joined by two physicians. Major Reginald Malone, the assistant director of the Haffkine Institute and a member of the Indian Medical

Service, organized the field tests of phage in the villages of the Punjab. Dr. M. N. Lahiri was an Indian physician (and hence, not eligible for the Indian Medical Service) who carried out the studies with patients in the Campbell Hospital. Their first work was to study both the cholera vibrio and the bacteriophages present in their patients in India. They studied 361 vibrio isolates in some detail. To understand the natural history of the disease and the possible role of bacteriophages they examined twenty-three hospitalized patients in Calcutta and ten more in Lahore. Of these thirty-three patients treated with the conventional injections of fluids and salts as recommended by Rogers, thirteen died (40 percent mortality). The Campbell Hospital group's mortality rate (30 percent, that is, seven of twenty-three) was comparable to the overall 1926 cholera mortality rate of 27 percent at the hospital. Against this control group, over the same period, Lahiri treated sixteen patients with two ounces of d'Herelle's most active phage preparation by mouth as early as possible in the course of the disease. There were no deaths in this group. These hospital studies continued until the end of June 1927.

By mid-July 1927 d'Herelle was in the Punjab with Major Malone with the plan to distribute phage ampules in the villages for use by the local dispensary doctors at the first sign of cholera. He was the guest of the Central Research Institute in Kasauli, where he was given a laboratory and help in preparation of the necessary phage stocks for distribution in the villages. The selection of cases to be treated was poorly controlled, perhaps reflecting some aspects of Gandhian non-cooperation, but after six weeks they had collected information on 198 cases of cholera in the villages under surveillance. Of these patients, 124 had not received bacteriophage treatment and 74 had been given the anti-vibrio phages. The mortality rate in the untreated group was 63 percent, whereas that in phage-treated group was 8 percent (FdH: 103, 88–121).

By the end of August 1927 d'Herelle felt that he had demonstrated the utility of anti-vibrio phages in both individual therapy and in epidemic control and prophylaxis, and he concluded his laboratory and field work in India. After a few days of vacation in the mountain resort town of Simla, he indulged his lifelong wanderlust and visited Agra, Peshawar, and the Khyber Pass. As he planned to remain in India to attend the Seventh Congress of the Far Eastern Association of Tropical Medicine to be held in Calcutta in December 1927, he accepted an invitation to spend six weeks at the Pasteur Institute in Kuala Lumpur, where he collected even more isolates of cholera vibrios.

In November 1927 an account of the cholera work appeared in a brief note in the *Indian Medical Gazette* (FdH: 91). At the Far Eastern Association for

Tropical Medicine (FEATM) Congress in Calcutta in December 1927 d'Herelle presented a brief report on his work on cholera along with a general talk on bacteriophage (FdH: 97; FdH: 98; FdH: 99). He returned to Alexandria about mid-January 1928.[17]

Results such as d'Herelle had reported for the dreaded disease cholera could not be ignored, and indeed, there was much discussion of his work. Even while he was still working in India he was attracting attention. Lt. Col. C. A. Gill, former Director of Public Health in the Punjab, wrote the following to Sir Leonard Rogers, the great cholera authority, in August 1927:

> A new light has appeared on the horizon in D'Herelle who has been working in the province [the Punjab]—and whose *bacteriophage appears likely to revolutionize both the prevention and treatment of cholera.* This is apparently a really good thing and the tests he is now carrying out are *most encouraging.* It is promised that all vaccines will go by the board in a few years. I have not read much of his work at present, but [Sir Rickard] *Christophers considers that he is on to the biggest thing in bacteriology since Pasteur.*[18]

In his presidential address to the FEATM Congress, T. H. Symons singled out Shiga and d'Herelle for special mention.[19] Meeting conjointly with the FEATM, the Expert Plague Committee of the League of Nations Health Organization called d'Herelle's work on plague an item of "particular importance" and recommended "further studies on antiplague bacteriophage and its practical application."[20] Five months later, at the May 1928 meeting of the Comité Permanent de l'Office International d'Hygiène Publique of the League of Nations, the discussion of cholera turned mainly on J. D. Graham's report of the work of d'Herelle, Malone, and Lahiri.[21]

Although many Indian cities had been beset with mass demonstrations against the visit of the Simon Commission, and nationalist fervor was increasing daily, the Government of India was interested in continued field trials of bacteriophage.[22] By the end of February 1928, the Secretary of State for India received a telegram from the Viceroy, Edward Wood, Lord Irwin, on behalf of the Department of Education, Health and Lands, requesting that d'Herelle be engaged for another six months on the same terms as his previous visit.[23] Again the bureaucratic channels were put to work: E. J. Turner, the medical adviser at the India Office, wrote to the Under Secretary at the Foreign Office asking that the Consul General in Alexandria (Heathcote-Smith) again be requested to approach the Conseil Quarantenaire and ask for d'Herelle's services.

By this time, however, d'Herelle had been in correspondence with Milton Winternitz at Yale and, anticipating an offer to join the Yale faculty, d'Herelle declined the invitation to return to India in 1928–1929. He did, however, want to see the Bacteriophage Inquiry go forward in trusted hands, and he recommended that the government of India secure the services of a Yugoslavian bacteriologist, Igor Asheshov. With d'Herelle's assurances that he would still participate in an advisory role, the Government of India through the India Office in London offered Asheshov a three-year contract to conduct phage research in India.

From this point forward, the Bacteriophage Inquiry followed two lines: basic laboratory studies directed by Asheshov and field trials conducted by Morison. Starting in January 1929, Asheshov and his group worked at a newly established bacteriophage laboratory in Patna, with the responsibility for providing phage for use in the province of Bihar, a region of high endemic cholera. This work was supported by the Indian Research Fund Association (IRFA) and was reviewed annually. In October 1927, after a year in Rangoon as director of the Pasteur Institute in Burma, Morison became the director of the King Edward VII Pasteur Institute and Medical Research Institute in Shillong in Assam Province, where he initiated a large scale field trial of phage prophylaxis. His work seems to have been supported in part by IRFA and in part by the Institute.

Asheshov and his group contributed to the classification of cholera vibrios and their phages. They seemed to be interested in laboratory bacteriology and lacked d'Herelle's vision and drive to practical applications. Prior to Asheshov's arrival, at the December 1928 conference of the IRFA, a plan for the Bacteriophage Inquiry was outlined and a resolution was voted: "This conference of medical research workers recommends that the whole question of the epidemiology of cholera should be the subject of enquiry under the direction of a first-class expert."[24] The first goal would be to classify both the phages and the vibrios found in Indian cholera patients with the aim of finding phages of highest virulence. In his first progress report to the IRFA, Asheshov noted that in addition to the diagnostic and taxonomic work, they had attempted trials of cholera prevention as well as cholera treatment. In an area where many pilgrims took up temporary lodging during a summer pilgrimage, they added anti-cholera phage to each of fifteen wells from which drinking water was drawn. This addition was repeated a week later. The incidence of cholera that summer in the region treated was four cases in about 10,000 pilgrims lodged there. In the entire region (untreated), the cholera incidence was about ten-fold higher with 231 cases in about 70,000 people. The trial of bacteriophage in hospitalized cases at the Puri Cholera Hospital was unsuccessful, however. The researchers cited the usual problems of hospital staff cooperation and compliance, inaccuracies of diagnoses, and another problem that would make it harder and harder to evaluate the effectiveness of phage therapy: the mortality rate in the control population was very low, about 5 percent. Against this low background, dramatic results are hard to observe and statistically significant results require very large sample sizes.[25]

Perhaps to work in a more cooperative environment, their next clinical trial was conducted in the hospital of the Patna Medical College. All patients were given alkaline intravenous fluid therapy following the method advocated by Rogers. In addition, patients were given bacteriophage preparations by mouth in small sips so as not to induce vomiting. The authors noted that they reduced the incidence of mortality "almost to nil," even in cases where the patient was "pulseless and severely collapsed."[26]

At the Annual All-India Conference of Medical Research Workers held in December 1929 and sponsored by the IRFA the most important topic was the Bacteriophage Inquiry, according to an editorial in the *Indian Medical Gazette.* Asheshov, Morison, Malone, and Lt. Col. J. Taylor of Rangoon presented reports to the conference. The Association voted to continue funding the three projects of Asheshov, Morison, and Malone. They noted that "Dr. Asheshov's investigation was of fundamental importance."[27]

After these reports of work carried out in 1929, Asheshov published no more work involving clinical trials or population-based studies. This direction of this research was in response to the advice of the IRFA Scientific Board: "The decision of the S.A.B., IRFA, limited the activity of this enquiry to pure basic research. In interpreting this decision the problems chosen were studied in such a way that the results obtained might directly help the practical application of bacteriophage."[28] The IRFA seemed less than pleased with Asheshov and in 1932 started reducing his grant funds in anticipation of the end of his contract in 1934: during 1932 he received 64,260 rupees; for 1933 he received 43,550 rupees, with the explicit notation that the budget was reduced because his activities were being confined to basic research only. For 1934 he was awarded only 8,500 rupees to suffice until his contract expired.[29]

In 1933 Asheshov and his group published three long articles in the *Indian Journal of Medical Research* in which they summarized their work over the previous four years. These articles appeared back-to-back and seem to represent a final report of their work. In addition to detailed description of the laboratory methods used to study cholera phages, they present extensive studies of the classification of cholera phages based on their host range specificity for various vibrio isolates. The final part of this report described biological studies on the various properties, such as agglutinability, of the different strains they had studied. While Asheshov determined the requirements needed to make good therapeutic strains and investigated the pitfalls involved in their use, he had not addressed the issue that seemed critical to the Bacteriophage Inquiry, namely, is bacteriophage therapy useful in treatment or prevention of cholera?

The Eleventh All-India Research Worker's Conference, which met in December 1933, seemed frustrated by the lack of results of the inquiry: "The subcommittee on cholera considered experiments in connection with the use of *bacteriophage* for the prevention and treatment of cholera, and came to the conclusion that, on the evidence available, it was not possible to express any definite opinion on the subject and recommended the appointment of an *ad hoc* committee to go into the data available."[30] The Scientific Advisory Board of the IRFA appointed such a committee which included A. J. H. Russell, A. D. Stewart, and H. H. King, all members of the Indian Medical Service. Their report, dated 27 April 1934 and adopted by the Scientific Advisory Board in December 1934, was also transmitted to the Comité Permanent de l'Office International d'Hygiène Publique of the League of Nations, on which Russell represented British India.

This special IRFA committee noted the deficiencies of previous work and reviewed the extensive data presented by Morison from his studies in Assam[31] as well as the preliminary alternate case trial of phage treatment by Pasricha in Calcutta. The uncertainties in the field tests frustrated the committee—"It is practically impossible to obtain reliable figures for comparable treated and untreated cases under field conditions"—yet they recommended continued support for the case-control study just started at Campbell Hospital. They also observed: "There is so far practically no conclusive evidence from Assam or elsewhere on the most important question of all, namely, should epidemics of cholera be treated by bacteriophage rather than by the accepted methods of disinfection and vaccination." The report concluded: "The necessity for the appointment of the Committee shows the need for the presence of a statistician in the Medical Research Department whose duty it would be not only to examine collected figures but, even more important, to advise all enquiries before hand as to the figures which should be collected and the methods of collections which should be adopted."[32]

While Asheshov's laboratory classification and bacteriophage collection would continue to be used by cholera workers, he did not continue with the Bacteriophage Inquiry. He published no more papers in India and left there in 1935.[33]

Morison, on the other hand, used his position as director of the King Edward VII Pasteur Institute in Assam to organize hundreds of villages in endemic cholera regions to try anti-vibrio phage therapy. He selected Naogaon and Habiganj, two widely separated but rather comparable regions in Assam for the test of phage prophylaxis. Both had histories of serious and repeated cholera outbreaks throughout the 1920s. In 1928 and 1929 Morison issued phage to "Tea Garden doctors [physicians employed to care for the workers on tea plantations], Civil Surgeons and Assistant and Sub-assistant surgeons of rural dispensaries," but there was little cooperation, perhaps reflecting the general attitudes fostered toward centralized authority by the past *satyagraha* campaigns. His next approach was to bypass the trained medical personnel and make the phage available directly to the village leaders, the headmen. The project worked as planned in the Naogaon region, but the district official in the Habiganj region objected for unknown reasons and so this region became the control group in Morison's study.

In December 1929 phage was issued along with instructions for its use to every village headman along ninety miles of the Kalang River. In the first six months sixty-three scattered cases of suspected cholera were treated this way. No epidemics occurred in Naogaon in 1930–1935, the duration of the study.[34] In contrast, in the Habiganj region, in both 1930 and 1931 there were spring and fall epidemics of cholera. In the first half of 1932 there were 474 deaths, at which time the government ordered the use of bacteriophage in the district. For the next three years the two districts had similar low death rates from cholera, that is, about ten per year. In the nearby district of Sunanganj, for example, where no phages were used, in 1933 1,505 people died from cholera.

Figure 8 shows the mortality data for one village for patients given bacteriophage and those who did not receive it. Figure 9 shows the cholera mortality in the two districts for the period during which phage was available in only one of the two areas.

The annual reports from the King Edward VII Pasteur Institute and Medical Research Institute give some indication as to the extent of Morison's bacteriophage trials. For the year 1928 more than 36,000 doses of cholera phage were produced.[35] In 1929 they made 130,823 doses of cholera phage; for 1931 they indicated they purchased the phage from the Laboratoire du Bactériophage in

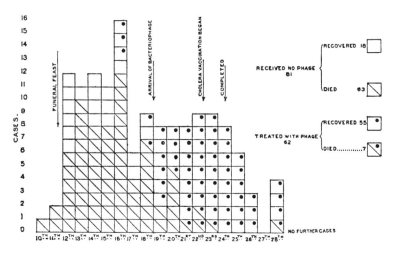

Figure 8. Daily case incidence and mortality during an epidemic of cholera in Jakrem village in Assam. Cases treated with anticholera bacteriophage are indicated with a dot. (Morison, 26; reprinted with permission of the publisher.)

Paris, and for 1934 they distributed 871,316 doses, presumably made in Shil-long.[36]

Morison seemed to have had more success in his field trials than Asheshov, perhaps because Assam province is somewhat culturally and ethnically distinct from the rest of India and hence less nationalistic in its fervor to go along with Gandhi's second *satyagraha* of 1930–1931. Nevertheless, Morison was still troubled by the lack of cooperation from the recipients of this material: "In spite of the wide and extending use of bacteriophage in Assam, few medical officers return the case sheets enclosed in every box [of bacteriophage]. It is not realized that though in Assam the bacteriophage has established itself through experiences not often possible in other places, others without such facilities await controlled figures capable of statistical examination. . . . On the other hand, numerous appreciative letters come to the Institute of which no statistical use can be made."[37] Later he conceded: "Phage is not a remedy in a city like Calcutta, nor is it a remedy where the source of infection can be traced and dealt with. It may have little interest for us as we push on with sanitary reforms. Indeed, very distinguished Directors of Public Health have done all they could to prevent its uses in their provinces. But the widespread epidemic of cholera in various provinces of India compared with its control, where this has not been attempted with phage in Assam, shows it is a weapon we cannot yet afford to discard."[38]

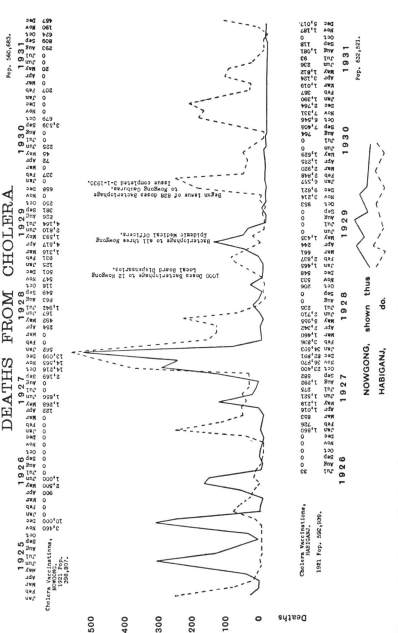

Figure 9. Monthly mortality from cholera in two districts in Assam between 1925 and 1932. In Nowgong district anticholera bacteriophage was widely distributed, whereas in Habiganj it was not generally available. (Morison, 28; reprinted with permission of the publisher.)

Although in 1934 Morison reached retirement age and a new director, L. A. P. Anderson, was brought in from the Haffkine Institute, the annual report for 1935 from the King Edward VII Pasteur Institute indicated that the Bacteriophage Inquiry was still in progress. Indeed, the annual grants from the IRFA continued to increase until 1937, the final year of the Bacteriophage Inquiry, in which it received 6,084 rupees.[39]

Bacteriophage was employed as an agent against cholera in three ways: *treatment* of active cases; *prophylaxis* during epidemics; *prevention* in potential epidemic areas. The initial studies of treating active cases by d'Herelle, Malone, and Lahiri suggested that phages were useful and effective when compared to no treatment or the rather ineffective conventional treatment. The Bacteriophage Inquiry itself was directed at the larger and more difficult problem of the utility of phage in prophylaxis and prevention. In these studies the comparisons were more difficult. The "control" groups were difficult to define, and probably most important, the results obtained with phage were compared with other approaches toward cholera control, that is, vaccination and sanitary reforms.

Vaccination and inoculation for smallpox in India have a long history (many accounts of inoculation date from the 1800s), and the popularity and acceptance of Haffkine's antiplague vaccine prepared the populace for the introduction of an anticholera vaccine for prevention in potentially epidemic areas.[40]

The general value of sanitary reforms for public health had become an article of faith with many authorities in India,[41] so any new approach to cholera prevention that reduced the apparent critical need for better water and sewer systems seemed threatening.

At least three factors can be noted that may have contributed to the ending of the Bacteriophage Inquiry: increasing political unrest in India and the attendant difficulties in provincial administration made large-scale field studies increasingly problematic; economic conditions seemed to constrain the budget of the IRFA; sanitary reforms in the major cities promised to reduce outbreaks not only of cholera but of other diseases as well; the field trials were disappointing and the statistical results uncertain because of flaws in the design of the studies.

With regard to treatment of cholera patients with bacteriophages, C. L. Pasricha and his colleagues at the Campbell Hospital in Calcutta noted the deficiencies in the past clinical tests of choleraphages in the treatment of hospitalized cholera patients. These deficiencies included the use of historical controls and the lack of randomization of the cases to be treated. They undertook a more controlled test of cholera phage therapy in the hospital patient population. "Two wards were set apart in the Campbell Hospital for cholera cases, and the admission of cases was alternately into the two wards. The treatment in the two wards was identical except that in one bacteriophage was used in addition to the usual treatment of cholera. Bacteriophage used was constantly 'refreshed' by passage with vibrios isolated during the different phases of the epidemic and was given mainly by the mouth. In 50 cases choleraphage was given intravenously and gave us satisfactory results."[42] Pasricha's studies of the clinical use of phage and his laboratory investigation of the vibrio itself continued to be supported as part of the Bacteriophage Inquiry by the IRFA.

His study of epidemic cholera for the years 1933–35 comprised 1,369 cases; 684 were treated with cholera phages (2 ml doses of phage every four hours) and 685 were not treated with cholera phages. All together, the mortality rate was 13.5 percent for the phage-treated group and 16.6 percent for the control group (Table 2). Pasricha noted that the control group was not entirely "untreated," otherwise the mortality rate might well have been significantly higher. Thus, the comparison was phage along with conventional treatment tested against conventional treatment alone. Conventional treatments were not specified in Pasricha's paper because "the usual hospital treatment is so well known that it is not necessary to give details here"; at this time they usually consisted of oral calomel, potassium permanganate, and essential oils, as well as injections of salt, water, and bicarbonate.

The results of overall mortality were not considered very significant. However, two other results of this study were emphasized by both Pasricha and others (Table 2). First, when the results were confined only to patients with a bacteriologic diagnosis of cholera—that is, the 841 patients from whom vibrios had been isolated—the addition of phage treatment offered significant improvement: 8.3 percent mortality versus 17.8 percent mortality. For the patients who were infected with "agglutinable," that is, the "standard" cholera vibrios, the survival with phage treatment was a little better, 6.8 percent mortality versus 20 percent. The very low mortality rates (3–8 percent) among patients from whom no vibrios could be isolated suggested that these patients were already on their way to recovery regardless of treatment, or else they had some other, less virulent, illness; the very high mortality rates (60–75 percent) among patients for whom no samples were examined suggested that patients in this group were too moribund for treatment. Thus, exclusion of these two groups of patients from the analysis of phage treatment seemed justified to these authors.

The second conclusion of this careful study was that phage offered significant reduction in morbidity, that is, the course of the illness was less severe among those patients who did survive.

> We have analyzed various other clinical data. We find that there is an appreciable difference in the phage-treated and control series of cases. The patients are less toxic, there is less dehydration and fewer 'salines' are required in the phage series than in the control series. Cases receiving phage are discharged sooner from the hospital, they secrete vibrios for a smaller number of days and in general run a clinically milder course. There is less tendency to develop pneumonia but these and other clinical conditions are not suitable for statistical analysis. The general impression of experienced workers in clinical charge of cases is that uraemia and other deadly complications are often averted, or, if they supervene, are milder in the phage-treated series.[43]

Pasricha and his colleagues also found that the incidence of uremia was 11 percent for the phage group and 23 percent for the control group.

This study from Campbell Hospital, along with the epidemiological statistics from Assam, formed the basis for the 1936 report of the Cholera Advisory Committee of the IRFA. Item II in their report was entitled: "To consider the present position in regards to the bacteriophage treatment and prophylaxis of cholera in light of recent report." As for the Bacteriophage Inquiry, this committee noted that the "Cholera Clinical Enquiry" at Campbell Hospital was "brought to a close in June 1936 with the conclusion that, for patients with bacteriologically confirmed cholera, phage therapy appeared to reduce mortality by about two and one-half fold." This committee stated: "It is recommended that this enquiry be now discontinued, a sufficiently extended series of cases of cholera having been treated with bacteriophage under controlled hos-

Table 2. Mortality Rates for Cholera Patients, With and Without Treatment by Anticholera Bacteriophage

Author	Percent Mortality	
	Without Bacteriophage	Bacteriophage
Lahiri	39 (13/39)	0 (0/16)
Malone	63 (78/124)	8 (6/74)
Pasricha		
All cases	16.5 (144/685)	13.5 (92/684)
Vibrio-positive	17.8 (79/443)	8.3 (33/398)
Agglutinin-pos/vibrio-pos	20.1 (49/244)	6.8 (15/219)

pital conditions to provide information as to the value of the method."[44] They reproduced in their report a note from Col. L. A. P. Anderson, the director of the King Edward VII Pasteur Institute in Assam, about the state of the field studies of phage in Assam.

> During the past year in which there was relatively little cholera in Assam, the results of bacteriophage control, taken as a whole, have not been sufficiently striking to permit us to modify the rather noncommittal attitude we adopted at this time last year. . . .
>
> One factor has seriously militated against the success of this experiment and is probably mainly responsible for the absence of conclusive results one way or the other. This is the failure to confine the use of bacteriophage strictly, to the experimental areas. Although inoculation and other special measures were entirely stopped from the outset in the experimental areas, the use of bacteriophage was unfortunately permitted elsewhere when cholera was prevalent and this measure has become so popular in recent years that a very considerable quantity is used in every district in Assam during the cholera season. This can only be described as disastrous from the point of view of the experiment.
>
> The original intention to make the rest of Assam as control for the bacteriophage-controlled areas was not carried through. Had the use of bacteriophage been strictly confined to the experimental area, we should, I believe, by now have reached a conclusive result. As it is, it appears unlikely that we shall ever do so by an experiment on these lines in Assam. It is now too late to withdraw bacteriophage from the other districts.[45]

The Committee on Cholera noted with some regret that they regarded it as "most unfortunate that this trial was not carried out as a strictly controlled experiment and that the issue of bacteriophage was not confined to the experimental areas only." Further, they concluded that "the balance of available evidence taken as a whole indicates that the widespread use of bacteriophage for the control of cholera and its treatment under village conditions has a certain value the precise degree of which they are not in a position to assess." At that point the IRFA stopped support for field bacteriophage work in Assam. They did, however, provide a reduced budget for continued work on cholera in Assam aimed at laboratory characterization of vibrio strains from various sources.[46]

With the departure of d'Herelle, Asheshov, and Morison, the rising nationalism in the struggle for Indian independence, and the beginning of World War II, renewal and reinvigoration of the Bacteriophage Inquiry in India seemed unlikely after 1935. D'Herelle's work during his five years at Yale focused on the role of bacteriophages in generation of bacterial diversity and mutations. This work was a direct outgrowth of his experience with cholera: he was puzzled by the variability of the cholera vibrio with respect to pathogenicity as well as agglutinability by specific sera. In d'Herelle's view, it was again bacteriophages which were central to the understanding of this basic biological phenomenon.

Chapter 10 Bacterial
Mutations and Phage Research
at Yale

Yale University, like many other institutions, developed the discipline of bacteriology along two parallel tracks, one having to do with medically related organisms and phenomena and the other more broadly focused on agricultural bacteriology with an occasional scientist interested in bacteria simply as biological organisms. In the 1920s Milton C. Winternitz, who had been recruited to Yale from William H. Welch's famous pathology department at Johns Hopkins University, led a major restructuring as dean of Yale School of Medicine. Although he was a pathologist, Winternitz was keenly interested in infectious diseases and published extensively on the pathology of natural and experimental infections.[1] Charles-Edward Amory Winslow, Leo Rettger, and George Hathorn Smith made up the bacteriological enterprise at Yale. Winslow came to Yale in 1915 as the first professor in public health. Although as a student of Sedgwick he had had extensive experience in sanitary bacteriology as well as the biological aspects of bacteria, at Yale Winslow became a leader in the broader development of public health, preventive medicine, and in the realm of social medicine.[2] Rettger, in contrast, "believed, preached, and practiced the idea that bacteriology could and should become an independent science and free itself of gross paternalism by those sciences which it has come to redeem."[3] The third bacteriologist at Yale in the 1920s was George H. Smith, who had been recruited by Winternitz to his own department of pathology, later joined Rettger as professor of immunology and bacteriology. Smith was interested in the immunology of bacteria, immunizations, the antibody response and anaphylaxis. He and Winternitz published joint papers frequently during the latter's tenure as dean. One colleague, Samuel Harvey, recalled their close relationship by citing an epigram coined by one wag who noted: "When Winter comes, can Smith be far behind?"[4]

As the result of an invitation from E. W. Schultz, professor of bacteriology at Stanford to give the Lane Lectures in the fall of 1928, d'Herelle began planning an extended visit to the United States. In previous correspondence Smith had issued his own invitation for d'Herelle to come to Yale and participate in the activities of his department. D'Herelle took the occasion to inquire slyly about the possibility of a permanent position at Yale: "On the subject of your offer to work at Yale, I would have great difficulty to accept. As you know, I have a permanent position in Alexandria; I have obtained a year's leave for the study of cholera [in India], I have requested a new leave to be able to give the conferences [Lane Lectures] in the United States; it is not possible to ask for more. The situation would evidently be different if one were to offer me a stable and suitable position in the United States: in that case I would accept."[5]

Smith seized this opportunity to attract a world-famous scientist to his fledgling department as well as to authenticate his own efforts in the translation of d'Herelle's three major works. Smith's research on the resistance to infectious disease would seem to be reason enough for him to take a keen interest in d'Herelle's theories about immunity and the role of bacteriophages in this process. The course of events that resulted in Smith's translation of d'Herelle's first monograph, however, are not known. By early February 1928, Winternitz had approached Yale's president, James Rowland Angell, for a budgetary increase to cover the expected cost of recruiting d'Herelle to Yale.[6] Angell's immediate response was to send Winternitz to Abraham Flexner of the General Education Board in New York (a Rockefeller philanthropy) with a request for support for d'Herelle.[7] After a personal conversation, Winternitz wrote Flexner on 6 March 1928: "You may recall I spoke with you sometime ago about the possibility of attracting Dr. d'Herelle here, on the basis of a letter received from him by my colleague, Dr. Smith. I have just written to Dr. d'Herelle to ascertain the details under which he would be willing to join us."[8] Winternitz, however, acted even more quickly; within two days he had written to d'Herelle in Egypt with a concrete offer of a position.[9] By 28 March Winternitz reported to Flexner, "Yesterday I got a cablegram from d'Herelle in which he accepts our proposal to come here."[10]

At its meeting of 24 May 1928 the General Education Board considered the Yale request for support of d'Herelle and voted to provide three years of funding, after which the university was expected to readjust its budget to accommodate d'Herelle's needs. Starting 1 July 1928, the board awarded $10,000 for the first year, $8,000 for the second year, and $6,000 for the third year.[11] The Yale administration was quite pleased: on 15 June 1928 the university issued a press release headed: "Famous scientist appointed to faculty of the Yale School of Medicine." This statement announced the appointment of d'Herelle, of Paris, France, as professor of bacteriology. It noted that the new construction of an addition to the former Anthony N. Brady Memorial Laboratory would provide space for d'Herelle as well as for consolidation of all the university's activities in bacteriology in one place, including Drs. Smith and Rettger.[12]

Finally, it seemed, d'Herelle was being welcomed into the Establishment: a professorship in a major American university, new laboratory space, and funding from the mainline New York moguls. D'Herelle's appointment at Yale seemed ill-fated from its inception, however. Although he was appointed to the Yale faculty on 1 July 1928, he did not arrive until after his trip to California for the Lane Lectures in October 1928. As part of this excursion he managed stops in San Francisco, Los Angeles, Riverside, California, Cleveland, Madison, and Albany. He had invitations from many more places such as Dubuque, Portland, Oregon, and Minñneapolis.[13] The interest shown in d'Herelle both by the academic community and by county medical societies suggests that his work and its practical applications were widely appreciated. Not only was this lecture trip useful to spread his message about phage therapy, but it must have been quite lucrative as well. The usual lecture fee or "honorarium" was $100, a substantial sum in 1928.[14]

No sooner had d'Herelle arrived in New Haven than he was off to address the Philadelphia Pathological Society and receive its William Wood Gerhardt Medal.[15] Already Winternitz had started to express his irritation at his new colleague: in his notes he observed that d'Herelle was in New Haven for only "a few days" in October 1928 before leaving again, this time for Stanford.[16] For Winternitz, d'Herelle's lengthy absences from New Haven were to become a source of increasing annoyance until they became intolerable.

Shortly after D'Herelle returned to New Haven in mid-December 1928, finally ready to begin work in earnest, he was hospitalized. D'Herelle's medical records for this illness give several interesting insights. Not a little hypochondria is suggested: "The patient had felt well up until the afternoon before admission when he developed general malaise, a slight non-productive cough, and found he had a little fever. No pain in the chest, no sputum. He enters the hospital not because he feels ill but rather as prophylactic."[17] For much of his adult life d'Herelle suffered from incapacitating illnesses that interrupted his plans, whether at work or during travel to give lectures. The nature of some of these illnesses can be deduced from his past medical history taken down in December 1928: "Amoebiasis twice in Orient. Malaria several times. Unknown fever six months before admission while in Egypt. Phrenic paralysis ten years previously following auto-inoculation with tetanus bacilli."[18] The physicians in New Haven finally diagnosed influenza, but its clinical course was unremarkable. However, as was noted, d'Herelle suffered from serious illnesses in the past, including one caused by self-inoculation. Recurrent bouts of malaria also troubled d'Herelle during his years at Yale, where he was treated by Dr. John R. Paul, later to become famous for his work on animal viruses.[19]

Although d'Herelle devoted significant effort to emphasize the value and potential of bacteriophage therapy, while at Yale he turned his attention to two related problems, the nature of bacterial variation and the isolation of phages useful against staphylococcus infections.

For the period 1928–1933 d'Herelle was, for the first time in his scientific career, able to concentrate on his research as his first priority. No longer was he obliged to do service work to justify his position, as had been case with the Conseil Quarantenaire in Egypt, the vaccine department at the Pasteur Institute in Paris, or the Mexican sisal growers. Given substantial resources and a secure position in a major American university, d'Herelle embarked on a timely and ambitious research program to understand the causes of bacterial variation.

The topic of bacterial variation had been of increasing general interest since the early observations of Massini and Neisser on the strain of colon bacillus called *B. coli mutabile* and the description of the phenomenon of bacterial dissociation by De Kruif.[20] At stake was the Koch-Cohn doctrine of monomorphism. This idea held that bacteria could be classified into distinct groups based on the fixity of their morphology. Thus, cocci (spherical bacteria) differed from bacilli (rod-shaped bacteria) in some taxonomically meaningful way, and one form did not transform into the other any more than dogs became cats. This notion was the basis for much of the work to classify and identify specific types of bacteria and to apply such classifications to medical diagnosis.[21] When it was found that supposedly pure cultures of a given bacterial "species" gave rise to variants, or that it could "dissociate" into two variants, the utility and reliability of the taxonomic criteria became problematic. Two more or less opposing explanations were offered: the view of Beijerinck, De Kruif, and Arkwright was that the dissociation or variation was a manifestation of the type of genetic instability called mutation in higher plants and animals; the explanation offered by Löhnis, Enderlein, and Hadley was that bacteria underwent complex life cycles and that bacterial morphology (and presumably the physiology) differed for the different phases of growth.

Soon after his discovery of bacteriophage d'Herelle confronted the phenomenon of bacterial resistance to the action of bacteriophages. Some cultures appeared to lyse completely, only to become turbid again a few days later with "secondary cultures." These secondary cultures were frequently resistant to the action of the original phage, having acquired resistance or "immunity." Not only was this phenomenon of practical importance to his theory of natural immunity, but he believed that it could give an understanding of the process of bacterial variation as well. From his first papers in 1920 and 1921 he conceived of bacterial mutations in terms of phage-induced modifications of the bacterium (FdH: 36; FdH: 43; *BIRI,* 84–92). D'Herelle's interest in this problem was a direct consequence of his studies on cholera in India. In particular, he was struck by the problem of variation in virulence of cholera as a disease and in the variability in properties of the cholera vibrios isolated from sick patients. His explanation for these phenomena was based on his work on bacteriophage; he believed that the variants classified as mutations were caused by the symbiosis of the bacterium and a bacteriophage. He thus embarked on a program of investigation of the variable properties of a specific bacterium upon survival after infection by bacteriophage.

Even before coming to Yale, d'Herelle had conceived of the cholera problem in terms of bacterial variability. In a paper published in March 1929 in the *Yale Journal of Biology and Medicine,* d'Herelle set out his definition of the problem: "Everyone who has written upon the subject of cholera has pointed out that however familiar we may be with respect of the characters of the pathogenic organisms discovered by Koch in 1883, with regard to its pathogenicity the single fact actually known is that the presence of this vibrio in the intestinal mucosa causes the disease. But why do the vibrios undergo modifications in the body? Why do they lose their virulence? Why do they disappear? Why does the patient recover? These questions remain unanswered. There is the same obscurity with regard to the epidemiology of the disease, and there is no explanation for the sometimes bizarre progress of epidemics" (FdH: 100, 195).

A major puzzle for the bacteriologist at the time was the nature of the El Tor vibrios. Although pathogenic strains of the cholera vibrio were positively identified by specific agglutination reactions with specific sera, the El Tor vibrio was an enigma. It was first isolated in 1906 from the bodies of pilgrims at Tor on the Gulf of Suez who died with dysentery-like symptoms at a time when there were no known cases of cholera in the area. These vibrios resembled cholera vibrios in most aspects, including specific agglutination, but produced an active hemolysin and a demonstrably different extracellular toxin. Because non-pathogenic, saprophytic vibrios were commonly isolated from soil, water, and healthy human beings, the role of the El Tor vibrio in cholera was puzzling: was it a "true" cholera, albeit a variant, or was it just another non-pathogenic passenger in patients made ill by some other organism?

Likewise, the presence of "non-agglutinable," non-pathogenic vibrios in healthy individuals was considered by some bacteriologists as a potential source of cholera in the event that these vibrios acquired pathogenic properties. Since true cholera vibrios sometimes lost their agglutinability (and pathogenicity for laboratory animals) upon passage in the laboratory, the complementary acquisition of agglutinability and virulence by non-pathogenic vibrios was considered a real possibility.

D'Herelle thought that both the peculiar El Tor strains and the variation in agglutination were manifestations of mutations induced by phage-bacterium symbiosis. He believed that this symbiosis and consequent avirulence accounted for the carrier state in several diseases, including typhoid and cholera. After reviewing the known epidemiology of cholera he concluded: "Carriers of the cholera vibrio, other than incubating and sick carriers, are not infectious. . . . There only remains a last question, namely, at what moment does the carrier cease to be infectious?" D'Herelle went on to supply his answer: "As may be shown, it is possible to demonstrate that the loss of virulence is coincident with the occurrence of bacteriophagy, from which it follows that only incubating and sick carriers are infectious. In the convalescent carrier bacteriophagy has taken place and he is no more infectious" (FdH: 109, 36–37).

In order to study the changes in bacterial virulence (and other properties) that accompany phage-bacterium symbiosis, d'Herelle turned to study of *Bacillus typhi-murium* (*Salmonella typhimurium*). This choice was not just for laboratory convenience but was entirely consistent with his philosophy of studying infection only in the "natural" host. "It was not possible to utilize the cholera vibrio, for there is, for this organism, no susceptible experimental animal" (FdH: 109, 38). In the same article he noted for typhoid:

> It is impossible to verify experimentally the variations of virulence in typhoid bacilli which are carrying bacteriophage, since an experimental animal naturally susceptible to these organisms is lacking.* To the end of ascertaining the possible variations in virulence in the typhoid bacillus I have recently made a study of a related disease— mouse typhoid, caused by a bacillus of the same group, *B. typhi-murium* of Loeffler. * An experiment of this type carried out on a refractory animal such as the guinea pig or rabbit, is without value and can only lead to erroneous conclusions. In so far as typhoid is concerned the only susceptible animal is the anthropoid ape, and unfortunately funds available for laboratory studies do not permit their utilization. (FdH: 109, 25)

D'Herelle's views on bacterial variation and the role of bacteriophage infection reflected his desire to provide broad and general explanations for biological phenomena and exhibited clear French neo-Lamarckian genetic concepts.[22] His experimental approaches to these questions, as he framed them, were simple and elegant. For example, in order to determine if the origin of bacteriophage-resistant mutants of *E. coli* resulted from selection of pre-existing mutants or phage-induced acquisition of resistance, he devised and carried out the type of experiment later to be christened the Luria-Delbrück fluctuation test. He distinguished experimentally between two types of phage-bacterium interactions, one of which gave rise to "immune" bacteria, which harbored latent bacteriophage, and the other resulted in complete lysis of the infected bacterium.

In his monograph of 1921, d'Herelle hinted that the origin of secondary cultures was in some way related to genetic changes in the bacteria. After a discussion of the phenomenon of secondary, resistant cultures, he noted that natural variations in resistance were observed among strains isolated from patients: "These differences in resistance arise, as will be demonstrated later, in hereditary factors which originated in the struggle which took place between the ancestors of this bacterium and the bacteriophage within the body of the infected animal. As is the case of the resistance acquired experimentally, this naturally acquired resistance disappears gradually with repeated culture on laboratory media" (*BIRI,* 88–89). In the summary to this monograph he concluded: "Although the bacteriophage is capable of acquiring a virulence for the bacterium, the bacterium on its side is capable of acquiring a resistance to the bacteriophage. The virulence of the one and the resistance of the other are not fixed, but are essentially variables, being enhanced or attenuated according to the inherited properties of each of the two germs, and according to the circumstances of the moment which favor the one or the other of the two antagonists" (*BIRI*, 294). The suggestion that "hereditary factors" and "inherited properties" underlie the acquisition of bacteriophage resistance was to be elaborated and refined in subsequent publications.

D'Herelle considered himself a true disciple of Lamarck and as such his concept of heredity and inheritance bear some investigation. Repeatedly d'Herelle used the term "adaptation" when describing changes in virulence or resistance. This concept he connected with the work of Lamarck, Geoffrey Saint-Hilaire, Alpheus Hyatt, Alpheus S. Packard, and Edward D. Cope:

> Since the time of Lamarck many theories have been brought forth to explain evolution, but analysis of these diverse theories immediately shows that, despite all care taken by their authors to avoid it, they are all dominated by the conception of Lamarck—adaptation to the environment. Natural selection, mutation, are only corollaries to the principle of adaptation. Lamarck certainly saw correctly when he attributed correctly to adaptation to the environment a preponderant rôle in the processes of evolution; at the basis of the fundamental cause of the survival of a line, of a species, rests the aptitude for its defense. Fundamentally, adaptation and survival are the consequences of defense, or, to speak more correctly, of a victorious "specific reaction." (*INID*, 74–75)

Lamarckism for d'Herelle, however, seemed to embody more of the ideas we associate with Lamarck, himself, rather than his nineteenth-century followers. D'Herelle described the survival of species in terms of those with the best power of defense or superior abilities to adapt to the environment.

The "inheritance of acquired traits" applied to traits "acquired" by processes such as De Vriesian mutation. D'Herelle cited the botanical work of the French biologist Noël Bernard, who attributed the results of De Vries on mutations in *Oenothera* to parasitism and the subsequent symbiotic relationship between host and parasite. Many curious examples of symbiosis were being discovered in the early part of the twentieth century, and symbiosis provided d'Herelle with a plausible mechanism for Lamarckian evolution: the changes were "acquired" by parasitism, and they were heritable so long as the symbiotic equilibrium remained intact.[23] In d'Herelle's conception of bacterial and bacteriophage variation the two notions of the process of change and the process of transmission are handled quite differently. With regard to the latter, it is clear that he accepted the gene theory of cellular heredity: in 1925 he wrote: "The only transmission of characters which we are concerned about here is that which takes place when a cell becomes two cells through division. Here, the transmission of *acquired* characters is beyond doubt" (*BIB,* 350, footnote).

His descriptions of the process of genetic transmission from parent to progeny are clear and unproblematic, unlike his discussions of the processes by which the parent cell becomes changed. Although this process of "mutation" was the focus of much of his attention, his almost invariable use of the term "acquired" without further explanation obscured or rendered ambiguous what he meant by this process. For example, in a discussion of an experiment to study the formation of secondary cultures he wrote: "That a selection [for resistant bacteria] takes place is precisely what I had shown previously by means of an experiment which has been presented in this present section. But it operates not through a selection of the bacteria naturally endowed with a resistance, but through a selection of those susceptible bacteria which are the more apt at acquiring resistance. This experiment shows definitely that what takes place is really an *acquisition,* in the strictest sense of the word, of resistance to the action of the bacteriophage" (*BIB,* 191). It seems then, that the preexisting variants subject to Darwinian selection are not phage-resistant bacterial variants, but *potentially* phage-resistant bacterial variants, a seemingly subtle distinction not further explored by d'Herelle. The notion that the secondary cultures arose as an adaptation to bacteriophage infection was theoretically attractive and amenable to experimentation.

The origin of these resistant bacteria became the focus of the ongoing confrontation between d'Herelle and André Gratia. While d'Herelle believed that the resistant cultures represented the symbiosis of phage and bacterium, Gratia proposed that preexisting phage-resistant variants in the culture simply grew out after the rest of the sensitive population had been killed by the phage.[24] D'Herelle described two results that he believed were convincing. First he carried out experiments on the formation of secondary cultures with phages of increasing virulence. In this context virulence was defined as the ability of a small inoculum of phage to lyse a turbid bacterial culture rapidly and completely, that is, so that it was clear to the eye.

> To state the situation briefly, the frequency of secondary cultures is strictly related to the virulence of the bacteriophage. With the bacteriophage of maximum virulence they [secondary cultures] do not occur when the conditions are optimal for the development of the bacteriophage corpuscles. . . . And finally, for races where the virulence is only moderate or weak, the bacteria acquire, within the first few hours, a resistance to enable them to develop in spite of the presence of bacteriophage. Under

such conditions clearing of the medium cannot take place. Coincident with the dissolution of those bacteria which are least capable of developing a resistance there occurs a multiplication of the bacteria which are the more apt to acquire a resistance. (*BIB*, 186–187)

When analyzing the course of events leading to development of resistant bacteria, d'Herelle asked, "How can this acquisition of immunity by a bacterium be explained?" He then described two possible outcome of phage infection:

Numerous experiments have shown that if a certain quantity of a *slightly active* culture of a bacteriophage is introduced into a relatively heavy (1000 to 2000 million per cubic centimeter) suspension of bacilli, the ultramicrobes, readily demonstrated at first by the presence of plaques on planting on agar, disappear from the medium after an interval of time varying from one hour to two or three days, and that they cannot later be demonstrated. Subcultures give normal cultures of bacteria. On the other hand, we have seen that with a very virulent bacteriophage the ultramicrobes disappear from the fluid between ten and twenty minutes after the introduction into a suspension, but that they reappear in about twenty times as great a number in from one to one and a half hours later—they have multiplied within the interior of the bacteria. In the case of a bacteriophage of low virulence it seems, therefore, that penetration of the bacterium takes place but that multiplication can not be effected. The bacterium resists and the ultramicrobe is actually destroyed *in vivo*. These parasitized bacteria which "recover" acquire by this an immunity. We will see later that they are even capable of producing antilysins.

Another fact has been sometimes observed which shows that certain bacteria are able to become "carriers." . . . The fact, demonstrated by experiment, of the penetration of virulent ultramicrobes into the bacteria, warrants us in thinking that this ultramicrobe (but slightly virulent) has been preserved in a latent state within the interior of the bacterium. At a given moment the resistance of the bacterium is broken down and infection results. (*BIB*, 194–95)[25]

These experiments, which suggested that the number of resistant cultures correlated with the virulence of the phage, were interpreted by d'Herelle to mean that the phage acted positively to *induce* the resistance. The alternative idea—that the phage just killed off the sensitive bacteria—predicted that there should be the same number of resistant cultures in any case, because the resistant bacteria were already there and their frequency should be unrelated to the action of the bacteriophage.

A second experiment to test this notion is of significant historical interest because it is similar in concept and design to the fluctuation test used by

Salvador Luria and Max Delbrück in 1943 to answer the same question.[26] As part of the analysis of the effect of virulence on the appearance of secondary cultures, d'Herelle tested several phages of differing "virulence" by determining the frequency of secondary cultures that developed in twelve replicate cultures. For the "most potent race of bacteriophage which I have yet isolated," he found that one culture out of twelve gave rise to a secondary culture. He repeated this experiment five more times and found the frequencies of secondary cultures to be 0/12, 2/12, 0/12, 3/12, and 1/12. For a less virulent bacteriophage, the frequencies of secondary cultures in six replicate experiments were 7/12, 9/12, 5/12, 10/12, 5/12, and 6/12 (*BIB*, 185–186).

When discussing the mechanism for the appearance of secondary cultures he noted:

> At first thought it appears strange that when secondary cultures develop with a race of bacteriophage of high potency, they appear in some tubes and not in others. The following experiment offers an explanation for this.
>
> Two flasks, each containing 200 cc. of a *B. dysenteriae* suspension (250,000,000 per cubic centimeter) are inoculated with 0.04 cc. of a culture of the bacteriophage (the same race as that used in the preceding experiments). Immediately after inoculation the contents of the first flask is distributed into 20 tubes, 10 cc. to each. In all of these dissolution takes place normally, being permanent in 19, showing a secondary culture in 1. The second flask is portioned out the next day, that is, after dissolution is completed, 10 cc. being placed in each of 20 tubes. None of these tubes become turbid. When this second part of the experiment is repeated, 18 remain clear and 2 tubes yield secondary cultures.
>
> Each flask of suspension contained 50,000 million bacilli, and the above experiments show that of this number but one or two were capable of acquiring an immunity to the very active bacteriophage. It is these "immune" bacilli which give rise to organisms that enjoy the same degree of resistance.
>
> Secondary cultures, then, have their origin in the operation of the phenomenon of natural selection, whereby some bacilli show a greater aptitude than others to the acquisition of a resistance to the bacteriophage.
>
> The phenomenon of secondary culture formation is governed by the individual properties of the bacterium and the bacteriophage. Against a single strain of bacterium the less virulent the bacteriophage the greater will be the proportion of secondary cultures, or, in other words, the greater is the number of bacilli in the suspension capable of acquiring a resistance. (*BIB*, 190–191)

D'Herelle noted the odd statistical result of the appearance of secondary cultures "in some tubes and not in others." His approach was to compare the results of the same large culture, divided into subcultures before and after the lytic growth of the phage in the host cells. The result, one secondary culture out of twenty tubes for the initially separated cultures and zero and two of twenty for the tubes prepared the next day from the mass lysate, suggested to him that very few, perhaps 1 or 2 bacteria in the entire original 200 ml culture, could respond to the bacteriophage attack, become resistant, and start produce a secondary culture three days later. He seemed to think that if the resistant bacteria already existed, they should have grown during the first day of the experiment and each of the twenty subcultures prepared the day after infection should have given rise to secondary cultures. His interpretation was consistent with the Pasteurian notion of attenuation and exaltation of virulence by re-peated passage under altered conditions. Thus, the few bacteria "more apt at acquiring resistance" are initially parasitized by the phage, but still manage to live. They slowly grow, their progeny are attacked by the phage, but little by little they acquire increased resistance and eventually (after the last division into the twenty subcultures), begin to grow rapidly as resistant variants, even in the presence of bacteriophage. This model also provides an explanation for the inverse correlation of the appearance of secondary cultures in relation to the virulence of the phage. The variation in the "threshold of aptitude" toward acquisition of resistance meant that increasing the virulence of the phage would eliminate many of the bacteria which, if infected with a less virulent phage, could eventually become resistant by repeated growth cycles in the presence of phage.

D'Herelle clearly appreciated the design of this experiment and its power to discriminate between the two hypotheses. However, the mathematical analysis of the statistical expectations for the number of secondary cultures and the realization that knowledge of the differential growth rate of the sensitive and resistant bacteria was essential to interpretation would await the attention of Salvador Luria and Max Delbrück twenty years later.[27]

In addition to his theoretical approaches to the mechanism of phage-pro-voked mutations, d'Herelle and his co-workers, Ruth Koester Beecroft and Tony Liebman Rakieten examined the more directly relevant question of the nature of the changes produced in the bacterium following exposure to bacte-riophage. As early as 1921 d'Herelle had wondered about the alterations in bacteria which had acquired resistance to phage (FdH: 43). At this time he reported only changes in cellular and colony morphology. A few years later, in 1925, he explicitly referred to the "bacteria-bacteriophage symbiosis" and noted that the cellular morphology was appreciably changed soon after infection but that with continued culture, some of the resistant, "secondary cultures" reverted to the original form while some maintained the altered forms which included small granules which d'Herelle supposed might be a "primitive bacterial form" (FdH: 88). By 1931 however, d'Herelle's focus seemed somewhat sharpened:

> In studies which I have made upon cholera it has been clear that the cholera vibrio entering into symbiosis with bacteriophage undergoes profound modifications. These arise without coordination, and thus present all the characteristics of mutations. Recently in this laboratory we have undertaken a more complete study of another bacterium, *Salmonella typhimurium,* this particular organism being selected because with it the virulence of the derived mutants for a naturally susceptible animal, the mouse, can readily be determined. (FdH: 120, 56)

This study, started in December 1929, involved the complete lysis of a culture of *S. typhimurium* by a very virulent, newly isolated phage, followed by development of a secondary culture of resistant bacteria. This culture was then spread on agar plates and five types of variant colonies were noted. Some of these colonies were picked and transferred to broth cultures and tested for complete resistance to bacteriophage. In this way twenty-one strains were obtained. Tests of filtrates from each of the twenty-one mutants exhibited phages active against the original parental *S. typhimurium;* thus, each mutant was a "carrier" of bacteriophage. The effects of continued passage were examined for eight of the twenty-one isolates. Not only did the ability to produce phage change with increased passage, but the specificity of the phage produced seemed to change in complex ways. Likewise, specific agglutination by antiserum against the parental strain was lost in about half the mutants, and the fermentation reactions on several sugars were altered in five of the eight mutants studied.

For d'Herelle, however, the experiments on animal virulence must have held the greatest interest. Normally, mice fed 0.01 ml of a twenty-four-hour broth culture of *S. typhimurium* all died within seven to thirteen days. He tested the virulence of all his phage-resistant mutants after 10, 100, and 150 daily subcultures. Three mutants (I, III, and IV) were essentially avirulent; three mutants (II, V, and VII) were slightly virulent, and two mutants (VI and VII) were as virulent as the parental strain. Interestingly, mutant III could be recovered months later in cultures of the spleens of infected animals, whereas another avirulent mutant (I) completely disappeared from the mice inoculated with this strain. From these experiments d'Herelle concluded: "In relation to the problem of carriers these experiments show us that not all the carriers are infective.

Some carry avirulent mutants, others mutants of low virulence, few of them carry mutants whose virulence is equal to that of the primitive strain, and finally some may carry mutants which may be hypervirulent. The latter are very rare in nature" (FdH: 124, 673).

D'Herelle had no doubt that he was studying mutations, not cyclogenic changes, in part because of the haphazard combination of changes observed in each mutant: "This investigation shows that the principal cause of variations among bacteria is a result of symbiosis and certainly not the result of a life cycle. The variations are not cyclic but appear in a very disorderly fashion. What is more characteristic is that each character may vary by itself as an entity, without having any repercussive effect upon the other characters. If we consider for example the three characters 'virulence,' 'agglutinability,' and 'fermentation,' we observe that there is no relation between the variation of one of them and the variation of the others" (FdH: 124, 673–674).

This study of virulence was followed in 1934 by an equally detailed and extensive analysis of the serological reactivity of mutants (FdH: 132). In this work d'Herelle and Rakieten showed that, just as for fermentations and virulence, not all the bacterial mutants were sensitive to complement, even in the presence of antiserum. They attributed this variation, of course, to the action of the bacteriophage.

The final paragraphs of this publication seem laden with significance far beyond the immediate results. Not only had d'Herelle come to the brink of his Lamarckian position, having found that the mutations are haphazard and "disorderly," but his very research methodology, employing the bacteriocidal action of complement and antiserum (that of his early bête noire, Jules Bordet), was what a decade earlier he had described as "the history of an error" (*INID*, 162). This paper turned out to be d'Herelle's final experimental work and his last paper from Yale. As he left North America for good, in the concluding lines of this paper he seemed to close a major chapter not only in his personal life, but also in his scientific life: "These experiments complete the study of the general behavior of bacteriophage in relation to immunity carried on by one of us (d'Herelle) during the last fifteen years" (FdH: 132, 338).

D'Herelle had been at Yale for five years, but trouble had appeared within a few months of his arrival in 1928. In late March 1929, for what were called "personal reasons" he had to leave for Paris.[28] Dean Winternitz noted at the time that d'Herelle apparently was running a clinical and commercial laboratory in Paris having to do with the practical applications of bacteriophage. That summer Winternitz deputized a Yale visitor in Paris to check up on his suspicions and he noted later that the visitor was rebuffed by d'Herelle, who refused to show him the laboratory.[29] Although d'Herelle returned to New Haven in late September 1929 and Winternitz noted that things went well, in the spring of 1930, d'Herelle requested and was granted a highly irregular half-time faculty appointment. Again he spent the summer in France. Upon his return to New Haven in October 1930 d'Herelle asked to see the dean and, in Winternitz's words, d'Herelle "did not greet me but burst forth at once in broken English, telling me that he had not been treated fairly here."[30] By 18 November 1930 a compromise had been reached. Apparently the issue was money. Winternitz noted that the school would meet d'Herelle's requirements, which included an annual salary of $10,000, retroactive to 1 July 1930, support for a research assistant at $3,750, and a technician at $1,200, as well as increases in support for his secretarial and janitorial expenses from $800 to $2,500 each year and an increase in laboratory expense budget from $1,300 to $3,000 per year. With the largess, however, came the "understanding that he will spend the entire year (academic) at Yale" and that d'Herelle "will agree that the budget now offered you must be regarded as a stable one, which in the future will not vary by reduction on our part or by requests for increases on your part."[31]

With this investment of scarce resources in the face of the Great Depression, Winternitz hoped for future stability in his relations with his excitable colleague, and indeed, the next two years apparently passed without incident. The record is sketchy for this period with only suggestions of D'Herelle overspending his laboratory supplies allowance. In July 1931 the University Treasurer cleared an overdraft on the department budget but raised the question as to whether d'Herelle was using salary money provided for the employment of bacteriology instructors for research expenses instead. By January 1932 he was informed that his expense account was in the red by $136.15, so he sent a personal donation to Yale University to cover these expenses. Further correspondence ensued to clear up the status of d'Herelle's contribution for his own work as a tax deduction.[32]

A year later, however, when d'Herelle was ready to leave, he received a well-timed invitation to work with a close friend and former Pasteur Institute colleague, Georgiy Eliava, a Georgian microbiologist and cofounder of the Tiflis Bacteriological Institute. On 10 May 1933 d'Herelle sent his resignation from the Yale faculty to president Angell, giving "continued misunderstandings" and the "economic situation" as reasons for his departure. The university press release put it somewhat differently: "While in residence here Dr. d'Herelle confined himself largely to the study of bacteriophagy as a laboratory phenomenon, since suitable clinical material was lacking. The control of infections by the use of bacteriophage has long been a primary interest with him, and it is the hope of elaborating his work in the clinical field, possibly at the new institute for infectious diseases at Tiflis, Russia, which now takes him abroad."[33] Once more d'Herelle was off on a new endeavor.

Chapter 11 To Tiflis and Back

In the USSR the period from 1921 to 1928 was a time of relative liberality and tolerance in the arts, social thought, and science. Non-political activities had not yet come under strict state control while the nation struggled in the aftermath of War Communism. The New Economic Policies, introduced in 1921 by Lenin, represented a pragmatic retreat from State Communism to State Socialism. At the same time, the government started to encourage broad education of the population and what might now be called "outreach" programs, such as workers' night courses. In a massive national effort to modernize and industrialize the USSR, government policies supported heavy industry and the development in the cities at the expense of consumer goods production and agricultural development.

In 1928, however, Stalin was able to consolidate his power in what has become known as the Stalin Revolution. The first of the Five-Year Plans dated from October 1928 and was declared so successful that it was completed in December 1932. One consequence of the Stalin Revolution was a new emphasis on "polytechnism," that is, on-the-job training, and emphasis on practical applications and skills. These

objectives resulted in a crackdown on intellectuals and centrally directed effort
to achieve certain goals and abandon others.

As part of the national drive to improve science and medicine, Georgiy
Grigor'yevich Eliava, a Georgian microbiologist working at the Pasteur Institute from 1918–1921, returned to Tiflis (Tbilisi)[1] to join the Tiflis Central
Laboratory in the Union of Cities Hospital. In 1923 he was one of the co-
founders of the Tiflis Bacteriological Institute, and in 1927 he was appointed to
the chair in hygiene at Tiflis University. Two years later he was made professor
of bacteriology.[2]

After serving as a bacteriologist in the Soviet army in a front line unit at
Trebizond (now Trabzond, Turkey), Eliava joined the Pasteur Institute in 1918
where he worked in the laboratory of Edouard Pozerski.[3] When d'Herelle lost
his laboratory at the Pasteur Institute in 1920 following his return from Indochina, Pozerski provided him with a small bit of space in his own laboratory
(literally "a stool," in Pozerski's words). During this time Eliava and d'Herelle
became close friends and collaborated on several bacteriophage studies (FdH:
51; FdH: 52).

Eliava returned to Tiflis in 1921 but came back to Paris to work again at the
Pasteur Institute from 1925 to 1927. In 1923 Eliava was instrumental in the
organization of the Tiflis Bacteriological Institute, where he introduced a research program on bacteriophage. He was particularly interested in the practical applications of bacteriophage in clinical medicine and public health, interests which coincided well with the practical goals of the central authorities in
the USSR. Eliava was able to command significant government support for his
plan to produce and test bacteriophages on a large scale in the Soviet Union,
and by 1936 he had created the All-Union Bacteriophage Institute in Tiflis. The
decree of the Council of People's Commissars, dated 14 April 1936, called for the
building of the institute, which was envisioned as the future world center of
bacteriophage research.[4]

In 1933 when d'Herelle decided to leave Yale, Eliava was in a position to offer
him everything he wanted: a new institute with congenial researchers dedicated
to his ideas, a governmental policy supportive of clinical trials of new technolo-
gies, and the attractions of the new scientific socialism.

As d'Herelle's relationship with Dean Winternitz deteriorated in New Haven,
he began to make plans to move to Tiflis. In his official report on d'Herelle's
departure, Winternitz noted that d'Herelle resigned "to be able to carry out
work in regions where clinical and field studies can be carried out more readily
than they can in this country."[5] After attending the Congress on Immunology

of the Royal Academy of Italy in Rome at the end of September 1933, d'Herelle arrived in Tiflis in October 1933 with supplies and equipment, purchased with his own funds, ready to set up work in Eliava's institute (*HM*).

In the early 1930s the USSR, in its attempt to modernize, was actively importing not only foreign technology but especially foreign expertise. D'Herelle was probably recruited under this rubric with payment in hard currency.[6] To employ the famous discoverer of bacteriophage must have been viewed as an important and prestigious advance for Soviet science. On the grounds of the Bacteriophage Institute was a duplex dwelling planned for Eliava, d'Herelle, and their families. For the first time in his life, d'Herelle enjoyed the real appreciation of his work. His laboratory was supported in grand style with able technical staff, and he enjoyed the personal attention of servants, including a chauffeur (*HM*).

D'Herelle was appointed as professor at the school for continuing education of physicians and was also consultant-general at the Institute of Bacteriophage.[7] The professorship may have been an appointment of convenience, made without the usual bureaucratic difficulties, or it may have been deliberate to allow him direct contact with practicing physicians who could be induced to try his phage therapy. In this position he was, indeed, able to influence some of the leading physicians in Tiflis to use phage therapy in clinical trials. Perhaps the most powerful ally in this work was Professor Alexandr Petrovich Tsulukidze, who had been appointed professor of general surgery at the Tiflis Medical Institute in 1930. Tsouloukidze championed the use of bacteriophages to treat surgical infections and published fourteen papers on the subject between 1935 and 1957.

After facing increasing resistance to his belief in bacteriophage therapy in the United States, d'Herelle found willing collaborators in the USSR. Infectious disease epidemics were still an important problem in the Soviet Union, and in Georgia, in particular, cholera outbreaks recurred frequently.

Even though he was setting up his new laboratory in Tiflis, d'Herelle continued his usual practice of a long summer visit to France. He left Georgia in April 1934 to return in November. Although d'Herelle had committed himself to the work in the Soviet Union, he continued to maintain his private commercial laboratory in Paris, the Laboratoire du Bactériophage. His scientific staff during this period consisted of Vladimir Sertic and Nikolai Bulgakov,[8] along with Théodore Mazure, who had married d'Herelle's daughter Huberte in 1922. Sertic and Bulgakov were microbiologists and Mazure was a pharmacist. This laboratory continued to make bacteriophages for commercial sale[9] as well as to carry out basic research on bacteriophages. Indeed, while d'Herelle was associated with the institute in Tiflis, his Paris operation was remarkably productive: Sertic and Bulgakov published seventeen papers in *Comptes Rendus de la Société de Biologie* between 1935 and 1937.

In 1934 d'Herelle attended the Second Congress of Azerbaijan Microbiologists in Baku and read a paper on the role of bacteriophages in immunity (FdH: 131). Although it contained no new data, this paper again gave him the occasion to enlist support for the clinical application of bacteriophages. Eliava also presented a paper about his work on bacteriophages.

D'Herelle himself published no research papers during his stay in Tiflis, but a report by Elena G. Makashvili and E.-G. Djanagowa in 1936 gives some insight into the experimental work of his laboratory during this period. Makashvili was a research associate in d'Herelle's laboratory, and the paper "On the significance of the presence in an animal organism of a given bacteriophage" was submitted from the "Institut de Bactériologie de Tiflis, URSS, Laboratoire de M. d'Herelle."[10]

This work was aimed at the practical goal of using bacteriophages as tools in clinical medicine. It had been suggested that the presence of bacteriophages that were specific for a given bacterial species could be used in diagnosis of pathogenic infection by that species. Thus, the tests for the specificity of phages from a sick person might rapidly diagnose the causative organism. Because some bacteria were hard to culture or took a long time to grow, the business of diagnostic bacteriology could be quite lengthy. The speed with which phages grew might hasten the diagnosis considerably. The reports of correlations of phage specificity with infecting organism could be explained by two hypotheses which d'Herelle saw as mutually exclusive. The first hypothesis is that there is a diversity of phages in the environment and that the phages with the required specificity are retained in the body and multiply since they are able to infect the offending bacteria—that is, sort of a *selection* hypothesis. The second hypothesis is that there is one fundamental, "polyvalent" type of bacteriophage that becomes *adapted* to increased virulence toward the offending micro-organism. The second hypothesis had been supported by d'Herelle since his early work and reflected his neo-Lamarckian ideas of induced adaptation. It also agreed with the basic notions of Trofim Lysenko, the agrobiologist who was beginning to gain ascendancy in Soviet science starting in 1935.[11]

Makashvili and Djanagowa examined the feces of ten horses, ten pigs, and ten chickens for phages active against four common strains of intestinal bacteria. Even after plaque purification (purification by the method of isolated plaques), every one of the isolates retained the virulence pattern toward the four species which was found for the initial sample before plaque purification. They concluded that the results supported the hypothesis that the specificities were observed because of the polyvalent nature of the bacteriophage rather than because there was a mixture of phages, each with its own specificity. Furthermore, they concluded that it was not possible to infer the identity of the predominant organism from the specificity of the phages present, as many of their isolates, even from healthy animals, exhibited specificities for a number of pathogenic strains of intestinal bacteria.

In addition to directing two laboratories half a continent apart, d'Herelle undertook to update his views on the subject of bacteriophage by writing his third general summary on the subject in the form of a monograph on the phenomenon of recovery in infectious diseases. This work was taking form even before he left Yale, because in his letter of resignation, he told Dean Winternitz that he was just about ready to publish a summary of the past four years of research in a book on the relationship of bacteriophages to immunity.[12] This monograph probably was drafted in the summer of 1934 at his country home in France and completed in the USSR because the introduction is dated 9 February 1935 in Tiflis. D'Herelle indicated that the audience for this work was to be "mainly hygienists, infectionists and therapists" not "only several dozen specialists." In outlining the chapters, he emphasized that "the phenomenon of bacterial mutations, arising as one of the possible consequences of the illness, presents the least studied, yet the most difficult of problems. To the systematic study of this phenomenon I have dedicated the last four years" (FdH: 133, 3–4). This monograph, written "for the scientists of the U.S.S.R., a remarkable country, which, for the first time in the history of mankind, chose as its guide not irrational mysticism, but a sober science without which there cannot be any logic or genuine progress" (FdH: 133, 6), appears to be d'Herelle's own scientific manifesto upon starting his life and work in the Soviet Union.

Bakteriofag i fenomen vyzdorovleniya [Bacteriophage in the phenomenon of recovery] was written in French and translated into both Russian and Georgian by Eliava. The Russian version was published in Tiflis in 1935, but the French edition (which except for the preface was identical to the Russian volume) did not appear until 1938. The fate of the Georgian version is obscure.

As usual, d'Herelle returned to France for the summer of 1935. Some time in the fall of 1935 he was injured in a train accident in Russia and spent several months of the winter of 1935–1936 in enforced recuperation on the French Riviera (*HM*). With the spring of 1936 came the establishment of the All-

Union Bacteriophage Institute. By then, however, the Stalinist purges had begun. With the assassination in December 1934 of Sergey Kirov, the Leningrad Party Secretary and second in command after Stalin, as a pretext, Stalin initiated a massive campaign of extermination of intellectuals and mid-level party and military officials. Eliava was caught up in the Terror and in 1937 he was arrested and executed. This tragedy ended d'Herelle's work in the USSR.

While Eliava had served his nation on the front lines in war and in its scientific development in peacetime, he incurred the wrath of a formidable enemy, Lavrenty Beria. In the early 1930s Eliava had been arrested as a "wrecker" (a term used for anti-party activity), and Beria, who was first secretary of the Georgian Communist party and head of the Georgian security police (OGPU), personally insisted on his prosecution. Only pressure from the leadership in Moscow, perhaps from Stalin himself, resulted in his release.[13] In 1937 Eliava was again arrested and accused of deliberately infecting children in the region of the Georgian town of Signakh. He was executed along with his wife, a Polish opera singer.[14]

Pozerski recorded the dramatic events surrounding Eliava's arrest as he heard it from some Georgian refugees in Paris a year later:

> One morning some soldiers burst into the Institute. They were commanded by an officer, who, when he entered the courtyard, saw from a distance the French thoroughbred in the stable through the open door. He entered.
>
> As a true Caucasian, he could not refrain from jumping on the horse. Under the action of a strike of the spurs, which she had never felt, this one reared up and suddenly rushed out of the stable at such a speed that the officer did not have time to lower his head. His forehead struck the frame of the open doorway. He fell backwards, stained with blood, his head shattered.
>
> All the soldiers rushed up to Eliava, took him away. His wife gave forth the cries: "they arrested him, they took him away."
>
> What became of her? I never knew anything. But this I did hear a year later, in Paris, from some Georgian refugees, that Eliava was tried and shot the same day . . . and the horse too, because both had caused the death of the commandant.[15]

False accusations of poisoning water supplies and wells or of deliberately infecting people were commonly used against bacteriologists and physicians during this reign of terror,[16] borrowing, of course from the tradition of the pogroms, and based on themes dating back to the Crusades. The reason for Beria's enmity toward Eliava, in particular, is unclear. Eliava did not seem to be overtly political but rather dedicated to advancement of his scientific work. Rumors of a love triangle involving Beria, Eliava, and an actress vie with a political affront to Beria as possible reasons.[17] Eliava's possible kinship with Shal'va Zurabovich Eliava, a well-known Soviet communist and Central Committee member who *was* Beria's enemy, may also have been a reason behind Eliava's execution.

In 1937 d'Herelle prepared the French edition of his monograph *Le phénomène de la guérison des maladies infectieuses,* which was published in early 1938.[18] Comparison of the 1935 Russian edition with the 1938 French edition gives some insight into d'Herelle's reasons for going to the Soviet Union and his reactions to subsequent events.

D'Herelle's political views were liberal, and he was fond of engaging in discussions of world events and politics over lunch with his students and co-workers.[19] He had just experienced the Great Depression in the United States and thought the government responses to be inadequate (*PM,* 756–770). Against this background, his introduction to the Russian edition must be viewed as more than the pro forma political puffery. As in all his books, he took the opportunity to philosophize, to rail against his enemies, and to set the record straight: "The history of epidemics and history in general may be studied using analogous methods. This should not seem unusual to a person who is used to grasping what is around him: the main characteristic of living material—protoplasm—is the ability to assimilate. From this results all other properties of living matter. It is clear then that all biological phenomena and occurrences may be studied as possessing, at their core, this fundamental ability" (FdH: 133, 5). For d'Herelle, assimilation seemed to be a metaphor, as well, for his adoption of the new "scientific" sociology of the USSR. Yet he was not uncritical in his position. He went on to discuss types of scientific error and the "experimental method."

Such considerations led, in turn, back to his basic arguments about the need to study immunity in the "natural host." With reference to "the established scheme," where one "limits oneself to the artificial constraints of the laboratory" he wrote:

Hundreds of scientists work according to the established scheme and the pooled results constitute "the study of immune responses" or immunology. I find it necessary to note that although all these experiments may be conducted in the most conscientious way and the obtained results may be real and valuable and may represent theoretical interest, the author does not deem them to be such.

Because all illnesses studied by significant authors were "artificial" illnesses (neither the rabbit not the guinea pig are affected by cholera or typhus in the natural environment) they have bearing only when talking about the artificial illness and not at all practical for application to real, natural illnesses which occur in humans. . . .

The second experimental method consists of studying an illness in its natural habitat and its progression within the confines of nature.

In order to establish the cause of Asiatic cholera, one must go to an area of epidemic propagation of this disease and study in natural conditions changes arising in humans who have recovered from cholera. If one wants to be convinced of the nature of the process and path of recovery from the plague, it must be studied in a environment of its natural occurrence—the midst of the plague.

This same path must be followed when studying all other acute infectious illnesses of man and animal which have the capacity of helping science strip the cover off of the natural process of recovery.

Both methods may be called experimental; however, I believe that only the second one is logical, expedient, and allows the building of a real dynamic which truly reflects the infectious processes in immunology.

I would be happy to see all hygienists and doctors in the USSR on the side of the real experimental method, a revolutionary method because it destroys set traditions and overthrows entrenched habitual opinions. (FdH: 133, 7)

D'Herelle's optimism for the future of science is glowing: "I dare hope that my book can serve as a stimulus for orientation on the new epidemiological frontiers. I wish for this even more so because an era of rebirth and unheard of enlightenment must originate in the USSR. Laboratories intended for biological findings are sprouting everywhere in our huge country; the scientific life is intensifying more and more at a time when in capitalist countries it has a growing tendency to slow down; science was doomed to be the first victim of worldwide economic crisis" (FdH: 133, 8).

In the name of science and logic d'Herelle took this opportunity to decry the publication of "mistaken experimental conclusions" resulting, he believed, from "lack of experimental experience, experimental training, and on hurried publication of inadequately checked observations" (FdH: 133, 8). With regard to his third source of error, premature publication, he notes:

This last cause of experimental mistakes is because of the usual method for evaluation of a scientist. In the evaluation not only the quality but the quantity of publication is taken into consideration. A scientist is compelled to write fast and to publish often. Alas, it is enough to leaf through any periodical of scientific publication to see where this leads.

For example, ulcer is a condition to which much attention ought to be focused in order to learn how to treat it. In a scientific work, its nature should be subjected to evaluation. In a government system properly organized, repeated publication of experimental errors should result in the author's disqualification.

At the present time there is not an institution in the entire world that specializes in the fight against experimental blunders. Another measure would be to compel authors to be in less of a hurry to publish and more willing to check their results, which might put a stop to the anarchy which is slowing down the progress of science and in creating disbelief in the masses.

Only in the Soviet Union is it possible, without fear of offending the habitual, to judge the erroneous method. The new socialist order can rightfully revise all that has been handed down by the predecessors. (FdH: 133, 8–9)

While some parts of his introduction contain contemporary political rhetoric, most of it is consistent with his earlier writings and his philosophic views on science and the logic of experimentation.[20]

In the Russian version, in addition to the introduction, there is included a dedication bound into the book just after the title page, printed on better quality paper, followed by d'Herelle's signature in script. This dedication reads as follows:

At the present time, no one can rightfully doubt that sociology represents a strong scientific discipline. The basis for this conclusion is the progress of social development.

Workers can be separated into two groups: (1) philosophers and (2) scientists who painstakingly, brick by brick, erect the great monument of experimental science.

However, "experimental" does not yet mean "infallible." An experiment may lead one along the wrong path; only the final conclusion serves as the supreme criterion of rightness or wrongness of the experimental route taken.

For a person who had dedicated his/her life to experimental medicine, the goal should be to minimize man's suffering; for the fighter for human causes, the goal is to fight for the welfare and happiness of mankind, to free it from poverty and ignorance.

In both cases the path taken is invariably to reach the intended goal.

This book, which summarizes twenty years of seeking new pathways in medicine, is dedicated to him who possesses ruthless and relentless logic of history and who stands at the threshold of society. I dedicate this book to him who has reached the top. I dedicate this book to Comrade STALIN. [Signed] F. d'Herelle

Its political jargon and its physical and typographical distinction from the rest of the book all suggest that this dedication, in contrast to the introduction, was a precondition for its publication.

Turning to the French edition of 1938, one finds mainly revisions in the text to incorporate recent findings, especially d'Herelle's own work and that of his colleagues. The chapter titles and subheadings in the Russian version were largely retained in the French edition, but several topics were deleted and some were added. A section on colloids and micellae was omitted from the French edition and a full chapter on the nature of bacteriophage was added. The introduction was revised to remove any reference to socialism and the Soviet Union. Instead, we read of the importance of Euripides, Bacon, and Jenner in the study of nature and epidemics by "natural" experimentation, and of Becquerel, Duclaux, Gibbs, and Donnan for the applications of chemical insight to biology.

Even though d'Herelle spent only three years associated with the institute in Tiflis, he exerted an immense influence in the USSR. Bacteriophage research institutes at Kiev and Kharkov were established, reportedly under his leadership,[21] and phage therapy became widely adopted in the USSR. In 1936 his old colleague from the Institute for Cancer Research at Villejuif, Edouard Peyre, edited a special number of the French journal *La Médecine* on the topic of therapeutic application of bacteriophage. D'Herelle wrote a brief historical introduction to this work, which included two papers from Tiflis. Alexandr Tsulukidze described the use of bacteriophage in peritonitis subsequent to intestinal perforation in cases of typhoid,[22] while a group headed by Charles Mikeladze presented their experience with bacteriophage treatment of typhoid fever and acute colitis.

In trying to evaluate the use of bacteriophages for treatment of advanced cases of typhoid fever, Mikeladze and his coworkers compared the mortality rate, complication rate, and recurrence rate for patients treated in the "usual way" (which was unspecified, but probably consisted of fluids and supportive therapy), with those receiving bacteriophage therapy. Sixty-four patients were treated as "usual" and twenty-one received bacteriophage therapy. The mortality was 15.6 percent with the conventional treatment and 4.8 percent with bacteriophage treatment. Unspecified "complications" were 56.2 percent and 13.0 percent, respectively. Recurrence of the disease was, however, higher with bacteriophage (9.5 percent) than with "usual" treatment (4.5 percent). Mikeladze found that patients tolerated the treatment by mouth much better than by intravenous injection. He reported that although many patients responded well to intravenous administration of bacteriophage, insofar as their typhoid was concerned, many exhibited "violent reactions" and shock-like symptoms. He recommended that young patients with a sound cardiovascular system should be given intravenous phage, but that in older patients the oral route of administration was safer.

Acute colitis, both amoebic and bacillary, was endemic in Georgia. In cases where protozoan causes had been excluded, they administered by mouth a preparation from d'Herelle's Laboratoire du Bactériophage, *Bacté-intesti-phage,* a mixture of phages with diverse specificities, selected to be active against the common dysentery organisms. They treated ninety cases this way, forty-seven with dysentery and forty-three with colitis, and pronounced the results as "excellent." Of the patients with dysentery, there were three deaths, which was twice the average mortality in their hospital; however, the symptoms, even in grave cases, were rapidly ameliorated and the patients recovered more rapidly than expected. The same favorable clinical course was observed in the patients with acute colitis, where there were no deaths. The researchers concluded: "If it [the bacteriophage] is administered at the beginning of the illness, it interrupts its course. If it is administered late, it always improves the grave state of the patient, diminishes the local symptoms and reduces the mortality."[23]

Tsouloukidze had tested bacteriophages, also obtained from d'Herelle as *Bacté-pyo-phage* and *Bacté-intesti-phage,* for their usefulness in treatment of patients with intestinal perforation as a complication of typhoid fever. Prior to the antibiotic era, this complication, resulting in generalized peritonitis, was rapidly fatal in the majority of patients. Even with surgery to repair the perforation, Tsulukidze cited the mortality rate in his institution as 89 percent by three days after the operation. He reported a series of forty-seven cases which were divided into two groups: twenty-seven patients received the standard treatment (consisting of supportive care and surgery) and twenty patients had bacteriophage treatment added to their regimen. In the control group the mortality was 24/27 or 89 percent. In the group receiving phage, the mortality was 7/20 or 35 percent. In circumstances where nearly all the patients died, this was clearly a dramatic finding. Tsulukidze described his method for use of bacteriophage therapy in typhoid fever, but suggested that this method was probably generally applicable to cases of acute peritonitis from other causes.[24]

Tsulukidze carried on his work on the application of bacteriophage in surgery even after Eliava's death and d'Herelle's departure. He headed a team that field-tested bacteriophage for control of infections in war wounds in 1939–1940 during the "Finnish events."[25] For this work, which was deemed successful, he was awarded the Order of the Red Star. Another of d'Herelle's colleagues, Magdalina Petronova Pokrovskaya, had started working with bacteriophage therapy in 1929; she, too, worked on methods to apply phage therapy to war wounds from 1940 until the end of World War II.[26]

By 1946 bacteriophage therapy had become firmly established in the Soviet

Union. Stuart Mudd, an American microbiologist reporting on a postwar visit to study programs for medicine and national health, noted that during the war polyvalent dysentery phage preparations had been scattered in soil, sewage, and food, as well as given by mouth.[27] Such preparations were also being given at ten-day intervals to children in kindergartens and summer camps between May and October. It was reported to Mudd that controlled studies showed the protective effects for the phage treatments. In addition to this work at the Central Institute of Epidemiology and Microbiology of the Ministry of Public Health, and the All-Union Institute of Biological Prophylaxis of Infections, both in Moscow, Mudd described the phage work being continued in the successor to Eliava's institute, the Institute of Microbiology, Epidemiology, and Bacteriophagy of the Ministry of Health of the Georgian Republic in Tbilisi. Both polyvalent dysentery phages and typhoid phages were prepared there and used for clinical and epidemiologic studies.

This tradition of the clinical and epidemiologic applications of bacteriophage therapy has continued to the present in Eastern Bloc nations. One center of this work has been the Institute in Tbilisi, founded by Eliava and at which d'Herelle worked.[28] With the resurgence of antibiotic-resistant infections, researchers in the West have again taken up the study of phage therapy, too.[29]

Although eclipsed by the worldwide success of antibiotic treatment of infectious diseases and sanitary improvements in the developed countries, phage therapy and prophylaxis remains an intriguing, yet uncertain idea which still attracts attention.[29]

Chapter 12 Reflections and Legacies

As with other European and American scientists who initially supported the "scientific" social experiments in the USSR, d'Herelle was shocked and confused by the events of 1936–1937. To an idealist such as d'Herelle, the cynical and brutal politics of Stalin must have been deeply disappointing. With the tragic death of his friend, Eliava, in Tiflis, d'Herelle decided to remain in Paris rather than return to Georgia in the fall of 1937 as planned. His family was living in Paris and his laboratory for making phages for therapy was located nearby and was running well.

D'Herelle continued to spend his summers at his country house in Le Nervost in the little village of Saint-Mards-en-Othe in the department of Aube (Champagne-Ardenne region). In the country he devoted mornings to reading and writing while he spent the afternoons with his family. These outings often included his daughter Marcelle as well as his two grandsons, Félix and Hubert Mazure, the sons of Bertha (Huberte) d'Herelle and Théodore Mazure. D'Herelle indulged his passion for automobiles in the form of a French Panhard.

The Laboratoire du Bactériophage occupied space in a modern

building at 75 rue Olivier-de-Serres in the fifteenth arrondissement, and was engaged in production of a variety of phage preparations marketed for d'Herelle by the reputable firm of Robert et Carrier (later acquired by Laboratoires Synthélabo France, a company mostly owned by a L'Oréal subsidiary). The laboratory was producing phages directed at common infectious diseases such as dysentery, carbuncles, sinusitis, and wound infections (Figure 10).

Involvement in a commercial venture such as the Laboratoire du Bacté-riophage was a source of tension as well as gratification for d'Herelle. On one hand, he was philosophically opposed to exploitation of science for personal gain. He concluded his 1926 monograph with a long footnote:

> As was remarked some two years ago by an English medical journal, in the prophylac-tic and therapeutic use of the bacteriophage there is a vast field for commercial exploitation. This has already begun. I can not witness it without apprehension. . . .
>
> Too often commercial firms mislead both physicians and the public by clever quotations (clever in the sense that they avoid conflict with the law) tending to make it appear that such and such a scientist supervises their products, or even controls them. I now declare that I am, and always will remain, a stranger to all commercial enterprises. I may even go further in this direction and state that every time I have treated a patient it has been done solely from a scientific motive. (*BIB,* 578)

On the other hand, he felt a responsibility to ensure that effective phage preparations were available for clinical trials and evaluation. He noted that it was not easy to make effective bacteriophage for therapy and that skill, experi-ence, and constant attention to detail are needed. Over the years he had examined more than twenty commercial preparations of phage made in Ger-many, Belgium, Italy, the United States, Argentina, India, Japan, and France. He concluded: "On the whole, none of the preparations on the market is capable of effecting recovery from infectious disease." D'Herelle noted that these preparations were all made in capitalist countries by profit-making com-panies. He then speculated: "When one considers these numbers, capitalism is disastrous" (*PM,* addendum 6). He felt he was the "guardian of the method" of general therapy that he had discovered (*PM,* 735), so when he was approached in the spring of 1928 with a proposal from a Parisian pharmaceutical firm and a medical bacteriologist who wanted to buy the exclusive rights to sell phages made under d'Herelle's supervision in a new laboratory to be established, he agreed. For this agreement, d'Herelle received a million francs. The cost of the new laboratory was about a million francs, but it is unclear if this expense was born by d'Herelle or the promoters of his bacteriophages (*PM,* 736). Although

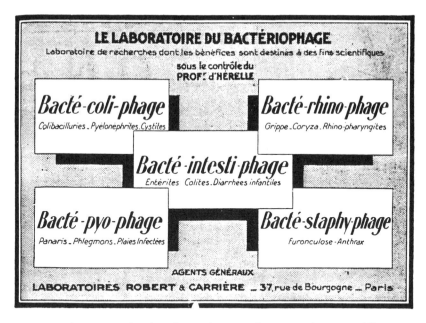

Figure 10. Advertisement for phage from Laboratoire du Bactériophage, 1936. This advertisement appeared in the supplementary issue of *La Médecine* devoted to phage therapy in 1936.

d'Herelle installed his son-in-law, a trained pharmacist, as head of the laboratory, the physician who proposed the venture was made the director of the company. Within the first year, the director violated the terms of the agreement that allowed d'Herelle to review and prohibit advertising that he did not approve of. Thus began six years of turmoil for d'Herelle which eventually brought him to the Supreme Court in France with his litigation against the commercial developer of bacteriophage therapy. Although he eventually managed to end his relationship with the offending parties and keep the laboratory functioning, he drew the moral of his experience: "Between a scholar, acting scientifically, without self-interest, and a rich company, up-to-date with all the procedural tricks, with the voting of the judges . . . it is a battle of a clay pot against an iron pot" (*PM,* 737). By the late 1930s, however, the Laboratoire du Bactériophage had come to function as a hybrid between a commercial producer of phages, making ten thousand doses per day, and a research laboratory that collaborated with scientists at the Institut Pasteur and the Institut du Radium to study the basic properties of bacteriophage (*PM,* addendum 5).

In addition to its commercial aspects, the Laboratoire du Bactériophage allowed d'Herelle and his colleagues to continue scientific research on phage. D'Herelle recruited Vladimir Sertic, a physician from Yugoslavia, and Nikolai Bulgakov, a Russian physician, and brother of the well-known dissident Soviet writer, Mikhail Bulgakov.[1] Sertic and Bulgakov described many new phage isolates and developed classification schemes for these phages. They also had collaborations with Pierre Lépine at the Pasteur Institute and Paul Bonét-Maury at the Radium Institute on the study of the physical properties of phage using the new techniques of sedimentation analysis and calibrated colloidon filters.[2] These studies, based on the use of the ultracentrifuge by Svedberg, and porous membranes by Elford and Andrewes,[3] were aimed at confirming the particulate, discontinuous nature of phage in the face of continued opposing claims for the continuous, "soluble ferment" concept of phage advocated by Northrop, Bordet, and others.

One of these isolates from the Laboratoire du Bactériophage went on to make history. It seemed to be quite small: it sedimented very slowly and easily passed through fine membranes.[4] This small phage, isolate number 174, designated ϕ, for its host range on several species of *Enterobacteriaceae,* and phage antigenic type X (Roman number 10), was later provided to Robert L. Sinsheimer by Bulgakov for Sinsheimer's pioneering studies on phage nucleic acid chemistry,[5] and eventually became the first biological organism for which a complete genomic DNA sequence was known.[6]

Certainly by the early 1940s, d'Herelle's conception of bacteriophages as particulate microbes began to attract more adherents as well as experimental support. As Ton van Helvoort has argued, the concept of filterable viruses was evolving from earlier microbiological paradigms to one based on physico-chemical ideas.[7] This evolution was especially clear in the case of tobacco mosaic virus, which was particularly amenable to chemical analysis, crystallization, and X-ray diffraction studies. Although bacteriophages were not yet fully under the rubric of "viruses," and eminent authorities such as John Northrop continued to support the Bordet model of phages as endogenous, autolytic enzymes, new methods and new investigators increasingly saw phage as yet another example of a filterable virus, particulate and infectious. The ability to "see" phages in the newly devised electron microscope, and the study of phage by scientists educated in physics and chemistry, rather than medicine and microbiology, completed this step in the evolution of the concept of phage to what Van Helvoort has called "the modern concept of a virus."

With the development of the electron microscope in Germany by Ernst Ruska and his colleagues, microbiologists were keen to look at the heretofore "invisible" agents known as filterable viruses. Two brief notes were published by his brother, Helmuth Ruska, in 1940 and 1941 in *Naturwissenschaften* which showed uniform particles attached to bacterial surfaces of bacteriophage-infected cells, as well as the same uniform particles in preparations of free bacteriophage.[8] Other publications from this same group, working with the German firm of Siemens and Halske, showed photographs of plant viruses and animal viruses. This new power to visualize the formerly invisible viruses transformed microbiology and conceptualization of the notion of filterable viruses.[9]

Constantin Levaditi and Paul Bonét-Maury, two French virus workers, reviewed the new evidence on the nature of "ultraviruses" in *La Presse Médicale* in early 1942.[10] They reproduced some of the German photographs, including one showing an *E. coli* cell covered with particles (phage) and "about to lyse." The clear interpretation from this new technique was that phages were particles, not "autolytic ferments." Levaditi and Bonét-Maury awarded the debate to d'Herelle: "The clear facts shown here speak in favor of the conception of d'Herelle."[11]

In addition to these direct physical studies, new research on the biological properties of phage during the late 1930s and early 1940s also contributed to clarification of the nature of phages as bacterial viruses. Eugène Wollman continued to work on phage at the Pasteur Institute and by his last of six papers in the series "Recherches sur le phénomène de Twort-d'Herelle," Wollman fully supported d'Herelle's view of the corpuscular nature of phage.[12] As early as 1927 Wollman had declared "It is certain that the discontinuous state of bacteriophages (d'Herelle) and not that of the substratum [bacterial lawn] (Bordet) that explains the phenomenon of plaques."[13] In collaboration with the physicist Fernand Holweck and Salvador Luria, both working at the Radium Institute in Paris, Wollman undertook the study of inactivation of phage by radiation. Their experiments were predicated on the belief that phages were infectious particles which were killed in an all-or-none way by the gamma rays they were using.[14] Prior to coming to Paris, Luria had worked in Rome and in the spring of 1938 collaborated with the microbiologist Geo Rita where he worked out the statistical relationship between the plaque-forming unit and the infectious unit of phage as determined by lysis of broth cultures.[15] Luria's analysis was predicated on d'Herelle's particulate concept of phage, and his statistical reasoning was based on a 1933 paper by Roy F. Feemster and W. F. Wells from Harvard.[16] These latter workers realized the power of d'Herelle's argument for the particulate nature of phage based on distribution of highly diluted phage, but recognized, as had Harry Clark in 1927, that the rather intuitive argument as advanced by d'Herelle and Bronfenbrenner and Korb could be greatly strengthened by rigorous statistical analysis.[17] Feemster and Wells seem to be the first to apply the Poisson distribution to analyze the unit of bacteriophage infectivity and its relationship to plaque formation.

Another approach to bacteriophage was under way at the California Institute of Technology in Pasadena, where in 1937 Emory L. Ellis decided that phage would be a good model for viruses that induce cancer.[18] Ellis accepted d'Herelle's view of phages as ultraviruses and his initial studies were aimed at replicating some of d'Herelle's observations, especially the step-wise growth of phage in infected bacterial cultures. In mid-1938 Ellis was joined by Max Delbrück, a German physicist looking for opportunities to extend his physical ideas into biology. Apparently unaware of the prior work by Feemster and Wells and by Luria and Rita, Delbrück derived mathematical expressions to fit Ellis's data which were designed to show that one plaque-forming unit in the solid-phase petri dish assay was equivalent to one unit of infectivity as measured by lysis of bacterial cultures. Ellis's experimental work, together with Delbrück's theoretical analysis, appeared in 1939 and has become one of the classics of molecular biology.[19] Although Ellis took up other research, Delbrück exploited the bacteriophage and became one of the founders of the American school that became known as the Phage Group.[20] By the end of the 1930s, then, new methods and new scientists increasingly confirmed d'Herelle's basic concept of phage as a particulate and infective ultravirus. For d'Herelle, however, important issues remained open: what was the biological organization of bacteriophage? Was it a true "microbe?" In 1942, in an article "Le Critère de la Vie" (FdH 140) he argued that his concept of phage as particulate was not enough; it must be "organized" in order to carry out its various actions as a living being. Thus, he was ensuring that bacteriophage was an element in the debates on the general place of viruses in the ladder of life, a debate which had received a major jolt with Stanley's crystallizations of plant and animal viruses.

Having finished the French edition of his third monograph, *Le Phénomène de la Guérison des maladies infectieuses,* explaining his concept of phage and its role in immunity in 1937, d'Herelle turned to more philosophical pursuits. He was sixty-four years old, apparently financially secure, and probably tired of the constant battles with the scientific establishment. D'Herelle's laboratory absorbed his attentions and his missionary zeal to proselytize for phage therapy was waning.

Against the background of Stalinist purges in the USSR, civil war in Spain, and German aggression in Austria and Czechoslovakia, life in France in 1938 was tranquil only by comparison. By September 1939, both Canada, d'Herelle's native country, and France, his adopted homeland, were at war with Germany. Up until the fall of Paris in June 1940 and the formation of the collaborationist Vichy French government, d'Herelle divided his time between supervision of his company in Paris and his country home in Saint-Mards-en-Othe. As a Canadian citizen, d'Herelle was liable to arrest or internment, yet he remained in France even though American friends urged him to return to the United States and offered him material help to do so.[21] He and his family, however, decided to remain in France and they moved to the spa town of Vichy, where his son-in-law had friends who found them lodging. Soon after this move, however, France fell to the German invasion and Vichy became the seat of the collaborationist government. While d'Herelle, his wife, and his daughter Marcelle remained in Vichy for the duration of the war, his son-in-law, Théodore Mazure, and his family returned to Paris, where Mazure continued to manage the affairs of the Laboratoire du Bactériopage. In February 1944, however, Mazure received clandestine warning that he was about to be arrested and deported to Germany, so he and his family fled to Saint-Mards-en-Othe for the rest of the war.[22]

The local authorities in Vichy recognized d'Herelle's international scientific reputation, and so he was able to continue his writing undisturbed, more or less under house arrest. He even attempted to carry on some laboratory work in collaboration with local health officials. His handwritten personal notes from this period, jotted on small pieces of paper, give the impression that d'Herelle was always on the look-out for opportunities to test his ideas about microbes and to apply bacteriophages in new ways.[23] When an idea occurred to him, he would write himself a short note describing an experiment to do, a hypothesis to test, or a reference to consult. One idea for a dermatologic preparation reads: "Pommade-Pyo-phage: Pyo + lanoline to saturation. + 1/3 glycerine (which functions as an antiseptic and does not kill the phage)." Another note: "Look for a phage for whooping cough bacteria;" yet another: "Large phages cannot penetrate bacteria—can they symbiose? Make secondary cultures with large and small phages on the same bacterial stock—Study the mutants." One amusing note describes d'Herelle's idea for isolating a phage to attack intestinal bacteria which produce flatulence. He included a recipe for making bacteriological media from beans, isolation of bacteria which produce hydrogen sulfide gas on bean bouillon, and then isolation of phage which attack these bacteria. He ends the note: "Test after eating cabbage."

In Vichy, perhaps as a result of his forced inactivity, d'Herelle started to write his autobiographical memoirs as well as his philosophical thoughts on science and its proper role in society and culture. His autobiography, *Les Péregrinations* [*sic*] *d'Un Microbiologiste,* was written in 1939 with emendations added after the war in 1946. This work is, indeed, a peregrination, with lengthy, discursive chapters on historical subjects, Eastern religions, and local customs related to places where d'Herelle had worked or traveled.

The table of contents of this 786-page manuscript lists thirteen chapters, the first ten of which are devoted to d'Herelle's accounts of his research, travels, and observations of his world. Chapter 11 is listed in the table of contents as "L'Agonie du Vieux Monde" (The agony of the Old World) but in the manuscript the chapter is entitled "La fin d'un Monde" (The end of one world). D'Herelle crossed out "Grandeur et Décadence" as the tentative title for this chapter, which describes his research program at Yale in the late 1920s and early 1930s and gives his account and interpretation of the Great Depression, World War II, and the postwar situation in Europe. He was not sanguine about the future. Just after the end of the war, in reference to the Marshall Plan, he wrote: "A new unbridled propaganda is raining down, not only in the U.S., but on the whole world: battle to the death against Communism. The notion of war is cultivated as the grand salvation: the U.S. starts up again as the manufacturers of war materiel and they arm all the countries who wish to submit to the power of the dollar" (*PM,* 780). "After dying Capitalism unleashes the next war, this time it will be the end: a new world will be born" (*PM,* 780).

In three more volumes, written during the war years, he elaborated his views of science under the title *La Valeur de l'Expérience: Essai de l'Expérimentalisme.* This work has a touching dedication to his wife, dated 2 February 1946, and probably was completed about the time of her death.[24] Volume I, "La Psychologie du Comportement," surveys experimental psychology: conditioning, reflexes, and various kinds of judgment and reasoning. Volume II, "Les Deux Méthodes Fondamentales," contrasts the methods in the arts with the methods in science. Volume III, "La Méthode Expérimentale," treats of the problem of induction and ends with a discussion of the axiomatic method and its relation to experimentation, using Euclidean geometry as an example. This work was d'Herelle's harsh critique of Descartes and his paean to Bacon and what d'Herelle believed to be the correct experimental method.

In 1946 d'Herelle summarized his long interest in epidemic infectious disease in *L'Etude d'une Maladie: Le Choléra, Maladie à Paradoxes,* a monograph prepared under the general editorship of Paul Hauduroy, professor of microbiology in Lausanne, and one of d'Herelle's proteges from the heady days of Paris in the 1920s (FdH: 141). In this book d'Herelle reviewed his philosophy of scientific investigation, presented a history of cholera, and described in detail his studies on cholera in India in the 1927 which led to the Bacteriophage Inquiry of 1927–1936.

After the war, recognition, if not acceptance, was finally coming to d'Herelle. Although the Wollmans had perished at the hands of the Nazis,[25] after the war the Pasteur Institute continued to support bacteriophage research and soon became the center of European phage research.[26] To commemorate the thirtieth anniversary of the publication of d'Herelle's first paper announcing his discovery of bacteriophage at the Pasteur Institute in 1917, the Pasteur Institute and the French Academy of Microbiology sponsored a lecture by d'Herelle in the Grand Amphitheatre of the Institute on 27 November 1947. D'Herelle's lecture was entitled "Bacteriophage in Nature." At this meeting d'Herelle was presented with the Medal of the Pasteur Institute. While this invitation caused distress to some older members of the Pasteur Institute, who recalled d'Herelle's turbulent time there, the younger staff apparently thought it unseemly to celebrate the discovery of phage but exclude its discoverer.[27] For this attempt to make amends, d'Herelle picked a seemingly neutral topic, but according to two observers he used the lecture to renew old controversies and once again raised the ire of the Pastorians.[28] He also was honored, probably more amicably, by the Society of Paris Surgeons, at their meeting on 4 July 1947. In what must have been written as a commemorative effort, d'Herelle recalled and reconstructed his work that led up to the discovery of bacteriophage in a memoir published in the French popular science journal *Atomes,* and which was subsequently translated into English and published in *Science News* (FdH: 142; FdH: 143). This latter publication juxtaposed Twort's recollections of his early work on phage with that of d'Herelle to give a sense of closure and finality to the old debates. The next year d'Herelle received the Prix Petit-d'Ormoy for natural science from the French Academy of Sciences. This prize was awarded 13 December 1948 and carried the sum of 50,000 francs (about $165).[29]

A Nobel prize, however, eluded him. At least some French scientists publicly questioned this possible oversight: in response to an article by The Svedberg, of the Nobel Committee, Etienne Wolff, professor on the faculty of science at Strasbourg, compared d'Herelle's work to that of Alexander Fleming (Nobel prize in 1945 for the discovery of penicillin), Paul H. Müller (Nobel prize in 1948 for the discovery of DDT as an insecticide), and Kendall, Reichstein, and Hench (Nobel prize in 1950 for discovery of cortisone). Although both Fleming and d'Herelle discovered agents of bacterial destruction, Wolff argued that "the existence of a destructive principle of bacteria, which was revealed to be a filterable virus, is very much more important from the general point of view than the discovery of penicillin, a bactericidal substance extracted from an organism. . . . Bacteriophage represent a scientific revolution, while penicillin is a particular case of chemotherapy."[30] Others speculated that d'Herelle's strained relations with the Pasteur Institute so compromised his stature with the Nobel Committee that he was effectively blocked from receiving this most prestigious of scientific awards.[31]

In the fall of 1948 d'Herelle developed obstructive jaundice and was diagnosed as having gallstones. Surgical exploration, however, revealed that he had cancer of the pancreas. He died in Paris on 22 February 1949.[32] He was buried alongside his wife in the village cemetery in Saint-Mards-en-Othe, the site of his country home where one of the two main streets now bears his name.

Bacteriophage, of course, became the organism of the molecular biological revolution. D'Herelle, however, seemed to pay scant attention to this path of investigation. He held fast to his quasi-Lamarckian ideas about heredity and did not follow up on his work on the role of phage in mutation and alteration of bacterial phenotype. His legacy in this direction was taken up by a new generation of scientists, often trained in physics and unschooled in biology, who saw phage as models for genes and as probes for cellular functions.

While d'Herelle had difficulty in bringing phage into the category of filterable viruses, in a complete turnabout, virologists now take bacteriophage as the paradigmatic case on which to base work on animal and plant viruses. D'Herelle was aware of the new work on phage being done in the early 1940s: phage genetics, physical properties of phage, and phage-host biology. Not only did his laboratory collaborate with the phage workers in Paris to study the physical and chemical properties of phages using the latest techniques,[33] but he had access to the new work coming out of America; for example, in 1947 Luria and Delbrück presented their work at the International Congress of Microbiology in Copenhagen in 1947, where several of d'Herelle's colleagues were in attendance.[34] Still, d'Herelle did not embrace the new direction of phage research; he hardly acknowledged the renewed interest in the biological nature of phage. Instead, his waning efforts were directed toward consolidating and publicizing his ideas and past research on phage therapy and epidemic infectious disease.

Phage therapy, of course, was suddenly confronted with the long-sought magic bullets of the antibiotic era, starting with sulfonamides and penicillin and later streptomycin, chloramphenicol, and tetracycline. Standards for evaluation of therapeutic agents were becoming sophisticated in the 1940s and chemotherapeutic agents were easier to test than complex biological agents such as bacteriophage. Even so, the most thorough and rigorous review of bacteriophage therapy could not find grounds for rejecting d'Herelle's approaches.[35] Compared to phage therapy, however, antibiotics were easier to administer, had a good shelf life, and were more "broad-spectrum."

Still, phage therapy has continued to have its advocates: d'Herelle's protégé André Raiga-Clemenceau in 1970 formed the Société des Amis de Félix d'Herelle, a French organization dedicated to promoting bacteriophage as a more natural therapy for infectious disease. Dr. Raiga-Clemenceau, nephew of the famous French premier (and physician) Georges Clemenceau, recruited French scientific, political and cultural luminaries to this organization.[36] In addition to publication of a journal, *Nouvelles Archives Hospitalières,* they succeeded in having a Parisian street named in honor of d'Herelle.[37] As if to complete d'Herelle's Pasteurian odyssey, in 1977, the year of the closure of the Laboratoire du Bácteriophage,[38] launched as yet unfulfilled plans for the Institut Félix d'Herelle.[39]

Appendix: On an Invisible Microbe Antagonistic to the Dysentery Bacillus

Félix d'Herelle

[Sur un microbe invisible antagoniste des bacilles dysentériques, *Comptes rendus Acad. Sci. Paris* 165 (1917): 373–375. FdH: 25]

From the feces of diverse patients convalescing from bacillary dysentery, and in one case from the urine, I have isolated an invisible microbe with the properties of antagonism to the bacillus of Shiga. This finding is particularly easy in the cases of common enteritis following dysentery; in convalescents who do not present this complication the disappearance of the anti-microbe quickly follows that of the pathogenic bacillus. In spite of numerous examinations, I have never found the antagonistic microbes either in the feces of dysenteritics during the disease period, or in the feces of normal subjects.

The isolation of the anti-Shiga microbe is simple: one inoculates a tube of bouillon with four to five drops of feces, incubates at 37°C for 18 hours, and then filters with a Chamberland L2 filter. A small quantity of the active filtrate added, either to a broth culture of Shiga bacillus, or to an emulsion of these bacillus in broth or even in physiological saline, provokes the arrest of the culture, the death of the bacillus then their lysis, which is complete after a period of time varying from hours to days depending on the amount of the culture and the quantity of the filtrate added.

The invisible microbe grows [*cultive*] in the lysed culture of Shiga bacillus because a trace of this liquid, placed in a new culture of Shiga, reproduces the same phenomenon with the same intensity: I have carried this out up to the present time with the first stock isolated for more than fifty successive transfers. The following experiment gives, moreover, the visible evidence that the antagonistic action is produced by a living germ: if one adds to a culture of Shiga a dilution of approximately one to a million of an already lysed culture, and if, immediately after, one spreads out on an agar slant a droplet of this culture, one obtains, after incubation, a coat of dysentery bacilli showing a certain number of circles about 1 mm in diameter, where the culture is void; these points can only represent the colonies of the antagonistic microbe: a chemical substance would not be able to concentrate at defined points. In working with measured quantities, I have seen that a lysed culture of Shiga contains five to six million of these filterable germs per cubic centimeter. One three-millionth of a cubic centimeter of the preceding culture from Shiga, or a single germ, introduced into a tube of broth, inhibits the culture of Shiga even when liberally inoculated; the same quantity added to a 10 cm³ culture of Shiga sterilizes it and lyses it in five or six days.

The diverse stocks of the antagonistic microbe which I have isolated were originally active only against the bacillus of Shiga; through symbiotic culture [*culture en symbiose*] with the dysentery bacilli of Hiss or Flexner, I could, after several passages, render them antagonistic to these bacilli. I have not obtained any results working with other microbes: typhoid bacilli, paratyphoid bacilli, staphylococci, etc. The appearance of antagonism against the bacillus of Flexner or of Hiss is accompanied by a diminution followed by a loss of power against Shiga, this power being recoverable with its original intensity after several symbiotic cultures; the specificity of antagonistic action therefore is not inherent in the nature of the invisible microbe, but is acquired in the sick organism by symbiotic culture with the pathogenic bacillus. In the absence of dysentery bacilli the anti-microbe does not grow in any medium, it does not attack heat killed dysentery bacilli; in contrast it grows perfectly in an emulsion of washed bacilli in physiological salt solution: it results from these studies that the antidysentery microbe is an obligate bacteriophage [*un bactériophage obligatoire*].

The anti-Shiga microbe does not show any pathogenic action on any of the animals tested. Cultures of Shiga lysed by the action of the invisible microbe, which are in reality cultures of the anti-microbe, possessed the property of immunizing a rabbit against a dose of Shiga bacilli which killed the controls in five days.

I have searched for evidence of such an anti-microbe from convalescents from typhoid fever: in two cases, one from the urine and the other from the feces, I have been successful in isolating a filterable microbe giving the clear lytic property with respect to bacillus of paratyphoid A, but always less marked than the anti-Shiga microbe. These properties are attenuated in successive cultures.

In summary, in certain convalescents from dysentery, I have shown that the disappearance of the dysentery bacillus coincides with the appearance of an invisible microbe endowed with antagonistic properties with respect to the pathogenic bacillus. This microbe, the true microbe of immunity, is an obligatory bacteriophage; its parasitism is strictly specific, but if it is limited to one species at a given moment, it may develop antagonism in turn against diverse germs by accustomization. It appears therefore that in bacillary dysentery, next to the anti-tonic [*sic*] homologous immunity, emanating directly from the organism under attack, there exists a heterologous antimicrobial immunity produced by the antagonistic microorganism. It is probable that this phenomenon is not special to dysentery, but of a more general order because I have shown it can be found likewise, though less marked, in two case of paratyphoid fever.

Notes

CHAPTER 1. PEREGRINATIONS OF YOUTH

1. D'Herelle's account of the treatments employed at the abbey in St. Hubert are corroborated, in the main, in Gaidoz, *La Rage et St. Hubert,* 41–42, 67–75; Baring-Gould, *Lives of the Saints,* 75–82; and Tricot-Royer, 273–290, 346–349. The stole was supposedly woven on the looms of heaven and presented to Hubert by the Virgin Mary herself. Baring-Gould lists several additional required rituals beyond those noted by d'Herelle.

2. LeBlanc, 3–11. See also Register of Marriages, Parish of Saint-Antoine de Padoue, Longueuil, Québec: 5 September 1899 Daniel Hérens dit d'Hérelle [*sic*] to Marie Euphémie Eudoxie Juliette Hurteau. Although his surname was often printed with an acute accent over the first vowel, Félix d'Herelle himself never used it in his autograph signatures or in typed letters. The ancient family name was Arles (*HM*).

3. Sir Henri Gustave Joly de Lotbinière (1829–1908) was Prime Minister of Québec (1878–79), Minister of Inland Revenue for Canada (1897–1900), and Lieutenant-Governor of British Columbia (1900–1906) (Wallace, *Dictionary of Canadian Biography,* 352–353).

4. While some sources indicate that d'Herelle received his schooling at the prestigious Lycée Louis-le-Grand in Paris, this was not confirmed upon inquiry by his grandson, Hubert Mazure (*HM*).

5. For comparison, the wages of day laborers in French vineyards at the time was 1.5–3 francs/day (Cocks and Feret, *Bordeaux and Its Wines*, 681).

6. The birth date and place of Louise Marcelle d'Herelle is given in her adult passport as 19 March 1894, Montreal. The timing of the winter sojourn in Greece is from *PM*. Neither source is contemporary with the events dated, and either or both may be in error. It seems strange that the d'Herelles would travel to Montreal in the dead of winter to have a baby. An alternate explanation, advanced by d'Herelle's grandson, Hubert Mazure, is that Marcelle was Marie's child by a former husband and that her passport birth date was a fiction to obscure this fact (*HM*). If one assumes that Marie's birth date on her passport is correct, however, she was only fifteen at the time and it seems unlikely that she would already have had a child.

7. Arthur Bernier (1873–?) graduated from Laval University Medical Department in 1897 and received his medical license the same year. After a year at the Institut Pasteur with Roux and Martin he became chief of bacteriology at the Hospital of Notre-Dame in Montreal. Later, he was professor of bacteriology at Laval University Medical Department, then located in Montreal. From 1918–1928 he was professor of bacteriology at the University of Montreal (Goulet, 110. American Medical Directory, 1927). According to d'Herelle he was the first to introduce the term "loop" (*boucle*) in bacteriology (*LPG*, 33).

8. Diary for 1899, 12 January entry (*dHFP*).

9. This evidence establishes that d'Herelle used the name Hoerens (or Haerens) until at least January 1899. By September 1899, however, he used Hoerens d'Herelle as a witness to his brother's marriage (see Register of Marriages, Parish of Saint-Antoine de Padoue, Longueuil, Québec). This same document gives d'Herelle's father's name as Félix Herens dit Hérelle and his mother's name as Augustine Worms dit Mect. By April 1901, however, he used "F. d'Herelle" on an application for insurance to the Identification and Protective Company of Canada (*dHFP*).

10. The property consisted of eight lots, each about 165 feet square (Bureau of Records of the Town of Longueuil, register B, volume 60, p. 607, no. 28 215 or consult records of M. Pierre Brais, notary, 17 August 1899, minute no. 11 255). It is situated adjacent to a former railway right-of-way, now a bicycle path, and across Chemin de Chambly from the Saint-Antoine parish cemetery in Longueuil.

11. Bureau of Records of the Town of Longueuil, register D, p. 210, no. 414, attested to by Robert Lararre. The original factory building has been enlarged and renovated and in 1989 was converted into a small business park, Place Hérelle, at 550 Chemin de Chambly, Longueuil, now occupied by a bank, an Italian restaurant, and some other businesses. The outlines of the original structure are still apparent.

12. His time of employment can be fixed to some extent by the existence of a document for a medical care and notification insurance policy with the Identification and Protective Company of Canada, dated 10 April 1901 in Montreal. For two dollars per year the company provided an identification "outfit" and further agreed "to bear the cost of a telegram notifying the Company of the death, serious injury, or sudden illness of the party registered, also to immediately notify the friends as specified in the application.

The Company will furnish, in case of notice, the best medical or surgical aid, protection, care, and attendance that can be obtained, as in the judgement of the Company the case may require, and will by reason of its power of attorney, take charge of the body or person of the party registered . . . until sufficient time has elapsed for friends to reach him after due notice." This registration described d'Herelle as age thirty (although other sources suggest he was twenty-seven), 5′7″ tall, 142 pounds, medium build, with brown eyes and dark hair. He wore a size 6 7/8 hat, size 6 shoes, and size 15 shirt. The attached photograph shows an earnest young man in full beard and mustache with rather short hair (*dHFP*).

13. Anonymous, *Les végétaux,* 98–99.
14. Geison, *Private Science of Louis Pasteur,* 38.

CHAPTER 2. FERMENTATIONS: GUATEMALA AND MEXICO

1. Registration certificate number 5560 dated 20 June 1901, recorded in Folio 133 of foreign registrants, office of the Secretary of State for Foreign Relations for the Government of Guatemala (*dHFP*).
2. Juan J. Ortega was professor of bacteriology, and sometimes dean, at the medical school of the University of San Carlos from 1882 until 1910, when he retired from hospital work to become the Minister of Guatemala to Mexico. He trained in Paris prior to his appointment in Guatemala and is credited with bringing antiseptic practice to Guatemala (Martínez-Durán, *Las ciencias médicas en Guatemala,* 650).
3. He indicated "l'Ecole de Médecine, l'Ecole Normale supérieure, l'Ecole d'Agriculture" (*PM,* 100).
4. D'Herelle is not listed in the faculty of the School of Medicine of the University of San Carlos, by Asturias, *Historia,* or by Duran, *Las ciencias médicas en Guatemala.*
5. Guérin, "L'Alcool de Banane," 76–79.
6. Guérin, "L'Alcool de Banane," 78.
7. In his memoirs d'Herelle indicates that the yellow fever in Guatemala was in 1904 (*PM,* 180–181). However, other evidence documents that the yellow fever epidemic in Guatemala, British Honduras, and Spanish Honduras occurred in the spring and summer of 1905 (Boyce, *Report,* 61–64).
8. *PM,* 115. D'Herelle's grandson confirmed that d'Herelle had what appeared to be a knife scar on his left hand; he regaled his grandchildren with this story of his youthful adventures (*HM*).
9. *PM,* 124; Letter from J. R. Paul to Steven Peitzman, 1969, undated (copy from Peitzman in author's files); Yale-New Haven Hospital Record 72262.
10. This account, from *PM,* 124–127, is corroborated in Boyce, *Reports,* 61–64.
11. Boyce reported that the disease struck somewhat earlier and that mortality in these villages had reached 2–5 percent by early June 1905 (Boyce, *Reports,* 61–64).
12. This experience with yellow fever, together with a later one in Mérida, Mexico (*PM,* 204), led d'Herelle to express in 1925 his skepticism of the recent claim by Hideyo Noguchi that *Leptospira icteroides* was the cause of yellow fever: "It would be strange if the

leptospira discovered by Noguchi is really the agent of yellow fever (a disease with which I am familiar from having studied it in Yucatán). I have spent weary days with my eye to the microscope examining slides of the organs and tissues of individuals dead of yellow fever, and never yet did I see a single leptospira" (*BIB*, 486n).

13. Delacroix, *Les maladies.*

14. The *Pyrenomycetes* and the *Basidiomycetes* are distinguished from each other by several defining characteristics. The former group includes *Neurospora sp.* and the latter *Ustilago sp.* (smuts) and *Coprinus sp.* (Gwynne-Vaughan and Barnes, *Structure and development of the fungi,* 243, 284).

15. Prillieux and Delacroix, "La gommose bacillaire," 31–60. See also Buchanan, Hold, and Lessel, *Index Bergeyana,* 179.

16. Passport issued to Félix H. d'Herelle and family for travel to Mexico. Number 2459, folio 122, dated 6 December 1907, valid for one month; from Secretary of State for Foreign Relations of the Republic of Guatemala (dHFP).

17. Sisal is named for a small port town in the Yucatán from which supplies of the fiber of the agave plant were shipped. The botanical name of sisal is *Agave sisalana* Perrine; older literature, including some of d'Herelle's papers, use the name *A. rigida* Miller for this species. Henequén, however is now recognized as a distinct species, *A. fourcroydes* Lemaire (Lock, *Sisal,* 17–30).

18. Zavala, 707.

19. Mexican Patent 7784 (Provisional); "For a procedure to recover alcohol and fuel from the waste and bagasse of henequén." D'Herelle's address at the time was listed as Tacubaya, D.F., a suburb of Mexico City (*Gaceta Oficial,* 36).

20. Later he recalled his disgust and sadness at the conditions of the Mayans (*PM*, 191–192).

21. Harald Seidelin was a Danish pathologist who later worked at the Lister Institute. See Gutiérrez Rivas, *Dr. Harald Seidelin.*

22. FdH: 6. Later, in October 1909 he became a member of this society.

CHAPTER 3. EPIZOOTICS: LOCUSTS IN ARGENTINA AND ALGERIA

1. Künckel d'Herculais, 238–239. Künckel d'Herculais was also the author of *Invasions des Acridiens, vulgo Sauterelles, en Algérie,* 1893–1905.

2. The organism was described as a short Gram-negative rod (one that failed to exhibit a characteristic deep violet color with Gram's staining method) which grows rapidly as a facultative anaerobe on usual laboratory media, such as nutrient agar and Liebig's bouillon. This organism was not pathogenic for chickens, guinea pigs, or rabbits. More recent authors have classified this organism as a variety of *Aerobacter aerogenes.*

3. Latour, *Pasteurization of France,* 75–100.

4. Larretta (1875–1961) was a well-known Argentine intellectual living in Paris and author of *La Gloria de Don Ramiro,* a novel of the life and times of Philip II of Spain, considered "one of the finest historical novels in Spanish-American literature."

5. Löwy, *Yellow Fever in Rio,* 144–147. Löwy, *La mission de l'Institut Pasteur,* 282. For a discussion of agricultural research in Puerto Rico and Venezuela, see McCook, 1996.

6. Bulloch, *History of Bacteriology,* 378.

7. Bryce, *South America,* 318, 346.

8. Ibid., 333–334.

9. Ibid., 334.

10. Ibid., 318.

11. In his late memoir (*PM,* 282 et seq.) d'Herelle recalled that it was during this three-week period that he first observe plaques of bacteriophages on cultures of coccobacilli: "It was during the course of this campaign at Chamical in the province of La Rioja that I saw for the first time the phenomenon which, on this first occasion, seemed strange and worthy of attention. . . . On two occasions in the course of the campaign the strange phenomenon which attracted my attention occurred in the plates where the microbes are so numerous that they form a continuous creamy layer. It consisted of clear spots where the culture appeared punched-out; some were small, very round, others very large, irregular in form, resembling the confluence of a great number of the small spots. To what can one attribute this singular aspect, which I had never observed in any other bacterial culture? My imagination wandered, I finally thought that the true microbe which was pathogenic for the locusts might not be the coccobacillus itself, but another microbe, very small, an infra-visible virus, associated with the coccobacillus.

"As it was impossible to study this new phenomenon in the field, with a rudimentary laboratory. Moreover, it was not possible for me to reproduce these spots at will since they appeared only in very rare cultures. Thinking that it was a phenomenon of biological importance, I returned to its study later, and I kept these initial findings to myself. One will see that it was this phenomenon, so simple in appearance, which was the origin of research which was to occupy me for the next thirty years, and which will occupy future generations of bacteriologists."

12. On the strain see Glaser, 19–42. For the summary publication see Kraus, 594–599.

13. Calmette, 129. Even today there are at least sixteen Pasteur Institutes outside of Paris, as well as at least eight associated institutes (Morange, *L'Institut Pasteur,* 15).

14. Dozon, 274.

15. Sergent and Lhéritier, 408–419.

16. Béguet, 651–653.

17. Paillot, *L'infection chez les insectes,* 441–452; Sweetman, *Biological Control of Insects,* 57–58; Steinhaus, *Principles of Insect Pathology,* 281–317, 671–709.

18. Steinhaus, *Disease in a Minor Chord,* 133.

19. Danysz, 193.

20. Pasteur, *Sur la destruction des lapins,* 1–8. Chaussivert, 242, 243.

CHAPTER 4. BACTERIOPHAGE DISCOVERED

1. Bertillon, 141–144.

2. The naming of the bacteriophage has been subject to some misinterpretation by recent authors, e.g., Stent, *Molecular Genetics,* 299; Brock, *Emergence of Bacterial Genetics,* 114, who have noted that the term derived from φαγειν (*phagein,* to eat or devour) and

assumed that d'Herelle meant to imply that the bacteriophage "devours" the bacterium. This interpretation probably comes as a natural extension of the terminology for cells that "eat" things, i.e., phagocytes. This aspect of cellular immunology had recently been popularized through the work of Metchnikoff in the early decades of the twentieth century. Brock distinguished this interpretation which he attributed to d'Herelle from that later suggested by Delbrück that the phage "attacked" the bacterium (Brock, *Emergence of Bacterial Genetics*, 120). In fact, d'Herelle used the term with the notion more akin to Delbrück's interpretation than to the related term, phagocytosis. In his monograph published in 1922, d'Herelle stated: "This introductory discussion should not be concluded without a word on the subject of the term 'Bacteriophage,' a term which has been criticized. The suffix 'phage' is *not* [emphasis added] used in its strict sense of 'to eat,' but in that of 'developing at the expense of'; a sense that is frequently used elsewhere in scientific terminology. Certain protozoa, for example, are parasitized by the *Nucleophaga* which develop within the interior of the nucleus. This is precisely the interpretation to be given to the term 'phage' in the word 'Bacteriophage'" (*BIRI*, 21).

In his autobiography d'Herelle suggested, however, that the gustatory connotations of the word played a role in its selection. In these memoirs, written between 1939 and 1946, he described his first observations of plaques: "That night, by the lamp, as I related to my family that which I had seen, the dysentery bacilli being devoured [*dévorés*] by a 'microbe of microbes,' my wife asked: 'What are you going to call it?' and we searched everywhere, proposing and rejecting again and again many names; finally, by this collaboration, it was 'Bacteriophage' which won out: a word formed from *bacteria* and *phagein*, to eat, in Greek. This was 18 October [1916]; I recall this because it was the day before the birthday of my younger daughter" (*PM*, 336).

3. D'Herelle was eventually reduced to working on a corner of a small table in the "minuscule" laboratory of his friend Pozerski (*PM*, 485). This account is corroborated in Pozerski's recollections (Pozerski, 45–47). At the same time d'Herelle started to work mornings at the Institute for Cancer Research in Villejuif on a project related to the viral origins of cancer. It was during this period without laboratory space that he wrote his first monograph on bacteriophage (FdH: 48).

4. Delaunay, *L'Institut Pasteur*, 177.

5. Liebenau and Robson, 56–57.

6. Delaunay, *L'Institut Pasteur*, 146–148.

7. Roux, 519.

8. Pfeiffer and Issaeff, 355–400; Bordet, 462–506.

9. FdH: 73. In a section headed "The theory of 'lytic' sera" he wrote: "If there is a history which presents a philosophical significance from the point of view of that which may be called 'the history of an error' it is indeed the history of the 'antibodies' . . . [he goes on to describe the work of Pfeiffer and Bordet on in vivo and in vitro "vibriolysis," i.e., lysis of cholera bacteria] . . . The magic of words. No one has ever observed the bacteriolysis of a single bacterium under the influence of a serum, but nevertheless, since then many impassioned controversies have been waged to explain the mechanism of this nonexistent phenomenon" (FdH: 73, 162).

10. The first description of the action of bacteriophage on confluent cultures of sensitive bacteria used the phrase "cercles d'environ 1 mm de diamètre où la culture est nulle" (FdH: 25). By 1918 (FdH: 29) the description was "taches parfaitement circulaires." Subsequently, *taches vierges* became the usual term: literally, *taches* means spots and *vierges* means virginal, blank. *Plaque* was a later introduction, in use by 1926 in the English edition of *BIB* (FdH: 89, 4). H.-W. Ackermann has suggested (personal communication) that *plaque* (patch, large spot) was preferred to *tache* (spot), which could be confused with the homonymic *tâche* (job, task).

11. De Schweinitz and Dorset, 41:1–4, 43:1–3; Clark, 490–514.

12. De Schweinitz and Dorset, 43:3.

13. FdH: 89, 2–3. Note that d'Herelle interpreted the work on hog cholera and his own work as involving the interaction of *two* agents.

14. In her analysis of the controversy with Frederick W. Twort over the priority for the discovery of bacteriophage, Duckworth suggested that the later recollection was perhaps unreliable and served, in retrospect, to strengthen d'Herelle's claim to priority (Duckworth, 799).

15. Bertillon, 141–144; FdH: 22.

16. Twort, *In Focus, Out of Step,* 188–192.

17. In 1925 d'Herelle recalled that in August 1916 he studied a patient who was under treatment at the Pasteur Hospital for severe bacillary dysentery and it was from this patient that the first phages were isolated (*BIB*, 3).

18. The papers of 1917 (Phage I, FdH: 25), 1918 (Phage II, FdH: 28), and 1919 (Phage IV, FdH: 30) describe the use of rabbits as the only experimental animals, yet his 1948 account (FdH: 143) indicates that both rabbits and guinea pigs were used. In his later work, d'Herelle included extensive lists of the various species used in order to argue for the generality of his findings. It seems unlikely that if he had data on guinea pigs in 1917 he would have ignored them in all of his publications.

19. Kabeshima, 1061–1064. Tamezo Kabeshima had worked with Kitasato in Japan and was very much interested in vaccines against dysentery. Kabeshima came to the Pasteur Institute just after the war and in December 1919 he started "working in my laboratory," according to d'Herelle (*BIRI,* 145). Kabeshima was to become d'Herelle's first colleague in phage work, but later they were to disagree over their conceptions of the nature of bacteriophage. See chapter 5, note 1.

CHAPTER 5. REACTION AND CONTROVERSY

1. *La Presse Médicale* (20 September 1917), 25:543.

2. Tamezo Kabeshima, a staff surgeon in the Imperial Japanese Navy, was assigned to Kitasato's institute in Tokyo about 1911. By 1915 he was working at the Maritime Hospital in the port city of Sasebo, and about 1918, probably at the end of the war, went to the Pasteur Institute in Paris. By 1925 he was back in Japan and in the Department of Preventive Medicine of the Tokyo Naval Medical College. In addition to the two papers he published on bacteriophage, he published work on cholera: "Ueber einen Häm-

oglobinextrakt-Soda-Agar als Elektivnährboden für Choleravibrionen," *Centralbl. f. Bakt. I Abt. Orig.* 70:202–208, 1913; "Le poisson de mer considéré dans ses rapports avec le vibrions cholériques qui peuvent exister dans l'eau," *Bull. Off. int. d'hyg. publ. Paris,* 10:908–915, 1918; "Notes sur la nature biologique des vibrions d'El Tor,'" *Comptes Rendus Soc. Biol.* 81:616–618, 1918; "Sur certaines propriétés du bacille cholérique en rapport avec l'immunité," *Comptes Rendus Soc. Biol.* 81:618–620, 1918; "Sur la pseudo-agglutination ou agglutination spontanée de vibrions cholériques," *Comptes Rendus Soc. Biol.* 81:687–689, 1918; and "Most simple method of preparation of cholera specific medium, haemoglobin extract-soda-agar," *Bull. Nav. Med. Assn. Tokyo* 15:5–8, 1926. In addition, he published on typhoid: "Importance des proportions de sang pour l'hémo-culture dans les fièvres typhoïd et paratyphoïd," *Comptes Rendus Soc. Biol.* 81:420–422, 1918; and yellow fever: "On the filtrability of Spirochaeta ictero-haemorrhagiae," *Bull. Nav. Med. Assn. Tokyo* 49:3–5, 1925.

3. Kabeshima, "Recherches expérimentale," 1061–1064.

4. Kabeshima, "Thérapie expérimentale," 71–72.

.5. Kabeshima, "Ferment d'immunité," 220.

6. Ibid., 221.

7. From 2 October 1919 through 17 February 1920 d'Herelle was carrying out his avian typhosis study 330 miles from Paris near Agen in the department of Lot-et-Garonne (*BIRI,* 243–244).

8. Entry in diary of Marcelle d'Herelle: "Papa part le 6 Mars par l'Armand Belise pour Saigon" (*dHFP*). In his memoir written twenty-five years later, d'Herelle recalled that he left Paris in January and sailed from Marseille aboard the *General Metzinger* (*PM,* 410).

9. Varley, *Living Molecules.*

10. I use the characterization "marginal" advisedly. D'Herelle was an unpaid staff member without his own lab, and Kabeshima was a visiting researcher from abroad.

11. Varley, *Living Molecules,* 108; Duckworth, 797; Van Helvoort, "Nature of the Bacte-riophage Phenomenon," 253.

12. That Bordet used cultures obtained from d'Herelle is supported by both Bordet's pub-lications and those of his student and collaborator, André Gratia (Gratia, "Lysis and Microbic Variation," 287).

As a footnote to this controversy, the phenomenon of lysogeny as discovered by Bordet and Ciuca confounded phage researchers for a long time. The ability of a virulent lytic virus to enter into a more symbiotic relation with a host, only to reemerge many generations later, was without precedent. Bacterial genes, viruses as genetic agents, and the nature of mutation were all concepts yet to be developed at the time when Bordet, Gratia, and d'Herelle were groping for a common understanding of fundamentally different phenomena. Later, d'Herelle speculated in his memoirs on the possible origin of the Bordet and Ciuca results. As he reconstructed events: Ciuca came to Paris in 1920 to obtain strains and phage, but d'Herelle was away for the year in Indochina: "I had left with my friend Salimbeni cultures of various bacteriophages, in sealed tubes, in case anyone wanted one. But I also left in the cold box in the laboratory for my personal use when I returned and to examine on my return, sealed tubes which contained various bacteria which I had rendered resistant to bacteriophage, that is to say, bacterial cultures containing phage particles. Salimbeni showed all the tubes to Ciuca who saw the labels 'Cultures de Bactériophages anti-dysentériques' 'Culture de Bactériophages anti-coli' etc., containing perfectly clear liquid, but during the course of exchanging pleasantries, he took one of the tubes which were not to be distributed and which contained a culture of bacillus coli which had acquired resistance to phage, that is to say, experimentally infected by me with phage particles possessing virulence against various bacteria. This tube was labeled Coli κ, that is: coli kappa: I had taken the habit designating by abbreviation each race of bacteriophage by a Greek letter expressing its actual virulence, 'kappa' designated bacillus coli. The inscription should have read '*Bacillus coli* contaminated with phage particles.' Ciuca took this tube by mistake and he read 'Coli x,' 'Coli ixe,' that ixe certainly represents the key to an enigma. Bordet believed this also and agreed with the deciphering. He followed a technique dear to the bacteriologists, and which infallibly leads to error, he inoculated a culture of Coli κ into the peritoneal cavity of a guinea pig; several hours later he removed the exudate from this cavity and he found a bacteriophage" (*PM*, 497–498).

D'Herelle noted that in the publications of Bordet and Ciuca and of Gratia, they explicitly stated that they worked with a strain of *Bacillus coli* obtained from him. The failure of d'Herelle as well as others to repeat the original observations of Bordet and Ciuca with regard to the induction of phage production by intraperitoneal injection of bacteria tends to support d'Herelle's conjecture as to the possible artifactual nature of their results. That they obtained a lysogenic strain from d'Herelle also is consistent with d'Herelle's later reconstruction. One way to make lysogens, we now know, is to infect sensitive strains and select for phage resistance, in modern terms, immune lysogens.

13. Pfeiffer and Issaeff, 355–400.
14. Varley, *Living Molecules,* 110.
15. Bordet and Ciuca, "Exudats leucocytaires," 1293–1295; "Le bactériophage," 1296–1298.
16 Varley, *Living Molecules,* 92.
17. Van Helvoort, "Nature of the bacteriophage phenomenon," 245; Van Helvoort, "Construction of bacteriophage," 91–139.
18. Bordet and Ciuca, "Le bactériophage," 1296.
19. Van Helvoort, "Nature of the Bacteriophage Phenomenon," 242–370.
20. D'Herelle was in Saigon on 16 November 1920 (*BIRI,* 225) and apparently was in Paris in January 1921 (*BIRI,* 254; *BIB,* 526).
21. FdH: 48. The original edition was in French and was published as a monograph of the Pasteur Institute. The English translation was published by Williams and Wilkins in 1922 (FdH: 56) and differs from the French edition mainly in having an expanded section on the nature of bacteriophage.
22. Bordet and Ciuca, "Remarques," 747.
23. Fildes, 505–517; A. Twort, *In Focus, Out of Step,* 1–340.
24. F. W. Twort, "Investigation," 1241.
25. F. W. Twort, "Investigation," 1241–1243.
26. A. Twort, *In Focus, Out of Step,* 66–76.

27. Ibid., 79.
28. Fildes, 510.
29. Varley, *Living Molecules,* 152.
30. Duckworth, 797.
31. Gratia, "Colonies de bactériophage," 753–754. Gratia was a lab mate and friend of Paul De Kruif, who was actively working on bacterial dissociation. This work contributed to the foundations of bacterial genetics (Summers, *Science in Arrowsmith,* 315–332; Amsterdamska, 191–222).
32. Kuttner, 49–101. Lisbonne and Carrère, 569–570. Bail, 447–449. Weinberg and Aznar, 833–834. Otto and Winkler, 383–384.
33. Bordet, "Theories," 296.
34. F. W. Twort, "The bacteriophage," 294.
35. Ibid., 294–295.
36. Gratia, *British Med. J.,* 296–297.
37. A. Twort, *In Focus, Out of Step,* 194–195.
38. Gratia, *British Med. J.,* 296.
39. Jaumain, 790–793.
40. F. W. Twort, "Ultramicroscopic Viruses," 359.
41. Ibid., 366.
42. Raettig, *Bacteriophage,* 2.
43. Gratia, "Le traîtement," 344–348.
44. André Raiga-Clemenceau, the nephew of the French statesman Georges Clemenceau, was the founder of the Société des Amis de Félix d'Herelle. This organization was set up in 1975 to promote the use of phage therapy, and it published several issues of its official journal, *Nouvelles Archives Hospitalières.* Raiga-Clemenceau recruited several medical and political luminaries to the board of this society. One of their goals was to have a Parisian street named for d'Herelle. The Council of Paris approved this request on 27 June 1975. The Avenue Félix-d'Herelle is a short road in the 16th arrondissement very near the Porte de St. Cloud.
45. D'Herelle probably arrived in Paris at the end of May 1930 as indicated in correspondence on Yale letterhead and dated 14 May 1930 (Letter 14 May 1930 from d'Herelle to L. Dalbis: Item D35/383, Archives of the University of Montreal: File on Professor d'Herelle); FdH: 105.
46. Letter from d'Herelle to Gratia, quoted in in Gratia, *L'identité du phénomène,* 16, note 11.
47. Gratia, "Discussion," 237–238.
48. Letter from Gratia to Twort, 27 January 1931 (A. Twort, *In Focus, Out of Step,* 200).
49. Gratia, "L'identité du phénomène," 1. Gratia's friend Paul De Kruif also recalled this discovery of Twort's paper in an article related to phage therapy: "I remember the very beginning of this discovery ten years ago, when the brilliant Belgian, André Gratia, rushed at midnight into my workroom in the Rockefeller Institute, shouting it was Twort—forgotten Twort—and not d'Herelle, who was the real father of this microbe suicide" (De Kruif, "Miracles of Healing," 3).
50. Gratia discussed this challenge in correspondence with Twort (A. Twort, *In Focus, Out of Step,* 202).

51. Flu and Renaux, 18.
52. Lépine, 196–199.

CHAPTER 6. THE NATURE OF PHAGE: MICROBE OR ENZYME?

1. Carter, 528–548.
2. Van Helvoort, "Nature of the bacteriophage phenomenon," 242–270.
3. Van Helvoort, "Nature of the bacteriophage phenomenon," 251–254.
4. Ellis and Delbrück, 365–384; Summers, "Phage Group," 255–267.
5. The term "plaque former" appeared first in 1926 (*BIB,* 98) and is the likely origin of the currently used terminology, "plaque-forming unit" or "pfu." Another interesting matter of terminology appears in this same passage; d'Herelle, or his translator, George Smith, introduced the word "bacteriophaged" to indicate the process by which a bacterium is attacked and lysed by an unspecified number of bacteriophage, as in "The number of corpuscles. . . . depends. . . . upon the number of bacteria bacteriophaged."
6. Van Helvoort, "Construction of bacteriophage," 91–139.
7. Ellis and Delbrück, 365–384.
8. Even in fiction this aspect of phage biology was recognized as crucial to the understanding of the nature of the lytic process. In *Arrowsmith* the first challenge put to young Martin Arrowsmith by his scientific mentor, Professor Gottlieb, was, "Why have you not planned to propagate it on dead staph? That is most important of all. . . . Because that will show whether you are dealing with a living virus" (Lewis, *Arrowsmith,* 326).
9. Wollman, "Sur le phénomène de d'Herelle," 3–5.
10. Occasional references to his colleagues indicate that d'Herelle considered Wollman and Salimbeni among his friends and supporters at the Pasteur Institute even after he left there in 1922 (*PM,* 376; *INID,* 318 footnote). D'Herelle and his family were neighbors of Eugène and Elizabeth Wollman in Square Frédéric Vallois, in Paris, in the 1920s; in addition, d'Herelle's son-in-law, Théodore Mazure, regularly played cards with Eugène Wollman (Elie Wollman, interview, June 1989).
11. Asheshov, "Quelques recherches," 120–121.
12. For a discussion of the influence of neo-Lamarckianism in French biology in the early twentieth century, see Buican, *Histoire de la génétique,* and Burian, Gayon, and Zallen, 357–402. For Bergson's explanation of the role of adaptation in evolution and *élan vital,* see Bergson, *Creative Evolution,* 112–114.
13. I prefer the more neutral term "biotype" rather than "species." For asexual, clonal organisms such as bacteria, the species concept is especially problematic. Early classification schemes for bacteria were based on simple morphological characters and, while they used Linnean binomials, were not intended to represent "natural" or "evolutionary" relationships.
14. See, for example, Amsterdamska, 191–222.
15. Van Helvoort, "Construction of bacteriophage," 91–139.
16. Morgan, *Theory of the Gene,* 309.
17. Goldschmidt, *Physiological Genetics,* 283.

18. Ibid., 60–62.
19. Muller, 48–49.
20. Bulloch, *History of bacteriology,* 230–231; Van Helvoort, "Construction of bacteriophage," 91–139.
21. See, for example, Summers, *Theorien der Verursachung,* 79–94.
22. Hall, *Ideas of Life and Matter,* 316–364.

CHAPTER 7. THE ORIGIN OF LIFE: COLLOIDS AND PROTOBES

1. In addition to the numerous references to Bacon and the experimental method in science which occur in d'Herelle's published work, he wrote a three-volume work, *La Valeur de l'Expérience* (FdH: 145), which was never published and which is devoted to a critique of Cartesian and Baconian approaches to knowledge. According to his grandson, d'Herelle kept a copy of *Novum Organum* open on his desk at all times. The family believed that d'Herelle was intrigued by the various encryption theories about Bacon's writings. For an example of one such theory, see Donnelly, *The Great Cryptogram.*
2. Article submitted to the Québec Francophone weekly newspaper *La Patrie,* 12 January 1899. FdH diary entry for 12 January 1899.
3. Morgan, "Strategy of biological research programmes," 143–147.
4. Ibid., 147, 149.
5. Osborn, 67–69; 80–99.
6. Quoted in Moore, 175–176.
7. Osborn, 67–71.
8. Farley, 159.
9. Haldane, 103–106.
10. Muller, 48–49.
11. Oparin, 197.
12. For a discussion of nineteenth-century theories of life and matter, see Hall, 316–364.
13. Wilson, 28–30.
14. Fruton, 136.
15. Kamminga, 103.
16. Oparin, 202–210.
17. Ibid., 244–245.
18. *Reports of the Directors of Laboratories and the Director of the Hospital. The Rockefeller Institute for Medical Research.* Vol. 13, 1924–1925, p. 181; vol. 14, 1925–1926, p. 84.
19. Asheshov, "L'accoutoumance du bactériophage," 1343–1344.
20. Wolff and Janzen, 1087–1088.
21. Bungenberg de Jong, 110–173; Oparin, 208–210. A coacervate is a condensation of droplets from an emulsion.
22. Dale, 599.
23. Simon, 532.
24. Stanley, 644–645.
25. Newman, 304–305.

26. Delbrück, 1312–1314.
27. Van Helvoort has analyzed these debates as case studies in the resolution of controversies in science (Van Helvoort, "Construction of bacteriophage," 91–139; "Controversy," 545–575; "Nature of the bacteriophage phenomenon," 242–270).
28. Levaditi and Bonét-Maury, 203–207; Ruska, "Die Sichtbarmachung," 45–46; Ruska, "Der bakteriophagen Lyse," 367–368; Pfankuch and Kausche, 46.

CHAPTER 8. THE HOPE OF PHAGE THERAPY

1. Van Helvoort, "Bacteriofaag-therapie," 118–131.
2. The original text can be found in FdH: 48, 127.
3. Delaunay, 186–187.
4. Summers, "Science in *Arrowsmith*," 315–332.
5. Paul Christian Flu (1884–1945); see Beukers, 21–22; Van Thiel, 1–11.
6. Record of appointment, Archives, Bibliotheek der Rijksuniversiteit te Leiden.
7. The title "conservator" has caused some confusion among d'Herelle's biographers. Lépine's obituary in the *Annales de l'Institut Pasteur,* which should be authoritative, describes d'Herelle's position in Leiden as "professeur extraordinaire;" Compton's obituary in *Nature* gives it as "visiting professor;" Théodoridès' biography in the *Dictionary of Scientific Biography* gives it as "assistant professor." D'Herelle, himself, reported his position as "lecturer" for biographical sketches in *American Men of Science* and *Who's Who.*
8. "Willem Storm van Leeuwen." Obit. *British Med. J.* ii:318–319, 1933. He translated some of d'Herelle's lectures for publication in Dutch (FdH: 72).
9. Archives of the University of Leiden. Letter 41087/L 41 from Silvia Vermetten, Douse-department in Bibliotheek de Rijksuniversiteit te Leiden, to the author, dated 17 January 1990.
10. Beukers, 27.
11. *PM,* 496–497. See also Compton, "Prof. Felix d'Herelle," 984–985.
12. Dobell, *Leeuwenhoek,* 356.
13. *PM,* 496–497. See also Compton, "Prof. Felix d'Herelle," 984–985.
14. Beukers, 25.
15. Félix d'Herelle to Emile Roux, 3 October 1923, Item 25.973 Pasteur Institute Museum.
16. Between 1920 and 1925 Madsen directed the doctoral research of Ernst Gjørup who worked on phage supplied by Bordet (Gjørup, *Investigation into d'Herelle's phenomenon,* 65).
17. Lagrange to Calmette, 14 September 1928, Pasteur Institute Archives.
18. The hajj pilgrimage to Mecca, which culminates in the Festival of the Sacrifice, spans the seventh to the tenth day of the last month of the Muslim calendar, *Dhū al-Hijja,* and took place from 10 to 13 July in 1924.
19. D'Herelle to George H. Smith, 2 June 1925, G. H. Smith file, Yale Medical Historical Library.
20. Compton, "Bacteriophage treatment," 719–720.

21. Edwin W. Schultz to Henry Allen Moe, Secretary, John Simon Guggenheim Memorial Foundation. 19 March 1926. Guggenheim Archives.

22. Schultz, 280–282.

CHAPTER 9. FIGHTING CHOLERA AND PLAGUE IN INDIA

1. A. Morrison to C. E. Heathcote-Smith, 4 December 1923, pp. 118–119, L/E/7 #1425, File 7616, India Office Records, The British Museum, London.

2. Medical Advisor to P. J. Patrick, 24 December 1925, pp. 113–114, L/E/7 #1425, File 7616, India Office Records, British Museum, London.

3. Secretary of State for India to Viceroy, 6 January 1926, p. 111, L/E/7 #1425, File 7616, India Office Records, British Museum, London.

4. R. H. Campbell to Heathcote-Smith, 26 January 1926, p. 105, L/E/7 #1425, File 7616, India Office Records, British Museum, London.

5. Heathcote-Smith to Foreign Office, 20 February 1926, p. 84, L/E/7 #1425, File 7616, India Office Records, British Museum, London.

6. Haffkine Institute, 5; 35–37.

7. Morison and Vardon, 48–54; Morison, *Treatment and prevention of cholera,* 12–13.

8. J. Morison, "Report of a trial of d'Herelle's antiplague bacteriophage with a note by Dr. F. d'Herelle, 23 June 1926," pp. 68–81, L/E/7 #1425, File 7616, India Office Records, British Museum, London.

9. D'Herelle to George H. Smith, 4 June 1926, G. H. Smith file, Yale Medical Historical Library.

10. John Morison (1879–1971), M.B. Ch.B. (hon.) 1901 (Glasgow), D.P.H. 1914 (Cantab.), Lieutenant Colonel, Indian Medical Service, 1906–34, Acting Director, Haffkine Institute, Director Pasteur Institute of Rangoon, Director King Edward VII Pasteur Institute and Medical Research Institute, Shillong, Assam (*Who was who,* 1971–1980).

11. Morison to Surgeon-General, 21–23 June 1926, pp. 61–62, L/E/7 #1425, File 7616, India Office Records, British Museum, London.

12. *Report on Indian Constitutional Reforms,* Publication Cd 9109, p. 5. 1918. London, His Majesty's Stationery Office. The Secretary of State for India was a Cabinet member with equivalent rank to the Foreign Secretary. The senior British official in India was the Governor General, who reported to the Secretary of State for India and at the same time represented the Crown as Viceroy. The Governor General, together with a Council, made up the central government of British India, which governed with the administrative help of the Indian Civil Service made up almost entirely of European-born British subjects. Provincial governments in British India were headed by Lieutenant Governors and their legislative councils. Not all of present day India and Pakistan was in British India; the nominally independent "Indian States" were ruled by Indian princes in an essentially feudal relationship to British India.

13. Pandy, *Breakup of British India,* 123.

14. Ibid., 118–121.

15. *Report of the Indian Sanatory Commission, Volume I, Survey.* Publication Cmd. 3568, pp. 278–279, 1930. London, His Majesty's Stationery Office.

16. Press clipping from *Times of India,* 21 May 1927, p. 38, L/E/7 #1425, File 7616, India Office Records, British Museum, London.

17. *PM,* 707; d'Herelle to Smith, 14 January 1927, G. H. Smith file, Yale Medical Historical Library.

18. C. A. Gill to L. Rogers, 18 August 1927, Item 58, Box C10, Leonard Rogers Correspondence, Wellcome Institute, London. In a footnote added later, Rogers commented: "I was also very hopeful that bacteriophage would prove to be valuable, but now (1949) it has proved to be a failure in cholera. LR."

19. Far Eastern Association for Tropical Medicine, part 2.

20. Far Eastern Association for Tropical Medicine, part 2, 71.

21. League of Nations: Office International d'Hygiène publique, Comité Permanent, Procès-verbaux. Meeting of May 1928, page 15.

22. The Simon Commission was a seven-man Indian Statutory Committee of the British Parliament, led by Sir John Simon, empowered by the Government of India Act of 1919 to review, within ten years, the government functions in India and recommend changes, if needed. Since, as a committee of Parliament, it had no Indian members, it was viewed with suspicion and offense by the Indian population. Mass demonstrations against the commission took place in Bombay, Delhi, Calcutta, Lucknow, Lahore, Patna, and Madras.

23. Viceroy to Secretary of State for India, 29 February 1928, p. 31, L/E//7 #1425, File 7616, India Office Records, British Museum, London.

24. *All-India Research Workers Conference,* 40.

25. Asheshov, Asheshov, Khan, and Lahiri, "Bacteriophage inquiry report," 54.

26. Asheshov, Asheshov, Khan, and Lahiri, "Treatment of cholera," 179–184.

27. Editorial, "The cholera bacteriophage," 91.

28. Asheshov, *Annual Report,* 1933–1934, 41.

29. *Annual Reports of the Scientific Advisory Board, Indian Research Fund Association* (Calcutta, n.p.), 1931–1932, p. 107; 1932–1933, p. 122; 1933–1934, p. 94.

30. *All-India Research Workers Conference,* 40.

31. Morison, Rice, and Pal Choudhury, 790–907.

32. Russell, Stewart, and King, 106.

33. A short biographical summary for Igor Nicholas Asheshov is in *J. New York Botanical Garden* 49:173–174, 1948.

34. Morison, *Treatment and prevention of cholera,* 28; Morison, "Bacteriophage in cholera," 563–570; *PM,* 652.

35. Morison, "Annual report for 1928," 472–474.

36. *Annual Reports of the King Edward VII Memorial Pasteur Institute and Medical Research Institute, Shillong, Assam for the Years* 1928, 1929, 1930, 1934. Shillong, n.p.

37. Morison, "Annual report for 1931," 53–54.

38. Morison, *Bacteriophage in Cholera,* 569.

39. *Annual Reports of the Scientific Advisory Board, Indian Research Fund Association,* 1931–1936.

40. Ramasubban, 55.

41. Ibid., 55.

42. Pasricha, de Monte, and O'Flynn, 61–68.
43. Ibid., 67.
44. *Annual Report of the Scientific Advisory Board, Indian Research Fund Association*, 1936, 128.
45. Ibid., 126–127.
46. Ibid., 127–129.

CHAPTER 10. BACTERIAL MUTATIONS AND PHAGE RESEARCH AT YALE

1. Liebow and Waters, 143–172.
2. Viseltear, "C.-E. A. Winslow," 137–151; Viseltear, "Public health education," 519–548. Watkins and Nelbach, 779–800; Winslow and Prescott, *Water Bacteriology*, 1–163; 1904; Winslow and Winslow, *Systematic Relationships of the Coccaceae*, 1–300.
3. Valley, 1–2.
4. Harvey, 300.
5. Félix d'Herelle to G. H. Smith, letter of 14 January 1928, G. H. Smith file, Yale Medical Historical Library.
6. M. C. Winternitz to J. R. Angell, letter of 8 February 1928, Dean's files, Presidential Papers, Yale University Library, Manuscripts and Archives Collection.
7. J. R. Angell to M. C. Winternitz, letter of 10 February 1928, Dean's files, Yale University Library Manuscripts and Archives Collection.
8. Winternitz to Flexner, 6 March 1928, J. R. Angell Presidential Papers, Yale University Library Manuscripts and Archives Collection.
9. Winternitz to d'Herelle, 8 March 1928, Dean's files, Yale University School of Medicine.
10. Winternitz to Flexner, 28 March 1928, J. R. Angell Presidential Papers. Yale University Library, Manuscripts and Archives Collection.
11. W. W. Brierley to J. R. Angell, 5 June 1928, J. R. Angell Presidential Papers, Yale University Library, Manuscripts and Archives Collection.
12. Yale University press release, 15 June 1928, Félix d'Herelle file, Yale Medical Historical Library.
13. E. W. Schultz correspondence, Schultz Family Papers, held by Dr. Robert B. Schultz. Copy in author's files.
14. E. W. Schultz correspondence, Schultz Family Papers, held by Dr. Robert B. Schultz. Copy in author's files.
15. FdH: 101, 37 footnote.
16. Dean's Files on Félix d'Herelle, Yale University School of Medicine.
17. Yale-New Haven Hospital Record 72262; admission note, 19 December 1928.
18. Yale-New Haven Hospital Record 72262; final summary, 25 December 1928.
19. J. R. Paul to S. J. Peitzman, Undated letter ca. Nov. 1969, copy from Peitzman in author's files.
20. Massini, 250–290. Neisser, 98–102. De Kruif, "Dissociation," 773–787.

21. For a recent discussion of the history of this controversy see Amsterdamska, 191–222.

22. Burian, Gayon, and Zallen, 357–402.

23. *INID,* 76–79. D'Herelle's ideas are discussed in the context of the development of the concept of symbiosis by Sapp, *Evolution by association,* 106–108.

24. FdH: 36; FdH: 43. Gratia, "L'adaptation héréditaire," 750–751. Gratia, "Colonies de bactériophage," 753–754.

25. This description seems to a classic case of lysogeny. In the absence of a precise notion of virulence, the notion of "weakly virulent" phage may have referred to lysogenic phage which can lysogenize with a high frequency so the lytic action is partially obscured. This description was to form the basis of a dispute between Lwoff and d'Herelle in which the latter's claim to have discovered lysogeny was denied by Lwoff (Lwoff to author, 5 February 1991).

26. Luria and Delbrück, 491–511.

27. The very low frequency of resistant bacteria, about 2×10^{-11}, observed in this experiment suggests that in the replicate 200 ml cultures there may have been no resistant cells because of the random distribution of such cells. Thus, this experiment, while sound in concept, was flawed because d'Herelle apparently failed to appreciate that his analysis required sufficiently frequent secondary cultures so that the implicit statistical argument was valid. That is, unless he was certain that there were some resistant, or potentially resistant, bacteria in each original 200 ml culture, the comparison of the initial aliquots with the delayed aliquots would be uninformative. Luria and Delbrück increased the power of this analysis by extending the statistical argument beyond the simple presence or absence of resistant cells to include an analysis of the variation in the sizes of the resistant populations among each of the secondary cultures.

28. During most of d'Herelle's time in New Haven, his wife and daughter Marcelle remained in the family home in Paris. While in New Haven, d'Herelle lived at several places, all close to his laboratory. His first address (42 College Street) was within 100 yards of his laboratory building. Subsequently, he lived in two apartments (220 Park Street and 228 Park Street) about a quarter mile from the laboratory. For a time his wife joined him in New Haven, as she was listed in the City Directory as a resident at 228 Park during 1932. Much of his summer visits to France were spent at his country home at Le Nervost in Saint-Mards-en-Othe in the department of Aube (*HM*).

29. Winternitz's notes in d'Herelle's file in Dean's Files, Yale University School of Medicine.

30. Winternitz's notes in d'Herelle's file in Dean's Files, Yale University School of Medicine.

31. Letter from Winternitz to d'Herelle, 18 Nov. 1930, Dean's Files, Yale University School of Medicine.

32. Correspondence: George Day, Lottie Bishop, Henry Farnam (Yale University officials), and d'Herelle; Dean's Files, Yale University Library, Manuscripts and Archives Collection.

33. Press release, undated. See also *New York Times,* 26 May 1933, *New Haven Register,* 27 May 1933 and *New Haven Journal Courier,* 26 May 1933. Clippings in Félix d'Herelle file, Yale Medical Historical Library.

CHAPTER 11. TO TIFLIS AND BACK

1. Tiflis was the Russian name for the city in Georgia which was designated the capital of the Georgian Soviet Socialist Republic in 1921. In the Georgian language it is called Tbilisi, the name which was officially adopted in 1936. D'Herelle always referred to the city by its Russian name.

2. Georgiy Grigor'yevich Eliava (1892–1937) (Schulz, Urban, and Lebed, *Who was who in the USSR*, 155; also Makashvili, *USSR great medical encyclopedia*, 130).

3. Pozerski, 46–47.

4. Letter from K. Rossiyanov to author, undated, September 1990.

5. Milton Winternitz, Report of the Dean, 1932–33, to James Rowland Angell, President Yale University. Dean's Papers, Yale University Library, Manuscript and Archives.

6. D'Herelle's family believed that he received sufficient compensation from the USSR, deposited in Switzerland, so that he could live comfortably from 1937 until his death in 1949 without financial concerns (*HM*).

7. These are the titles given in FdH: 135 and FdH: 136.

8. Nikolai Bulgakov (1898–1966) was the brother of the dissident Soviet writer Mikhail Bulgakov (Curtis, *Manuscripts don't burn*).

9. The Laboratoire du Bactériophage advertised five preparations: *Bacté-coli-phage*, *Bacté-rhino-phage*, *Bacté-intesti-phage*, *Bacté-pyo-phage*, and *Bacté-staphy-phage*. The preparations were marked by the reputable French firm of Robert et Carrière, which was subsequently acquired by the French conglomerate L'Oréal. The advertisements described the Laboratoire du Bactériophage as "A research laboratory whose benefits are directed to scientific ends" which is "under the control of Professor d'Herelle." See *La Médecine* 17 (Supplement 2): 35, 1936.

10. Makashvili and Djanagowa, 38–40.

11. Huxley, *Heredity east and west*, 29–33.

12. Letter d'Herelle to Winternitz, 10 May 1933; microfiche in d'Herelle's personnel folder, Dean's office, Yale University School of Medicine.

13. Published recollections of a former Georgian NKVD officer (Gazarian, 20–27).

14. Schulz, Urban, and Lebed, *Who was who in the USSR*, 155. Eliava was posthumously rehabilitated. A slightly different version is recounted by Shrayer, 94.

15. Pozerski, 47.

16. Letter from K. Rossiyanov to author, undated, September 1990. Berg, *Acquired traits*, 467.

17. Shrayer, 94.

18. FdH: 139. The Yale Medical Library copy is inscribed by d'Herelle and dated 14 January 1938.

19. Nathan Rakieten, interview 14 March 1989. Rakieten was a graduate student at Yale, and his brother, Morris Rakieten, was d'Herelle's assistant.

20. *INID*, 7–9; *CMP*, 9–18; FdH: 115.

21. In several of d'Herelle's obituary notices his involvement with bacteriophage research institutes in Kiev and Kharkov is mentioned. Only his activities in Tiflis, however, are described in the Russian sources, e.g., *The USSR great medical encyclopedia*.

22. Arshba, Murvanidze, and Kuparadze, "Alexandr Petrovich Tsulukidze," 103–106.

23. Mikeladzé, Nemsadzé, Alexidzé, and Assanichvili, 33–38.

24. Tsouloukidzé, 41–42.

25. Arshba, Murvanidze, and Kuparadze, "Alexandr Petrovich Tsulukidze," 103–106. The "Finnish events" refer to the invasion of Finland by the Soviet Union.

26. Kuznyetsova and Vyeger, 6–26.

27. Mudd, 71–81.

28. Radetsky, 50–58. As an example of recent work from Tbilisi, see Gachechiladze, Balardshishvili, Adamia, Chanishvili, and Kruger, 101–106.

29. Marcuk et al., 77–83; Dixon, 1168; Travis, 350–351.

CHAPTER 12. REFLECTIONS AND LEGACIES

1. Nikolai (Kolya) Bulgakov [Nicolai Boulgakov] (1898–1966). See also Curtis, *Manuscripts don't burn.*

2. Sertic and Boulgakov; Sertic "Sur la différence d'action des électrolytes"; Sertic, "Sur l'action inhibitrice des cations monovalents"; Bulgakov and Bonét-Maury; Bonét-Maury and Bulgakov; Frilley et al.; Lépine et al.

3. Elford and Andrewes.

4. Sertic and Boulgakov.

5. Sinsheimer.

6. Sanger et al..

7. Van Helvoort *Research styles in virus studies,* chapter 2.

8. Ruska "Die Sichtbarmachung der bakteriophagen Lyse in Ubermikroskop"; "Uber ein neues bei der bakteriophagen Lyse auftretendes Formelement."

9. Van Helvoort, *History of virus research,* 162. Also Van Helvoort, "Construction of bacteriophage," 121.

10. Levaditi and Bonét-Maury, 203–207.

11. Ibid., 207.

12. Wollman and Lacassagne.

13. Wollman, "Recherches sur la bactériophage."

14. Luria, "Action des radiations," 1939; Wollman et al. "Effects of radiations on bacteriophage C_{16}."

15. Luria, "Sur l'unité lytique." In his autobiography Luria provides a charming account of his introduction to bacteriophage: while he was studying physics in Rome in 1938 he read a paper by Max Delbrück on using radiation to measure the size of the gene in fruit flies. A chance conversation on a stalled tram car between Luria and a bacteriologist, Geo Rita, introduced Luria to bacteriophages, which Rita was studying for their potential therapeutic effect. Luria ended up spending a little time in Rita's laboratory learning to work with phage. See Luria, *A slot machine,* 20.

16. Feemster and Wells.

17. Clark, "On the titration of bacteriophage." Bronfenbrenner and Korb.

18. Ellis; Summers "How bacteriophage came to be used by the Phage Group."

19. Ellis and Delbrück.

20. Cairns, Stent and Watson, ix–x. Also Mullins.

    Ellis was constrained in his work on phage by the terms of his cancer research fellowship from Mrs. Seeley W. Mudd. In 1941 he joined the Caltech war effort, played a key role in the Caltech rocket project, and subsequently moved to the Pentagon when Harold Brown went from the Caltech presidency to become Secretary of War. He ended his government career as a U.S. representative to NATO in London. See Institute Archives web pages (06/16/97): http://www.caltech.edu/archives/bios/EllisEL.html.

    During the 1940s Max Delbrück, Salvador Luria, and Alfred Hershey gathered a group of researchers focused on phage as the experimental organism and genetics as the major problem. This informal group held periodic meetings, circulated a newsletter, and organized summer courses at the Cold Spring Harbor Laboratory.

21. Morris Rakieten to FDH, 10 September 1940. (dHFP)

22. Mazure and Mazure, 10.

23. Félix d'Herelle. Handwritten notes: two sheets (about 15 × 20 cm) written on two sides. The latest reference is to a paper in the December 1943 issue of *Comptes Rendus de la Société de Biologie de Paris* which suggests that these notes were made in early 1944 or sometime thereafter. (dHFP)

24. The dedication concludes: "She is coming to the end, her work finished, but something of her lives on in these pages, for the established thought is the only reality which survives us." Marie Caire d'Herelle died in 1946 according to the inscription on the family gravestone in Saint-Mards-en-Othe.

25. Nicolle, "Eugène Wollman."

26. For a detailed account of work at the Pasteur Institute in this period, see Delaunay, chapter 7.

27. Elie Wollman to author, letter dated 26 December 1988; interview, 6 June 1989.

28. Wollman interview, 7 June 1989; Raymond Latarjet interview, 20 August 1993.

29. Cited in *Comptes Rendus Acad. Sci. Paris* 227:1301, 1948.

30. Wolff.

31. Elie Wollman interview, 7 June 1989; Raymond Latarjet to WCS, letter 13 August 1991.

32. Hubert Mazure interview, 6 June 1989.

33. See, for example, Girard and Sertic; Bulgakov and Bonét-Maury; Lépine et al.

34. Report of Proceedings, Fourth International Congress for Microbiology, 1947; D'Herelle was listed as a participant in this congress and a member of the Scientific Council of the "Centre de Collection de Types Microbiens." However, he did not attend and was represented by his protégé Paul Hauduroy who was professor of microbiology in Lausanne and director of the Centre.

35. Eaton and Bayne-Jones.

36. Founded 27 May 1970, cited in *Nouvelles Archives Hospitalières,* no. 2, 1975, p. 29.

37. Conseil de Paris, Meeting of 27 June 1975. Avenue Félix-d'Herelle, Paris XVIe, cited in *Nouvelles Archives Hospitalières,* no. 3, 1976, p. 72.

38. *Nouvelles Archives Hospitalières,* no. 1, 1978. p. 6.

39. *Nouvelles Archives Hospitalières,* no. 3, 1976, p. 72.

Bibliography

The following list gives the major sources, published and unpublished, that were used in this study. Some are cited in the text by the abbreviations given here. "FdH" followed by a number indicates a citation from the chronologically numbered publications of d'Herelle listed below.

BCA: *The bacteriophage and its clinical applications* (FdH: 108)

BIB: *The bacteriophage and its behavior* (FdH: 89)

BIRI: *The bacteriophage: Its role in immunity* (FdH: 56)

CMP: *L'étude d'une maladie: Le choléra, maladie à paradoxes* (FdH: 141)

dHFP: D'Herelle Family Papers

HM: Interviews with Herbert Mazure, grandson of Félix d'Herelle, 6 June 1989 (Troyes, France) and 27 October 1989 (New Haven, Connecticut)

INID: *Immunity in natural infectious disease* (FdH: 73)

LPG: *Le phénomène de la guérison des maladies infectieuses* (FdH: 139)

LVE: *La valeur de l'expérience* (FdH: 145)

PM: *Les pérégrinations [sic] d'un microbiologiste* (FdH: 144)

British Museum, India Office Records: L/E/7 #1425, File 7616

Institut Pasteur, Paris, Museum

Institut Pasteur, Paris, Archives

Wellcome Institute, London, Leonard Rogers Correspondence

Yale University Library, Manuscripts and Archives. Deans' Files; Presidential Papers

Yale University School of Medicine, Deans' Files

PUBLISHED WORKS OF FÉLIX HUBERT D'HERELLE

1a. Hoerens, F. 1899. "Comment le monde finira-t-il? Quatorze fins du monde." *La Patrie* 14 January 1899, page 7, continued on 21 January 1899, page 1.

1. d'Herelle, Félix. 1901."De la formation du Carbone par les végétaux." *Le Naturaliste Canadien* 28:70–75.

2.———. 1908. "Experimentos relativos al alcohol obtenido del bagazo del henequén." *El Agricultor: Organo de la Caméra Agrícola de Yucatán* 2:73.

3.———. 1908. "Les aloès (Furcraea) au Mexique et dans l'Amérique centrale." *J. d'Agriculture tropicale* 8:256.

4.———. 1909. "Maladie du Caféier au Guatemala." *Bulletin de la Société mycologique de France* 25:171–185.

5.———, and Seidelin, H. 1909. "Sur deux microfilaires du sang de serpents." *Comptes rendus Soc. biol. Paris* 67:409–411.

6.———. 1909. "Lettre sur le Sisal au Yucatan." *Bulletin de la Société de Géographie Commerciale de Paris* 31:441–443.

7.———. 1910. "Informes sobre los ensayos hechos para la utilización de los desperdicios de henequén." Appendix No. 38, pp. 311–326 in Olegario Molina, *Memoria de la Secretaría de Fomento, Colonización e Industria de la República Mexicana, 1908–1909.* Mexico: Imprenta y Fototipia de la Secretaría de Fomento.

8.———. 1910. "Utilisation des résidus de la défibration des Agaves pour la production de l'alcool." *J. d'Agricult. tropicale* 10:161–167.

9.———. 1910. "Note sur une maladie des Sauterelles au Yucatan." *J. d'Agricult. tropicale* 10:237–238.

10.———. 1911. "Alcool de Nipa." *J. d'Agricult. tropicale* 11:123.

11.———. 1911. "L'alcool de Hennequen." *J. d'Agricult. tropicale* 11:219.

12.———. 1911. "Sur une épizootie de nature bactérienne sévissant sur les sauterelles au Mexique." *Comptes rendus Acad. Sci. Paris* 152:1413–1415.

13.———. 1911. "Sur une épizootie de nature bactérienne sévissant sur les sauterelles au Mexique." *J. d'Agricult. tropicale* 11:238–240.

14.———. 1912. "Sur la propagation, dans la République Argentine, de l'épizootie des sauterelles du Mexique." *Comptes rendus Acad. Sci. Paris* 154:623–625.

15.———. 1912. *Utilización industrial del bagazo del Agave rigida.* Mexico: Secretaría de Fomento.

16.———. 1914. "Le coccobacille des sauterelles." *Ann. de l'Institut Pasteur* 28:280–328.

17.———. 1914. "Le coccobacille des sauterelles." *Ann. de l'Institut Pasteur* 28:387–407.

18.———. 1915. "Sur le procédé biologique de destruction des sauterelles." *Comptes rendus Acad. Sci. Paris* 161:503–505.

19.———, and Géry, L. 1915. "Choc anaphylactique provoqué par le sang de femme chez des cobayes sensibilisés par des albuminoïdes du placenta." *Comptes rendus Soc. biol. Paris* 78:55–58.

20.———. 1915. "La campagne contre les sauterelles en Tunisie en 1915." *Bulletin de la Société de Pathologie exotique* 8:629–633.

21.———. 1916. "Campagne contre les *Schistocerca Peregrina* en Tunisie par le méthode biologique." *Arch. de l'Institut Pasteur de Tunis* 9:135–148.

22.———. 1916. "Sur un bacille dysentérique atypique." *Ann. de l'Institut Pasteur* 30:145–147.

23.———. 1916. "Contribution à l'étude de l'immunité." *Comptes rendus Acad. Sci. Paris* 162:570–573.

24.———. 1916. "Contribution à l'étude de la dysentérie. Nouveaux bacilles dysentériques, pathogènes pour les animaux d'expérience." *Bulletin de l'Académie de Médecine* 76:425–428.

25.———. 1917. "Sur un microbe invisible antagoniste des bacilles dysentériques." *Comptes rendus Acad. Sci. Paris* 165:373–375.

26.———. 1918. "Intoxication gastro-intestinale suraigue expérimentale." *Comptes rendus Soc. biol. Paris* 81:717–719.

27.———. 1918. "Essais de bactériothérapie expérimentale." *Comptes rendus Soc. biol. Paris* 81:937–939.

28.———. 1918. "Sur le rôle du microbe filtrant bactériophage dans la dysentérie bacillaire." *Comptes rendus Acad. Sci. Paris* 167:970–972.

29.———. 1918. "Technique de la recherche du microbe filtrant bactériophage (*Bacteriophagum intestinale*)." *Comptes rendus Soc. biol. Paris* 81: 1160–1062.

30.———. 1919. "Du rôle du microbe filtrant bactériophage dans la fièvre typhoide." *Comptes rendus Acad. Sci. Paris* 168:631–634.

31.———. 1919. "Sur une épizootie de typhose aviaire." *Comptes rendus Acad. Sci. Paris* 169:817–819.

32.———. 1919. "Sur le rôle du microbe bactériophage dans la typhose aviaire." *Comptes rendus Acad. Sci. Paris* 169:932–934.

33.———. 1919. "Sur le microbe bactériophage." *Comptes rendus Soc. biol. Paris* 82:1237–1239.

34.———. 1920. "Le processus de défense contre les bacilles intestinaux et l'étiologie des maladies d'origine intestinale." *Comptes rendus Acad. Sci. Paris* 170:72–75.

35.———. 1920. "Sur la culture du microbe bactériophage." *Comptes rendus Soc. biol. Paris* 83:52–53.

36.———. 1920. "Sur le résistance des bactéries à l'action du microbe bactériophage." *Comptes rendus Soc. biol. Paris* 83:97–99.

37.———. 1920. "Sur le microbe bactériophage." *Comptes rendus Soc. biol. Paris* 83:247–249.

38.———. 1920. "Sur le microbe bactériophage." *Comptes rendus Soc. biol. Paris* 83:1318–1319.

39.———. 1920. "Sur la nature du principe bactériophage." *Comptes rendus Soc. biol. Paris* 83:1320–1322.

40.———. 1921. "Le microbe bactériophage, agent d'immunité dans la pest et le barbone." *Comptes rendus Acad. Sci. Paris* 172:99–100.

41.———. 1921. "Sur la nature du bactériophage (*Bacteriophagum intestinale* de d'Herelle, 1918). *Comptes rendus Soc. biol. Paris* 84:339–340.

42.———. 1921. "Le bactériophage." *La Nature (Paris)* 49:219–222.

43.———. 1921. "Phénomènes coïncidant avec l'acquisition de la résistance des bactéries à l'action du bactériophage." *Comptes rendus Soc. biol. Paris* 84:384–386.

44.———. 1921. "Rôle du bactériophage dans l'immunité." *Comptes rendus Soc. biol. Paris* 84:538–540.

45.———. 1921. "Sur l'historique du bactériophage." *Comptes rendus Soc. biol. Paris* 84:863–864.

46.———. 1921. "Sur la nature du bactériophage." *Comptes rendus Soc. biol. Paris* 84:908–909.

47.———. 1921. "L'ultramicrobe bactériophage." *Comptes rendus Soc. biol. Paris* 85:767–768.

48.———. 1921. *Le bactériophage: Son rôle dans l'immunité.* Paris, Masson et Cie.

49.———. 1921. "Das bakteriophage Virus. Seine Rolle in des Immunität." *Zeitschr. f. ärztl. Fortbild.* 18:664–667.

50.———. 1921. "Le bactériophage. Son rôle dans l'immunité." *La Presse méd.* 29:463–464.

51.———, and Eliava, G. 1921. "Sur le sérum anti-bactériophage." *Comptes rendus Soc. biol. Paris* 84:719–721.

52.———, and Eliava, G. 1921. "Unicité du bactériophage; Sur la lysine du bactériophage." *Comptes rendus Soc. biol. Paris* 85:701–702.

53.———, and Pozerski, É. 1921. "Action de la température sur le bactériophage." *Comptes rendus Soc. biol. Paris* 85:1011–1013.

54.———, and Le Louet, G. 1921. "Sur la vaccination antibarbonique par virus atténué." *Ann. de l'Institut Pasteur* 35:741–744.

55.———. 1922. "The nature of the bacteriophage." *Brit. Med. J.* 2:289–293.

56.———. 1922. *The bacteriophage: Its role in immunity.* Baltimore: Williams and Wilkins.

57.———. 1922. *Der Bakteriophage und seine Bedeutung für die Immunität.* Braunschweig, F. Vieweg und Sohn.

58.———. 1922. "Sur les anti-lysines d'origine bactérienne." *Comptes rendus Soc. biol. Paris* 86:360–361.

59.———. 1922. "Sur la présence du bactériophage dans les leucocytes." *Comptes rendus Soc. biol. Paris* 86:477–478.

60.———. 1922. "Sur la prétendue production d'un principe lytique sous l'influence d'un antagonisme microbien." *Comptes rendus Soc. biol. Paris* 86:663–665.

61.———. 1922. "Sur une cause d'erreur pouvant intervenir dans l'étude bactériophage." *Comptes rendus Soc. biol. Paris* 87:665–666.

62.———. 1923. *Les défenses de l'organisme.* Paris, E. Flammarion.

63.———. 1923. "Action du fluorure de sodium sur le bactériophage." *Comptes rendus Soc. biol. Paris* 88:407–408.

64.———. 1923. "Sur un 'principe bactériolysant' non bactériophage, existant dans l'intestin des cholériques." *Comptes rendus Soc. biol. Paris* 88:723–724.

65.———. 1923. "Observations au sujet des expériences concernant le phénomène de bactériophagie." *Comptes rendus Soc. biol. Paris.* 89: 231–233.

66.———. 1923. "Sur la nature du bactériophage." *Comptes rendus Soc. biol. Paris* 89:914–916.

67.———. 1923. "La nature du bactériophage." *Nederl. Maandschr. v. Geneesk.*. 3:737–746.

68.———. 1923. "La nature du bactériophage." *Nederl. Tijdschr. v. Geneesk.* 67:2969–2970.

69.———. 1923. "Autolysis and bacteriophagis." *J. State. Med.,* London. 31:461–466.

70.———. 1923. "Le bactériophage." *Revue de pathologie comparée et d'hygiène générale* 23:595–620.

71.———. 1923. "Culture du bactériophage sans intervention de bactéries vivantes." *Verhandl. v. kon Akad. v. Wetensch., Amsterdam* 26:486.

72.———. 1924. *Drie voordrachten over het verschijnsel der bacteriophagie.* Groningen: J.B. Wolters.

73.———. 1924. *Immunity in natural infectious disease.* Baltimore, Williams and Wilkins.

74.———. 1924. "Sur l'autonomie du bactériophage." *Comptes rendus Soc. biol. Paris* 90:25–27.

75.———. 1924. "Sur l'état physique du bactériophage." *Comptes rendus Soc. biol. Paris* 90:27–29.

76.———. 1924. "Sur la constance des propriétés du bactériophage." *Comptes rendus Soc. biol. Paris* 90:481–482.

77.———. 1924. "De bakteriophaag." *Nederl. Tijdschr. v. Geneesk.* I:1598–1603.

78.———. 1924. "La nature du bactériophage." *Tijdschr. v. Vergel. Geneesk.* Vol. 10. [Reprinted in *Acta Leidensia* 1:167–184, 1926].

79.———. 1925. "Sur la nature du bactériophage." *Comptes rendus Soc. biol. Paris* 93:509–511.

80.———. 1925. "La théorie de l'autolyse microbienne transmissible de Bordet et Ciuca." *Comptes rendus Soc. biol. Paris* 93:1206–1208.

81.———. 1925. "La nature du bactériophage." *Bull. techn. d. sci. med., Genève.* I:11ff.

82.———. 1925. "Die Natur des Bakteriophagen." *Centralbl. f. Bakt. I. Abt. Orig.* 96:385–398.

83.———. 1925. "Les ultravirus et l'immunité antivirulique." *Nederl. Maandschr. v. Geneesk.* 13:33–110.

84.———. 1925. "Essai de traîtement de la peste bubonique par le bactériophage." *La Presse méd.* 33:1393–1394.

85.———. 1925. "On the relationship of clover and planaria to malaria." OHIP (League of Nations) *Malaria Commission Reports.* CH/Malaria/#49; CH/Malaria/51)1925.

86.———, and Hauduroy, P. 1925. "Sur les caractères des symbioses 'Bactérie-bactériophage'." *Comptes rendus Soc. biol. Paris* 93:1288–1290.

87.———. 1926. "Sur la théorie de l'autolyse microbienne transmissible de Bordet et Ciuca." *Comptes rendus Soc. biol. Paris* 94:973–974.

88.———. 1926. *Le Bactériophage et Son Comportement.* Paris, Masson et Cie.

89.———. 1926. *The Bacteriophage and Its Behavior.* Baltimore, Williams and Wilkins.

90.———. 1927. "La bactériophagie en hyperaérobiose." *Comptes rendus Soc. biol. Paris* 96:451–452.

91.———, and Malone, R. H. 1927. "A preliminary report of work carried out by the cholera bacteriophage inquiry." *Indian Med. Gazette* 62:614–616.

92.———, and Peyre, E. 1927. "Contribution à l'étude des tumeurs expérimentales." *Comptes rendus Acad. Sci. Paris* 185:227–230.

93.————, and Peyre, E. 1927. "Contribution à l'étude des tumeurs spontanées." *Comptes rendus Acad. Sci. Paris* 185:513–515.

94.————. 1928. "The nature of the ultrafilterable viruses." *Harvey Lectures* 24:45–71.

95.————. 1928. "Bacteriophage, a living colloidal micell." 535–541 in J. Alexander. *Colloid Chemistry: Theroretical and Applied.* Vol II. New York, Chemical Catalog Company.

96.————. 1928. "Le choléra asiatique." *La Presse méd.* 36:961–964.

97.————. 1928. "Bacteriophagy and bacteriophage." pp. 278–283, in *Transactions of the Seventh Congress held in British India, December,* 1927, *Far Eastern Association of Tropical Medicine.* Vol. II. Calcutta, Thacker.

98.————, Malone, R. H., and Lahiri, M. 1928. "The pathology and epidemiology of infectious diseases of the intestinal tract and of cholera in particular." pp. 284–287 in *Transactions of the 7th Congress held in British India, December,* 1927, *Far Eastern Association of Tropical Medicine.* Vol. II. Calcutta, Thacker.

99.————, Malone, R. H., and Lahiri, M. 1928. "The treatment and prophylaxis of infectious diseases of the intestinal tract and of cholera in particular." pp. 288–293 in *Transactions of the 7th Congress held in British India, December,* 1927, *Far Eastern Association of Tropical Medicine.* Vol. II. Calcutta, Thacker.

100.————. 1929. "Studies upon Asiatic cholera." *Yale J. Biol. Med.* 1:195–219.

101.————. 1929. "The bacteriophage in relation to the phenomenon of recovery." *International Clinics* 39:37–59.

102.————. 1929. [Untitled abstract.] *New Engl. J. Med.* 200:409–410.

103.————, Malone, R. H., and Lahiri, M. 1929. *Etudes sur le choléra.* Alexandria, Conseil Quarantenaire d'Egypte, Impr. Arturo Serafini.

104.————. 1930. "A propos d'une communication de M. André Gratia sur le bactériophage." *Bulletin et Mémoires de la Société Nationale de Chirurgie* 56:588–590.

105.————. 1930. "Le phénomène de Bactériophagie et sa signification biologique." *Bulletin et Mémoires de la Société Nationale de Chirurgie* 56:986–994.

106.————. 1930. "Le bactériophage: Ses applications à la dermatologie." *Arch. dermatol. syphiligr. Hop. St. Louis* 2:369–394.

107.————. 1930. "Elimination du bactériophage dans les symbioses bactérie-bactériophage." *Comptes rendus Soc. biol. Paris* 104:1254–1256.

108.————. 1930. *The bacteriophage and its clinical applications.* Springfield, Ill.: C. C. Thomas.

109.————. 1930. "The carrier problem." *Yale J. Biol. Med.* 3:21–38.

110.————, and Sertic, V. 1930. "Formation, par adaptation, de races de bactériophages thermo-résistantes." *Comptes rendus Soc. biol. Paris* 104:1256–1258.

111.————, Malone., R.H., and Lahiri, M. 1930. "Studies on Asiatic Cholera." *Indian Medical Research Memoirs* 14:1–161.

112.————. 1930. "Le bactériophage et la bacteriophagie." *La Science Moderne* 11:503–509.

113.————. 1931. "La bactériophagie et le bactériophage." pp. 138–145 in Vol. I, *First International Congress of Microbiology, Paris* 1930. Paris, Masson.

114.————. 1931. "Le choléra." pp. 432–437 in Vol. I, *First International Congress of Microbiology, Paris* 1930. Paris, Masson.

115.————. 1931. "Bacteriophage as a treatment in acute medical and surgical infections." *Bull. New York Acad. Med.* series 2; 7: 329–348.

116.————. 1931. "Le phénomène de Twort et la bactériophagie." *Ann. de l'Institut Pasteur* 46:616–618.

117.————. 1931. "Le phénomène de Twort et la bactériophagie." *Ann. de l'Institut Pasteur* 47:241–242.

118.————. 1931. "Le phénomène de Twort et la bactériophagie." *Ann. de l'Institut Pasteur* 47:470–471.

119.————. 1931. "Bacteriophagy and recovery from infectious diseases." *Canadian Med. Assn. J.* 24:619–628.

120.————. 1931. "Bacterial Mutations." *Yale J. Biol. Med.* 4:455–461.

121.————. 1932. "Bacterial mutations." *Yale J. Biol. Med.* 4:556.

122.————. 1932. "The practical application of bacteriophage." *Yale J. Biol. Med.* 4:738–738.

123.————. 1932. "Clover and Malaria." *Am. J. Hyg.* 16:609–617.

124.————, and Beecroft, Ruth. 1932. "Bacterial Mutations." *J. Lab. Clin. Med.* 17:667–674.

125.————, and Beecroft, Ruth. 1932. "Bacterial Mutations." *J. Bacteriol.* 23:17–18.

126.————. 1933. "Recherche de la nature des virus infravisible traitée comme un problème physiologique." *Archivo di Scienza Biologiche* 18:117.

127.————. 1933. "Prophylaxie collective du choléra par le bactériophage." pp. 485–488 in Vol. 1, *Hygiène méditerranéenne, Premier Congrès international, Marseille, Sept. 20–25, 1932, Paris, Baillière.*

128.————. 1933. "Le bactériophage et ses applications thérapeutiques." pp. 30ff. in *La Pratique médicale illustrée.* Paris, Doin.

129.————, and Rakieten, M. L. 1933. "The susceptibility of hemolytic staphylococci to bacteriophage." *J. Am. Med. Assn.* 100:1014–1014.

130.————. 1934. "Le bactériophage dans ses relations avec l'immunité." pp. 84–99 in *Convegno di Immunologia, Atti Dei Convegno III.* Rome, Reale Accadèm. d'Italia, Fond. Alessandro Volta.

131.————. 1934. "Bakteriofag i immynitet." *Proc. Second Cong. Azerbaijan Microbiol. Soc. Baku.* pp. 15–19

132.————, and Rakieten, T. L. 1934. "Mutations as governing bacterial characters and serologic reactions." *J. Inf. Dis.* 54:313–338.

133.————. 1935. *Bakteriofag i fenomen vyzdorovleniya.* Tiflis, Tiflis National University Publications.

134.————, and Rakieten, M. L. 1935. "The adaptation of a staphylococcus bacteriophage to an artificially produced antibacteriophagic serum." *J. Immunol.* 28:413–423.

135.————. 1936. "Le bactériophage dans ses relations avec l'immunité." *La Médecine* 17 (Supplement #2): 11–20.

136.————. 1936. "Traitement et prophylaxie par le bactériophage des maladies épidémiques de nature bactérienne." *La Médecine* 17 (Supplement #2): 23–32.

137.————, and Peyre, E. 1936. "Le bactériophage en stomatologie." *Revue Odontologique* 58:359.

138.————. 1937. "Bacteriophage and recovery from infectious diseases." pp. 287–301 in G. M. Piersol, ed., *The Cyclopedia of Medicine,* Vol. 2. Philadelphia, F. A. Davis.

139.————. 1938. *Le phénomène de la guérison des maladies infectieuses.* Paris, Masson and Cie.

140.————. 1942. "Le critère de la vie." *La Presse méd.* 50:447–448.

141.————. 1946. *L'étude d'une maladie: le choléra, maladie à paradoxes.* Lausanne, Rouge.

142.————. 1947. "Bactériophagie et chirurgie." *Bull. et Mémoires de la Soc. de Chirurgiens de Paris* 38:241–252.

143.————. 1948. "Le bactériophage." *Atomes* 3:399–403. English translation reprinted in *Science News* (West Drayton, London) 14:44–59, 1949.

144.————. 1940–1946. *Les Périgrinations* [sic] *d'Un Microbiologiste.* Unpublished manuscript.

145.————. 1940–1946. *La Valeur de l'Expérience.* Unpublished manuscript, three volumes.

SECONDARY LITERATURE

Ackermann, H.-W., Martin, M., Vieu, J.-F, and Nicolle, P. 1982. "Felix d'Herelle: His life and work and the foundation of a bacteriophage reference center." *ASM News* 48:346–348.

Amsterdamska, Olga. 1991. "Stabilizing instability: The controversy over cyclogenic theories of bacterial variation during the interwar period." *J. Hist. Biol.* 24:191–222.

"Annual report, Eleventh All-India Research Workers Conference, December 1933." 1934. *Indian Med. Gazette* 69:40.

Anonymous. 1901. "Les végétaux font-ils du Carbone?" *Le Naturaliste Canadien* 23:98–99.

————. "Editorial: The cholera bacteriophage." 1934. *Indian Med. Gazette.*

Arshba, S., Murvanidze, D., and Kuparadze, G. 1973. "Alexandr Petrovich Tsulukidze." In Russian with English and Georgian summaries. Tbilisi, Metsneyereba.

Asheshov, Igor N. 1922. "L'accoutumance du bactériophage." *Comptes rendus Soc. biol. Paris* 87:1343–1344.

Asheshov, Igor N. 1923. "Quelques recherches sur la nature des plages de bactériophage." *Comptes rendus Soc. biol. Paris* 89:120–121.

————. 1934. In: *Annual Report of the Scientific Advisory Board, Indian Research Fund Association for the Year* 1933–1934. Calcutta, n.p.

Asheshov, Igor N., Asheshov, Inna, Khan, Saranjan, and Lahiri, M. N. 1929. "Bacteriophage inquiry report on work during the period from 1st January to 1st September 1929." In: *Annual Report of the Scientific Advisory Board, Indian Research Fund Association for the Year* 1928–1929. Calcutta, n.p.

————. 1931. "The treatment of cholera with bacteriophage." *Indian Med. Gazette* 66:179–184.

Asturias, Francisco. 1902. *Historia de la medicina en Guatemala.* Guatemala, Tipografía Nacional.

Bail, Oskar. 1921. "Bakteriophagen Wirkungen gegen Flexner- und Koli-Bakterien." *Wien. klin. Woch.* 34:447–449.

Baring-Gould, S. 1914. *The Lives of the Saints.* New and revised ed. Edinburgh, John Grant.

Béguet, M. 1914. "Essais de destruction du *Stauronotus maroccanus* Thun. en Algérie, au moyen du *Coccobacillus acridiorum* d'Herelle." *Bull. soc. path. exot. Paris* 7:651–653.

Berg, Raissa L. 1988. *Acquired traits: Memoirs of a geneticist from the Soviet Union.* New York, Viking Penguin.

Bergson, Henri. 1911. *Creative evolution.* Trans. Arthur Mitchell. New York, Random House, The Modern Library.

Bertillon, Georges. 1916. "Une épidémique de dysentérie hémorragique dans un escadron de dragons." *Ann. de l'Institut Pasteur* 30:141–144.

Beukers, Harm. 1989. "The development of tropical medicine in Leiden." *Acta Leidensia* 58:3–43.

Bonét-Maury, Paul, and Boulgakov, Nicolai. 1944. "Recherches sur la taille et la structure du bactériophage φ.γ.174: Action de rayons du radon." *Comptes rendus Soc. biol. Paris* 138: 499–500.

Bordet, Jules. 1895. "Les leucocytes et les propriétés actives du sérum chez les vaccinés." *Ann. de l'Institut Pasteur* 9:462–506.

———. 1922. "Concerning the theories of the so-called 'bacteriophage'." *Brit. Med. J.* 2:296.

Bordet, Jules, and Ciuca, Mihai. 1920. "Exsudats leucocytaires et autolyse microbienne transmissible." *Comptes rendus Soc. biol. Paris* 83:1293–1295.

———. 1920. "Le bactériophage de d'Herelle, sa production et son interprétation." *Comptes rendus Soc. biol. Paris* 83:1296–1298.

———. 1921. "Remarques sur l'historique de recherches concernant la lyse microbienne transmissible." *Comptes rendus Soc. biol. Paris* 84:745–747.

Boulgakov, Nicolai, and Bonét-Maury, Paul. 1944. "Recherches sur la taille et la structure du bactériophage φ.X.174: Méthode de titrage." *Comptes rendus Soc. biol. Paris* 138:497–499.

Boyce, Rubert. 1906. *Report to the Government of British Honduras upon the outbreak of yellow fever in that colony in 1905.* London, Waterlow and Sons.

Brock, Thomas. 1990. *The emergence of bacterial genetics.* Cold Spring Harbor, N.Y., Cold Spring Harbor Laboratory Press.

Bronfenbrenner, Jacques J., and Korb, Charles. 1925. "Studies on the bacteriophage of d'Herelle. III. Some of the factors determining the number and size of plaques of bacterial lysis on agar." *Journal of Experimental Medicine* 42:483–498.

Bryce, James. 1912. *South America—Observations and impressions.* New York, Macmillan.

Buchanan, Robert E., Hold, John G., and Lessel, Ervin R., Jr. 1966. "*Bacterium gummis* (Comes) Trevisan 1899." *Index Bergeyana.* Baltimore, Williams and Wilkins.

Buican, Denis. 1984. *Histoire de la génétique et de l'évolutionnisme en France.* Paris, Presses Universitaires de France.

Bulloch, William. 1938. *The history of bacteriology.* London, Oxford University Press.

Bungenberg de Jong, H. G. 1932. "Die Koazervation und ihre Bedeutung für die Biologie." *Protoplasma* 15:110–173.

Burian, Richard M., Gayon, Jean, and Zallen, Doris. 1988. "The singular fate of genetics in the history of French biology." *J. Hist. Biol.* 21:357–402.

Cairns, John, Stent, Gunther S., and Watson, James D. (eds.). 1966. *Phage and the Origins of Molecular Biology.* Cold Spring Harbor, N.Y., Cold Spring Harbor Laboratory of Quantitative Biology.

Calmette, Albert. 1912. "Les missions scientifiques de l'Institut Pasteur et l'expansion coloniale de la France." *Revue Scientifique* 89:129.

Cancela, Arturo. 1922. *El coccobacilo de Herrlin. Tres relatos porteños.* Madrid, Calpe.

Carter, K. Codell. 1991. "The development of Pasteur's concept of disease causation and the emergence of specific causes in nineteenth-century medicine." *Bull. Hist. Med.* 65:528–548.

Chartrand, L. 1981. "Un aventurier de la science." *Que. Sci.* 19:50–51.

Chaussivert, Jean. 1991. "L'Institut Pasteur d'Australie." in Michel Morange, ed., *L'Institut Pasteur: Contributions à son histoire.* Editions La Découverte, Paris, 1991. pp. 242–252.

Clark, Harry. 1927. "On the titration of bacteriophage and the particulate hypothesis." *Journal of General Physiology* 11:71–81.

Clark, Paul F. 1959. "Theobald Smith, student of disease (1859–1934)." *J. Hist. Med. Allied Sci.* 14:490–514.

Cocks, Charles, and Feret, Edouard. 1899. *Bordeaux and its wines.* 3rd English edition, improved. Bordeaux, Feret et Fils.

Compton, Arthur. 1949. "Prof. Felix d'Herelle." *Nature* 163:984–985.

———. 1942. "Results of bacteriophage treatment of bacillary dysentery at Alexandria." *Brit. Med. J.* i:719–720.

Curtis, J. A. E. 1991. *Manuscripts don't burn: Mikhail Bulgakov. A life in letters and diaries.* London, Bloomsbury.

Dale, H. H. 1931. "The biological nature of the viruses." *Nature* 128:599–602.

Danysz, Jean. 1900. "Un microbe pathogène pour le rats et son application à la destruction de ces animaux." *Ann. de l'Institut Pasteur* 14:193–201.

De Kruif, Paul H. 1931. "Miracles of Healing." *Ladies Home Journal* 46:3, 74.

———. 1921. "Dissociation of microbic species: I. Coexistence of individuals of different degrees of virulence in cultures of the bacillus of rabbit septicemia." *J. Exptl. Med.* 33:773–787.

Delacroix, Georges. 1900. *Les maladies et les ennemis du caféier.* 2nd ed. Paris, A. Challame.

Delaunay, Albert. 1962. *L'Institut Pasteur: Des origines à aujourd'hui.* Paris, Editions France-Empire.

Delbrück, Max. 1970. "A physicist's renewed look at biology: Twenty years later." *Science* 168:1312–1314.

de Schweinitz, E. A., and Dorset, M. 1903. "A form of hog cholera not caused by the hog-cholera bacillus." *Bureau of Animal Industry: Circular* 41:1–4; 43:1–3.

Dixon, Bernard. 1987. "Scientifically speaking." *Brit. Med. J.* 294:1168.

Dobell, Clifford. 1958. *Antony van Leeuwenhoek and his "little animals."* New York, Russell and Russell.

Donnelly, Ignatius. 1888. *The great cryptogram: Francis Bacon's cipher in the so-called Shakespeare plays.* London, R.S. Peale.

Dozon, Jean-Pierre. 1991. "Pasteurisme, médecine militaire et colonisation en Afrique noire." In Michel Morange, ed., *L'Institut Pasteur: Contributions à son histoire.* Paris, Editions La Découverte, 1991. pp. 269–278.

Duckworth, Donna. 1976. "Who discovered bacteriophage?" *Bacteriolog. Reviews* 40:793–802.

Eaton, Monroe D., and Bayne-Jones, Stanhope. 1934. "Bacteriophage therapy." *J. Am. Med. Assn.* 103:1769–1776; 1847–1853; 1934–1939.

"Editorial: The cholera bacteriophage." 1934. *Indian Med. Gazette* 65:91.

Elford, William J., and Andrews, Christopher H. 1932. "The sizes of different bacteriophages." *Brit. J. Exptl. Path.* 13:446–456.

Ellis, Emory L. 1966. "Bacteriophage: One-step growth." In John Cairns, Gunther S. Stent, and James D. Watson, eds., *Phage and the Origins of Molecular Biology.* Cold Spring Harbor, N.Y., Cold Spring Harbor Press,

Ellis, Emory L., and Delbrück, Max. 1939. "The growth of bacteriophage." *J. Gen. Physiol.* 22:365–384.

Far Eastern Association for Tropical Medicine. *Report of the Seventh Congress in British India, December 5, 10, 24th, 1927.* Part 2. Calcutta, Government of India Press.

Farley, J. 1977. *The spontaneous generation controversy from Descartes to Oparin.* Baltimore, Johns Hopkins University Press.

Feemster, Roy F., and Wells, W. F. 1933. "Experimental and statistical evidence of the particulate nature of the bacteriophage." *Journal of Experimental Medicine* 58:385–391.

Fildes, Paul. 1951. "Frederick William Twort, 1877–1950." *Obituary Notices of the Fellows of the Royal Society of London* 7:505–517.

Flu, Paul-Christian, and Renaux, E. 1932. "Le phénomène de Twort et la bactériophage." *Ann. de l'Institut Pasteur* 48:15–18.

Frilley, M., Bulgakov, Nicolai, and Bonét-Maury, Paul. 1944. "Recherches sur la taille et la structure du bactériophage φ.X.174: Action des rayons X (K du molebdène)." *Comptes rendus Soc. biol. Paris* 138:726–727.

Fruton, J. S. 1972. *Molecules and life.* New York, Wiley.

Gaceta Oficial de la Oficina de Patentes y Marcas. [Mexico] 1908. Vol. 6 (I), p. 36, 1908.

Gachechiladze, K. K., Balardshishvili, N. S., Adamia, R. S., Chanishvili, T. G., and Krüger, D. H. 1991. "Host controlled modification and restriction as a criterion of evaluating therapeutic potential of *Pseudomonas* phage." *J. Basic Microbiology* 31:101–106.

Gaidoz, Henri. 1887. *La Rage et St. Hubert.* Paris, Alphonse Picard.

Gazarian, Surian. 1989. "It should not happen again." (In Russian.) *Zvezda* 1:3–80.

Geison, Gerald. 1995. *The private science of Louis Pasteur.* Princeton, Princeton University Press.

Girard, Pierre, and Sertic, Vladimir. 1935. "Action de hauts champs centrifuges sur diverse celles bactériennes, sur différents bactériophages et la lysine diffusible d'un bactériophage." *Comptes rendus Soc. biol. Paris* 118:1286–1288.

Gjørup, Ernst. 1925. *Investigation into d'Herelle's phenomenon.* Thesis, Copenhagen, Busck.

Glaser, Rudolf William. 1918. "A systematic study of the organisms distributed under the name of *Coccobacillus acridiorum,* d'Herelle." *Ann. Entomol. Soc. Amer.* 11:19–42.

Goulet, Denis. 1993. *Histoire de la Faculté de Médecine de l'Université de Montréal (1843–1993).* Montréal, VLB Editeur, 1993.

Gratia, André. 1921. "De l'adaptation héréditaire du colibacille à l'autolyse microbienne transmissible." *Comptes rendus Soc. biol. Paris* 84:750–751.

———. 1921. "De la signification des 'colonies de bactériophage' de d'Herelle." *Comptes rendus Soc. biol. Paris* 84:753–754.

———. 1921. "Autolyse transmissible et variations microbiennes." *Comptes rendus Soc. biol. Paris* 85:251–252.

———. 1922. [Untitled paper: Commentary on d'Herelle's paper.] *Brit. Med. J.* 2:296–297.

———. 1922. "The Twort-d'Herelle phenomenon. II. Lysis and microbic variation." *J. Exptl. Med.* 35:287–302.

———. 1930. "Le traîtement des infections à staphyloccoques par le bactériophage et le mycolysats staphylococciques." *Bulletin et mémoires de la Société nationale de chirurgie* 56:344–348.

———. 1931. "Sur l'identité du phénomène de Twort et du phénomène de d'Herelle." *Ann. de l'Institut Pasteur* 46:1–16.

———. 1931. "Discussion sur le rapport de M. d'Herelle." *First International Congress of Microbiology. Paris.* 1930. Volume 1, pp. 237–238. Paris, Masson.

Gratia, André, and Jaumain, D. 1921. "Identité du phénomène de Twort et du phénomène de d'Herelle." *Comptes rendus Soc. biol. Paris* 85:880–881.

Guérin, René. 1909. "L'Alcool de Banane: Résults industriels obtenus au Guatémala." *J. d'Agricult. tropicale* 9 (No. 93):76–79.

Gutiérrez Rivas, Efraim. 1951. *Dr. Harald Seidelin: Su obra en Yucatán y algunas de sus actividades científicas en otros lugares.* Mérida, Mexico, Dias Massa.

Gwynne-Vaughan, H. C. I., and Barnes, B. 1937. *The structure and development of the fungi.* 2nd ed. Cambridge, Cambridge University Press.

Haffkine Institute Annual Report for the year 1927. 1928. Bombay, n.p.

Haldane, John B. S. 1929. "The origin of life." *Rationalist Annual.* Reprinted in John Maynard Smith, ed., 1985. *On being the right size and other essays,* pp. 101–112. Oxford: Oxford University Press.

Hall, Thomas S. 1969. *Ideas of life and matter.* Volume 2. Chicago, University of Chicago Press.

Harvey, S. C. 1952. "G. H. Smith." *Yale J. Biol. Med.* 25:299–308.

Helvoort, Ton van. 1985. "Felix d'Herelle en de controverse rond het Twort-d'Herelle Fenomeen in de jaren 1920: Ultrafiltreerbaar virus of lytisch ferment." *Tsch. Gesch. Gnk. Natuurw. Wisk. Techn.* 8:58–72.

———. 1986. "Felix d'Herelle en de bacteriofaag-therapie: De laboratoriumtafel naast het ziekbed." *Tsch. Gesch. Gnk. Natuurw. Wisk. Techn.* 9:118–131.

———. 1991. "What is a virus? The case of tobacco mosaic virus." *Studies in Hist. Phil. Sci.* 22:557–588.

———. 1992. "Bacteriological and physiological research styles in the early controversy on the nature of the bacteriophage phenomenon." *Medical Hist.* 36:243–270.

———. 1992. "The controversy between John H. Northrop and Max Delbrück on the formation of bacteriophage: Bacterial synthesis or autonomous multiplication?" *Annals of Science* 49:545–575.

———. 1992. "Bacteriological and physiological research styles in the early controversy on the nature of the bacteriophage phenomenon." *Medical Hist.* 36:242–370.

———. 1993. *Research styles in virus studies in the twentieth century: Controversies and the formation of consensus.* Thesis, University of Limberg. Enschede, Sneldruk.

———. 1994. "History of virus research in the twentieth century: The problem of conceptual continuity." *History of Science* 32:185–235.

———. 1994. "The construction of bacteriophage as bacterial virus: Linking endogenous and exogenous thought styles." *J. Hist. Biol.* 27:91–139.

Huxley, Julian. 1949. *Heredity east and west: Lysenko and world science.* New York, Henry Schuman.

International Congress for Microbiology. 1949. *Report of Proceedings: Fourth International Congress for Microbiology,* Copenhagen, 20–26 July 1947. Copenhagen: Rosenkilde and Bagger.

Jaumain, D. 1922. "Autolyse microbienne en tubes scellés." *Comptes rendus Soc. biol. Paris* 87:790–793.

Kabeshima, Tamezo. 1919. "Recherches expérimentale sur la vaccination préventive contre le bacille dysentérique de Shiga." *Comptes rendus Acad. Sci. Paris* 169:1061–1064.

———. 1920. "Sur un ferment d'immunité bactériolysant, du méchanisme d'immunité infectieuse intestinale, de la nature du dit 'microbe filtrant bactériophage' de d'Herelle." *Comptes rendus Soc. biol. Paris* 83:219–221.

———. 1920. "Thérapie expérimentale de porteurs de germes." *Comptes rendus Acad. Sci.* 170:71–72

Kamminga, Harmke. 1991. "The origin of life on earth: Theory, history and method." *Uroboros* 1:95–110.

Kraus, Rudolf. 1916. "Zur Frage der Bekämpfung der Heuschrecken mittels des Coccobacillus acridiorum D'Herelle." *Centralbl. f. Bakt. Abt. II B* 45:594–599.

Künckel d'Herculais, Jules. 1910. "Observations on note by M. d'Herelle." *J. d'Agricul. tropicale* 10 (No. 110): 238–239.

Kuttner, Anne Gayler. 1923. "Bacteriophage phenomena." *J. Bacteriol.* 8:49–101.

Kuznyetsova, P. S., and Vyeger, E. M. 1983. "The life and scientific contributions of Magdalina Petrovna Pokrovskaya." (In Russian.) In: *Cellular and molecular mechanisms of immunity against infections.* Moscow, Ministry of Preventive Medicine of the Russian SSR.

Lapresle, Claude. 1991. "Le rôle de l'hôpital de l'Institut Pasteur dans l'application à la médecine de découvertes fondamentales." In Michel Morange, ed., *L'Institut Pasteur: Contributions à son histoire.* Paris, Editions La Découverte, pp. 45–51.

Latour, Bruno. 1988. *The Pasteurization of France.* Cambridge, Harvard University Press.

LeBlanc, Diane. 1989. "La chocolaterie des frères d'Herelle à Longueuil." *Cahiers de la Société d'histoire de Longueuil* 19:3–11.

Leibow, A. A., and Waters, L. L. 1959. "Milton C. Winternitz." *Yale J. Biol. Med.* 32:143–172.

Lépine, Pierre. 1949. "Félix d'Herelle (1873–1949)." *Ann. de l'Institut Pasteur* 76:457–460.

———. 1951. "André Gratia (1893–1950)." *Ann. de l'Institut Pasteur* 80:196–199.

Lépine, Pierre, Bonét-Maury, Paul, Bulgakov, Nicolai, and Giuntini, J. 1944. "Recherches sur la taille et la structure du bactériophage φ.X.174: Ultracentrifugation." *Comptes rendus Soc. biol. Paris* 138:728–729.

Levaditi, Constantin, and Bonét-Maury, Paul. 1942. "Les ultravirus: Considérés à travers le microscope électronique." *La Presse méd.* (24 February), 17:203–207.

Lewis, Sinclair. 1925. *Arrowsmith.* New York, Harcourt and Brace.

Liebenau, Jonathan, and Robson, Michel. 1991. "L'Institut Pasteur et l'industrie pharmaceutique." In Michel Morange, ed., *L'Institut Pasteur: Contributions à son histoire*. Paris, Editions La Découverte, pp. 52–61.

Lisbonne, M., and Carrère, L. 1922. "Antagonisme microbien et lyse transmissible du Bacille du Shiga." *Comptes rendus Soc. biol. Paris* 86:569–570.

Lock, George Winslow. 1969. *Sisal*. 2nd ed. London, Longmans, Green and Co.

Löwy, I. 1990. "Yellow fever in Rio de Janeiro and the Pasteur Institute mission (1901–1905): The transfer of science to the periphery." *Medical Hist.* 34:144–163.

Löwy, I. 1991. "La mission de l'Institut Pasteur à Rio de Janeiro: 1901–1905." In Michel Morange, ed., *L'Institut Pasteur: Contributions à son histoire*. Paris, Editions La Découverte, pp. 279–295.

Luria, Salvatore. 1939. "Action des radiations sur le *Bacterium coli*." *Comptes rendus Acad. Sci. Paris,* 209:604–606.

———. 1939. "Sur l'unité lytique du bactériophage." *Comptes rendus Soc. biol. Paris* 130:904–908.

———. 1940. "Méthodes statistiques appliquées à l'étude du mode d'action des ultravirus." *Ann. de l'Institut Pasteur* 64:415–438.

Luria, Salvador E. 1984. *A slot machine, a broken test tube*. New York, Harper and Row.

Luria, Salvador E., and Delbrück, Max. 1943. "Mutations of bacteria from virus sensitivity to virus resistance." *Genetics* 28:491–511.

Makashvili, E. K. 1986. In: *The USSR great medical encyclopedia*. Volume 28.

Makashvili, Elena G., and Djanagowa, E.-G. 1936. "Sur la signification de la présence dans un organisme animal, d'un bactériophage donné." *Comptes rendus Soc. biol. Paris*. 122:38–40.

Marcuk, L. M., Nikiforov, V. N., Scerbak, Ja. F., Levitov, T. A., Kotljarova, R. I., Naumsina, M. S., Davydov, S. U., Monsur, K. A., Rahman, M. A., Latif, M. A., Northrup, R. S., Cash, R. A., Huq, I., Dey, C. R., and Phillips, R. A. 1971. "Clinical studies of the use of bacteriophage in the treatment of cholera." *Bull. World Health Org.* 45:77–83.

Martínez Durán, Carlos. 1964. *Las ciencias médicas en Guatemala*. 3rd ed. Guatemala, Editorial Universitaria.

Massini, Rudolf. 1907. "Uber einen in biologischer Beziehung interessanten Kolistamm (*Bacterium coli mutabile*): Ein Beitrag zur Variation bei Bakterien." *Arch. Hyg.* 61:250–290.

Mazure, Félix, and Mazure, Hubert. 1946. *Deux lycéens français chez les fantômes de PATTON*. Fasquelle Editeurs, Paris.

McCook, Stuart George. 1996. *The agricultural awakening of Latin America: Science, development, and nature*. Ph.D. diss., Princeton University.

Mikeladzé, Ch., Nemsadzé, E., Alexidzé, N., and Assanichvili, T. 1936. "Sur le traîtement de la fièvre typhoïde et des colites aiguës par le bactériophage de d'Herelle." *La Médecine* 17 (suppl. 2): 33–38.

Moore, Benjamin. 1913. *The origin and nature of life*. London: Williams and Norgate.

Morgan, Neil. 1990. "The strategy of biological research programmes: Reassessing the 'dark age' of biochemistry, 1910–1930." *Annals of Science* 47:139–150.

Morison, John. 1930. "Twelfth annual report for 1928. King Edward VII Pasteur Institute and Medical Research Institute, Shillong." *Indian Med. Gazette* 60:472–474.

————. 1932. "Annual report for the year 1931. King Edward VII Memorial Pasteur Institute and Medical Research Institute." *Indian Med. Gazette* 67:53–54.

————. 1932. *Bacteriophage in the treatment and prevention of cholera.* London, H. K. Lewis.

————. 1935. "Bacteriophage in cholera." *Trans. Roy. Soc. Trop. Med. Hyg.* 28:563–570.

Morison, John, Rice, E. Milford, and Pal Choudhury, B. K. 1934. "Bacteriophage in the treatment and prevention of cholera." *Indian J. Med. Res.* 21:790–907.

Morison, John, and Vardon, A. C. 1929. "A cholera and dysentery bacteriophage." *Indian J. Med. Res.* 17:48–54.

Mudd, Stuart. 1947. "Recent observations on programs for medicine and national health in the USSR, Part 2." *American Rev. of Soviet Med.* 5:71–81.

Muller, Herman J. 1922. "Variation due to change in the individual gene." *American Naturalist* 56:48–49.

Mullins, Nicholas C. 1972. "The development of a scientific specialty: The Phage Group and the origins of molecular biology." *Minerva* 10:52–82.

Neisser, Max. 1906. "Ein Fall von Mutation nach de Vries bei Bakterien und andere Demonstrationem." *Centralbl. Bakt. Abt. I. Ref.* 38 Suppl.:98–102.

Newman, Barclay Moon. 1937. "The smooth slide up to life. Editorial comment." *Scientific American* 156:304–306.

Nicolle, Pierre. 1946. "Eugène Wollman." *Ann. de l'Institut Pasteur* 72:855–858.

————. 1949. "Félix d'Herelle." *La Presse méd.* 57:350.

————. 1949. "Le bactériophage." *Biologie Médicale* 38:233–306.

————. 1967. "Cinquantième anniversaire d'une grande découverte anglo-franco-canadienne en biologie: Le bactériophage." *Bull. Acad. Natl. Med. Paris* 151:404–409.

"Obituary: F. d'Herelle." 1949. *J. Am. Med. Assn.* 140:907.

"Obituary: F. d'Herelle." 1949. *Brit. Med. J.* 1:782.

"Obituary: F. d'Herelle." 1949. *J. Intl. Coll. Surg.* 12:597–598.

"Obituary: F. d'Herelle." 1949. *Lancet* 1:715–716.

"Obituary: F. d'Herelle." 1949. *Can. Med. Assn. J.* 61:86.

Oparin, Alezandr I. 1953. *Origin of life.* 2nd ed. Trans. Sergius Morgulis. New York, Dover.

Osborn, Henry Fairfield. 1917. *The origin and evolution of life.* New York, Charles Scribner's Sons.

Otto, R., and Winkler, W. F. 1922. "Uber die Natur des d'Herelle'schen Bakteriophagen." *Deut. med. Woch.* 48:383–384.

Paillot, A. 1933. *L'infection chez les insectes.* Trévoux, G. Patissier.

Pandy, B. N. 1969. *The breakup of British India.* London, Macmillan.

Pasricha, C. L., de Monte, A. J. H., and O'Flynn, E. G. 1936. "Bacteriophage in the treatment of cholera." *Indian Med. Gazette* 71:61–68.

Pasteur, Louis. 1888. "Sur la destruction des lapins en Australie et dans la Nouvelle-Zélande." *Ann. de l'Institut Pasteur* 2:1–8.

Peitzman, Steven J. 1969. "Felix H. d'Herelle and bacteriophage therapy." *Transactions and Studies of the College of Physicians of Philadelphia* 37:115–123.

Pfankuch, E., and Kausche, G. A. 1940. "Isolierung und übermikroskopische Abbildung eines Bakteriophagen." *Naturwissenschaften* 28:46.

Pfeiffer, Richard, and Issaeff, V. I. 1894. "Ueber die specifische Bedeutung de Choleraim-munität." *Zeitschrift für Hygiene und Infektionskrankheiten* 27:355–400.

Pozerski, Edouard Alexandre. n.d. In *Souvenirs d'un demi-siècle à l'Institut Pasteur.* Typescript in Pasteur Museum. pp. 45–47.

Prillieux, Edouard Ernest, and Delacroix, Georges. 1896. "La gommose bacillaire, maladie de vignes." *Ann Inst. nat. agron.* (Paris) (1891–92) 14:31–60.

Radetsky, Peter. 1996. "The good virus." *Discover* (November): 50-58.

Raettig, Hansjürgen. 1958. *Bacteriophagie: 1917 bis 1956.* Vol. I. Stuttgart, Gustav Fischer.

Raiga, A. 1949. "Obituary: Felix d'Herelle la Vie méd." *Vie méd.* 5: 37–38.

Ramasubban, Radhika. 1988. "Imperial health in British India, 1857–1900." In *Disease, medicine and empire: Perspectives on western medicine and the experience of European expansion,* ed. Roy McLeod and Milton Lewis. London, Routledge.

Roux, Emile. 1891. "De l'immunité—immunité acquise et immunité naturelle." *Ann. de l'Institut Pasteur* 5:517–533.

Ruska, Helmuth. 1940. "Die Sichtbarmachung der bakteriophagen Lyse im Uber-mikroskop." *Naturwissenschaften* 28:45–46.

———. 1941. "Uber ein neues bei der bakteriophagen Lyse auftretendes Formelement." *Naturwissenschaften* 29:367–368.

Russell, A. J. H., Stewart, A. D., and King, H. H. 1934. "Report of the *ad hoc* Bacteriophage Committee." *Annual Report of the Scientific Advisory Board, Indian Research Fund Association for the Year* 1933–1934. Appendix III, pp. 103–110. Calcutta, n.p.

Sanger, Frederick, Air, Gillian M., Barrell, Bart G., Brown, N. L., Coulson, Anthony R., Fiddes, John C., Hutchinson, Clyde A., III, Slocombe, P. M., and Smith, Michael. 1977. "Nucleotide sequence of bacteriophage φ.X174 DNA." *Nature* 265:687–695.

Sapp, Jan. 1994. *Evolution by association: A history of symbiosis.* New York, Oxford University Press.

Schultz, Edwin W. 1928. "Inactivation of staphylococcus bacteriophage by trypsin." *Proc. Soc. Exptl. Biol. Med.* 25:280–282.

Schulz, H. E., Urban, P. K., and Lebed, A. I., eds. 1972. *Who was who in the USSR.* Metuchen, N.J., Scarecrow Press.

Sergent, Edmond, and Lhéritier, Albert. 1914. "Essai de destruction des sauterelles en Algérie par le 'Coccobacillus acridiorum' de d'Herelle." *Ann. de l'Institut Pasteur* 28:408–419.

Sertic, Vladimir. 1937. "Sur la différence d'action des électrolytes sur le développement des diverses races de Bactériophages." *Comptes rendus Soc. biol. Paris* 124:98–100.

———. 1937. "Sur l'action inhibitrice des cations monovalents sur la multiplication d'une race de bactériophage." *Comptes rendus Soc. biol. Paris* 124:14–15.

Sertic, Vladimir, and Boulgakov, Nicolai. 1935. "Classification et identification des typhi-phages." *Comptes rendus Soc. biol. Paris* 119:1270–1272.

Shrayer, David P. 1996. "Felix d'Herelle in Russia." *Bull. Inst. Pasteur* 94:91–96.

Simon, Charles E. 1928. "The filterable viruses." In *Colloid chemistry,* vol. II. Ed. Jerome Alexander. New York, Chemical Catalog Co., pp. 525–533.

Sinsheimer, Robert L. 1959. "Purification and properties of bacteriophage φ.X174." *Journal of Molecular Biology* 1:37–42.

Stanley, Wendell. 1935. "Isolation of a crystalline protein possessing the properties of tobacco mosaic virus." *Science* 81:644–645.

Steinhaus, Edward A. 1949. *Principles of insect pathology.* New York, McGraw-Hill.

———. 1975. *Disease in a minor chord.* Columbus, Ohio State University Press.

Stent, Gunther S. 1971. *Molecular genetics: An introductory narrative.* San Francisco, W. H. Freeman.

Stepan, Nancy. 1976. *The beginnings of Brazilian science: Oswaldo Cruz, medical research and policy,* 1890–1920. New York: Science History Publications.

Summers, William C. 1991. "On the origins of the science in *Arrowsmith:* Paul de Kruif, Felix d'Herelle and phage." *J. Hist. Med. Allied Sci.* 46:315–332.

———. 1991. "From culture as organism to organism as cell: Historical origin of bacterial genetics." *J. Hist. Biol.* 24:171–190.

———. 1993. "Cholera and plague in India: The bacteriophage inquiry of 1927–1936." *J. Hist. Med. Allied Sci.* 48:275–301.

———. 1993. "How bacteriophage came to be used by the Phage Group." *J. Hist. Biol.* 26:255–267.

———. 1998. "Theorien der Versursachung, ihre Rechtfertigung und de expérimentelle Wissenschaft: Daniel E. Slamon und die Schweinepest." In Christoph Gradmann and Thomas Schlich, eds., *Strategien der Kausalitaet. Konzeptionen der Krankheits Versursachung im 19. und 20. Jahrhundert.* 79-94.

Sweetman, Harvey L. 1936. *The biological control of insects, with a chapter on weed control.* Ithaca, N.Y., Comstock.

Théodoridès, J. 1952. "Herelle, Félix d'." In *Dictionary of scientific biography,* vol. 6. New York, Scribner, pp. 297–299.

Thiel, P. H. van. 1946. "Prof. dr. P. C. Flu. His life and work." *Acta Leidensia* 17:1–11.

Tricot-Royer. 1925. "Bilan du traîtement de la rage à l'intercession de Saint Hubert." *Bull. Soc. Fr. d'Hist. Méd.* 19:273–290, 346–349.

Tsouloukidzé, Alexandr. 1936. "Sur l'application du bactériophage dans le péritonite par perforation au cours de la fièvre typhoïde." *La Médecine* 17 (suppl. 2): 41–42.

Twort, Antony. 1993. *In focus, out of step: A biography of Frederick William Twort F.R.S.,* 1877–1950. Phoenix Mill, UK, Alan Sutton.

Twort, Frederick W. 1915. "An investigation on the nature of ultra-microscopic viruses." *Lancet* 2:1241–1243.

———. 1922. "The bacteriophage: The breaking down of bacteria by associated filter-passing lysins." *Brit. Med. J.* 2: 293–296.

———. 1923. "The ultramicroscopic viruses." *J. State Med.* 31:351–366.

Valley, George. 1955. "Leo Frederick Rettger. 1974–1954." *J. Bacteriol.* 69:1–2.

Varley, Alan W. 1986. "Living molecules or autocatalytic enzymes: The controversy over the nature of bacteriophage, 1915–1925." Ph.D. diss., University of Kansas.

Viseltear, A. J. 1982. "C.-E. A. Winslow and the early years of public health at Yale." Yale J. Biol. Med. 55:137–151.

———. 1988. "The emergence of pioneering public health education in the United States." *Yale J. Biol. Med.* 61:519–548.

Wallace, W. Stuart. 1963. *Macmillan Dictionary of Canadian Biography.* 3rd edition, revised and enlarged. London, Macmillan.

Watkins, E. M., and Nelbach, J. H. 1947. "Bibliography of C.-E. A. Winslow." *Yale J. Biol. Med.* 19:779–800.

Weinberg, M., and Aznar, P. 1922. "Autobactériolysines et le phénomène de d'Herelle." *Comptes rendus Soc. biol. Paris* 86:833–834.

Wilson, E. B. 1923. *The physical basis of life.* New Haven, Yale University Press.

Winslow, C.-E. A., and Prescott, S. C. 1904. *Elements of water bacteriology with special reference to sanitary water analysis.* New York, J. Wiley and Son.

Winslow, C.-E. A., and Winslow, A. F. 1908. *Systematic relationships of the Coccaceae, with a discussion of the principles of bacterial classification.* New York, J. Wiley and Son.

Wolff, Etienne. 1951. "Le prix Nobel." *Les Nouvelles Littéraires* 1222 (1 February): 5.

Wolff, L.-K., and Janzen, J.-W. 1922. "Action de divers antiseptiques sur le bactériophage de d'Herelle." *Comptes rendus Soc. biol. Paris* 87:1087–1088.

Wollman, Eugène. 1921. "Sur le phénomène de d'Herelle." *Comptes rendus Soc. biol. Paris* 84:3–5.

———. 1927. "Recherches sur la bactériophage (Phénomène de Twort-d'Herelle). II." *Ann. de l'Institut Pasteur* 41:883–918.

Wollman, Eugène, and Lacassagne, A. 1940. "Recherches sur le phénomène de Twort-d'Herelle. VI. Evaluation de dimensions des bactériophages au moyen des rayons X." *Ann. de l'Institut Pasteur* 64:5–39.

Wollman, Eugène, Holweck, Fernand, and Luria, Salvador. 1940. "Effects of radiations on bacteriophage C_{16}." *Nature* 145:935–936.

Zavala, Gonzalo Camara. 1977. "Historia de la industria henequénera." *Enciclopedia Yucatanense.* Vol. III. Mexico, Gobierno de Yucatán, 707.

Index

Bacteriophages (continued)
99, 118, 119, 123, 178, 194*n12*, 197*n8;*
virulence, 59, 91, 153, 155, 203*n25;* early
publications about, 61, 185; particulate
nature of, 73, 93, 106, 177; one step
growth of, 86, 178; life cycle of, 87;
variations of, 88, 89, 90, 91, 123, 148,
151; as virus, 91, 96, 105, 176, 177, 182;
structure of, 93; as colloidsm, 94; metabolism and, 95, 105; origin of life
and, 102; antiplague, 128; naming of,
191*n2,* 197*n5*
Barbone, 68; in Indochina 115, 116
Beauceville, Québec, 5
Bernier, Arthur, 5, 189*n5*
Bertillon, Georges: and dysentery outbreak at Maisons-Laffitte, 47
Birth: Félix d'Herelle, 3
Bordet, Jules, 61; phage research of,
64; controversy with d'Herelle,
75, 99, 192*n9,* 194*n12;* invitation to
d'Herelle to 1st Internatl. Cong.
Microbiol., 78
Bovine hemorrhagic fever. *See* barbone
Bronfenbrenner, Jacques, J.: phage respi-
ration studies, 105; on phage structure,
178
Bulgakov (Boulgakov), Nicolai: collab-
oration with d'Herelle, 163, 176

Calmette, Albert: d'Herelle's conflict
with, 66, 118
Cancella, Arturo: fictional account of
d'Herelle in Argentina, 42
Cancer, Laboratory of (Villejuif):
d'Herelle's work on cancer and viruses, 67, 118, 123
Carbon cycle: d'Herelle's research on 8–
10, 97
Chemistry: d'Herelle's lack of interest in,
94
Chocolate factory: Longueuil (Québec),
6, 188*n10,* 188*n11;* bankruptcy, 7
Cholera: in Indochina, 115, 116; in India,

129, 131–144, 210*n18;* variation, 149; El
Tor strain, 150; monograph on, 178
Coccobacillus: in locust control, 33, 36,
40, 45, 190*n2;* possible bacteriophage
in, 54, 191*n11*
Coffee blight: in Guatemala, 16
Colloids: micellar theory of life and, 93,
103, 104; immunity and, 98
Controversies: carbon cycle, 8–10; locust
pathology, 31, 32; hive sickness in
bees, 40; locust control in Argentina,
41–42; priority dispute on phage discovery, 55, 70, 72, 76–81, 181, 193*n13,*
196*n49;* nature of phage, 62,64, 69,
99; with Calmette on BCG vaccinations, 66; cholera in India, 143; at
Yale, 147, 158, 159; on phage-resistant
bacteria, 153, 203*n25,* 203*n27;* on commercial phage therapy, 174, 175
Cyclogeny. *See* monomorphism

De Kruif, Paul H.: bacterial dissociation
and, 148; relation to André Gratia,
196*n31,* 196*n49*
Death and burial, 182
Delbrück, Max: early interest in viruses,
106, 178; "fluctuation test" for phage
resistant mutants, 156, 182
d'Herelle, Marie Adèle Caire, 4, 206*n24*
d'Herelle, Louise Marcelle: birth, 5,
188*n5*
d'Herelle, Daniel: 3, chocolate factory, 6,
188*n10,* 188*n11;* marriage of, 187*n2*
Dysentery: research at Pasteur Institute, 47,
109; at Maisons-Laffitte, 48; phage and
recovery, 58, 109, 114; in Egypt, 122

Ecological concept of disease: coffee
blights, 20; in epizootics, 40, 113; in
cholera, 150
Einstein, Albert: on the particulate nature of phage, 85
Electon microscopy: particulate nature of
phage and, 106

Parasitology: filaria in snakes, 28

Particulate nature of phage, 73, 93, 106, 177

Pasricha, C. L.: cholera phage studies in Campbell Hospital, Calcutta, 136, 141

Pasteur, Louis: comparisons with, 13, 120

Pasteur Institute: d'Herelle's first job at, 29, 33, 48; serological studies at, 38; in Algeria, 42; vaccine production in World War I, 43, 49, 52; in Lille, 61; in Indochina, 114; trials of dysentery phages, 114; in Kuala Lumpur, 132; in Shillong Assam, 134; in Rangoon, 134; Medal of Pasteur Institute, 181

Philosophy of experimentation, 38, 180, 198*nl*

Plague: in Indochina, 115, 117, 118; in Egypt, 124, 125

Plaques: phage, 58, 193*n10,* 197*n5;* particulate nature of phage and, 73, 83; Poisson distribution and, 85; correlations with lysis in liquid culture, 86, 177

Politics, 165, 167, 168, 180; Eliava's arrests and, 166

Pozerski, Edouard: as d'Herelle's host, 69, 162, 192*n3*

Priority disputes: Bordet's claim for Twort, 70

Protobes, 101, 102

Rabies: St. Hubert and, 1, 187*n1*

Raiga-Clemenceau, André: and phage therapy, 78, 183; Société des Amis de Félix d'Herelle, founder, 196*n44*

Recovery: phage and, 58; 109, 109, 117, 165

Renaux, Ernest: arbiter in d'Herelle-Gratia dispute, 80

Residences: Beauceville (Quebec), 5; Le Nervost (France), 173; New Haven (Connecticut), 203*n28*

Roux, Emile: as d'Herelle's patron, 50, 118, 120

Saigon: Institut Pasteur in, 115,194*n8,* 195*n20*

Salimbeni, A. T.: on the nature of phage, 67

Sauterelles. *See* Locusts

Schultz, Edwin W.: Guggenheim fellowship with d'Herelle in Egypt, 123; Lane Lectures by d'Herelle, 146

Secondary cultures, 65, 68, 151, 157, 203*n27*

Seidelin, Harald, 190*n22;* collaborations in Mexico, 28

Sertic, Vladimir: collaboration with d'Herelle, 94, 163

Sisal: industry in Yucatán, 21, 190*n17;* bagasse fermentation, 22; bagassse fermentation: talk on in Paris 29

Société des Amis de Félix d'Herelle, 183, 194*n44*

South America: early travels by d'Herelle, 3, 4

St. Hubert: patron saint of rabies victims, 1, 187*n1;* d'Herelle's interest in, 2

Stalin, Joseph: 161; "Terrors," 166; role in Eliava's death, 166; d'Herelle's dedication to, 169

Stanley, Wendell: crystalline tobacco mosaic virus, 106, 178

Steinhaus, Edward: evaluation of d'Herelle's work, 45

Storm van Leeuwen, Willem: friendship with d'Herelle, 119

Suez Canal: League of Nations Quarantine Laboratory, 121

Symbosis: bacterium-phage, 150, 152, 154, 156

Tbilisi. *See* Tiflis

Tiflis, 204*n1;* All Union Bacteriophage Institute, 162, 172; d'Herelle's arrival at, 163; work at, 164

Tsulukidze, Alexandr Petrovich: collaboration with d'Herelle, 163, 171

Tuberculosis: d'Herelle's research on, 123